Cisco® Access Lists

Field Guide

Cisco®
Access Lists

Gilbert Held
Kent Hundley

McGraw-Hill
New York   San Francisco   Washington, D.C.   Auckland   Bogotá
Caracas   Lisbon   London   Madrid   Mexico City   Milan
Montreal   New Delhi   San Juan   Singapore
Sydney   Tokyo   Toronto

Library of Congress Cataloging-in-Publication Data

Held, Gilbert
    Cisco access lists field guide / Gilbert Held, Kent Hundley.
        p.   cm.—(McGraw-Hill technical expert series)
        includes index.
    ISBN 0-07-212335-4
    1. Computer networks—Security measures.   2. Computer networks—
Access control.   I.
Title: Access lists field Guide.   II. Hundley, Kent.   III. Title.   IV. Series.
TK5105.59.H4497 1999
005.8—dc21   99-058030

McGraw-Hill

A Division of The McGraw·Hill Companies

    2 3 4 5 6 7 8 9 0   AGM/AGM   0 5 4 3 2 1 0

ISBN 0-07-212335-4

The executive editor for this book was Steven Elliot, the editing supervisor was Ruth W.
Mannino, and the production manager was Claire Stanley. It was set in Stone Serif by
Priscilla Beer of McGraw-Hill's desktop composition unit.

Printed and bound by Quebecor/Martinsburg

This book is printed on recycled, acid-free paper containing a minimum
of 50% recycled de-inked fiber.

Contents

Preface

This book focuses on Cisco IP access lists, and we will both review the operation and utilization of access lists and provide more than 100 examples you can tailor to satisfy specific operational requirements.

Access lists represent the first line of defense for a network. In addition, they are a mechanism for controlling the flow of information through a router interface. Thus, the use of router access lists gives you the capability to tailor the operation of a network and control the flow of data. This, in turn, provides you with the ability to establish certain network-related policies that can be controlled via the use of router access lists.

This book, which represents the first in a series of Cisco-related field guides, as well as subsequent ones being developed by the authors, is oriented toward providing the knowledge and real-life examples of how to do things. We will review the basics of different types of access lists and include their format, use of keywords, creation, and application to an interface. In addition, each chapter is focused on a specific type of access list, and we will provide numerous examples in a standard format. This format provides an overview of a network application or requirement to be implemented via an access list, a network schematic diagram, necessary Cisco *Internet online service* (IOS) statements to satisfy the application or requirement, and an explanation of the use of IOS statements. The authors' intention is to provide real-life examples that can be easily tailored to satisfy specific organizational requirements.

As professional authors, we place a high value on reader feedback. If you wish to share your thoughts concerning the scope and depth of topics covered in this book, subjects you would like to see covered in a future edition, or a different Cisco-related topic you would like the authors to cover in a new professional field guide, you can contact us either through our publisher or directly via email.

—Gilbert Held
Macon, Georgia
gil_held@yahoo.com

—Kent Hundley
Stanford, Kentucky
kent.hundley@prodigy.net

Acknowledgments

Although you might not realize it, a book is very similar to many sports, representing a team effort. Without the effort of an acquisitions editor with the knowledge and foresight to back a proposal, it would be difficult, if not impossible, to publish a manuscript. It is always a pleasure to work with a knowledgeable acquisitions editor, and Steve Elliot is no exception. Thus, we would be remiss if we did not thank Steve for backing this new project.

As an old-fashioned author who spends a significant amount of time traveling to various international locations, Gil Held long ago recognized that pen and paper are far more reliable than a laptop that is difficult to recharge. Converting his writings and drawings into a professional manuscript is a difficult assignment, especially when balancing the effort with family obligations. Once again, Gil is indebted to Mrs. Linda Hayes for her fine effort in preparing the final manuscript for this book.

Writing is a time-consuming effort, requiring many weekends and evenings that would normally be spent with family. Thus, last but not least, we truly appreciate the support and understanding of our families and friends as we wrote this book, checked proofs, and verified the techniques presented in this book.

Gil would like to thank his wife Beverly for her patience and understanding while he hibernated in his office on many evenings and weekends working on this book.

Kent would like to extend thanks to his family, friends, and coworkers who have provided assistance and encouragement over the months leading to the completion of this work. He would especially like to thank his mother and father for their guidance and love and his wife Lori for her understanding and support.

Cisco® Access Lists

CHAPTER 1

Introduction

In the preface we noted that a router's access list is a network's first line of defense. We also noted that an access list provides a mechanism for controlling the flow of information through different interfaces of a router. This capability allows use of access lists to regulate the flow of information as a mechanism to implement organizational network-related policies. Such policies can represent security functions and affect the prioritization of traffic. For example, an organization may wish to enable or disable access from the Internet to a corporate Web server or allow traffic generated by one or more stations from an internal *local area network* (LAN) to flow onto an ATM-based communications backbone *wide area network* (WAN). Both of these situations, as well as other functions, can be accomplished by the use of access lists.

This chapter's goal is to acquaint you with the contents of the book. First we will introduce you to the concept of the Cisco Professional Field Guide Series, of which this book is the first, followed by a brief review of the role of routers and some basic information concerning Cisco access lists. Then we will provide a preview of the book, briefly focusing attention on material presented in succeeding chapters. The introduction, along with the index, will enable you to find topics of interest.

The Cisco Professional Reference Guide

The Cisco Professional Reference Guide Series provides information and a series of practical examples covering the operation of Cisco equipment that you can easily tailor to your specific organizational requirements.

This first book in the reference guide series is focused upon access lists, and provides detailed information on the use of different types of access lists, their formats and creation, application to interfaces, and operation. We provide a series of examples for each distinct type of access list that follows a common format, which includes an overview of an application or problem, a network schematic diagram illustrating the basic structure of a router with respect to its WAN and LAN interfaces, and appropriate IOS statements for effecting an access list that satisfies the application or problem. Each access list example concludes with an explanation of the rationale for key IOS statements required to implement the access list.

The Role of Routers

From an operational perspective the major function of a *router* is to transfer packets from one network to another. Routers operate at the network layer that represents the third layer of the *open systems interconnection* (OSI) reference model. By examining the network address of packets, routers are programmed to make decisions concerning the flow of packets, as well as the creation and maintenance of routing tables. Such protocols as the *routing information protocol* (RIP), *open shortest path first* (OSPF), and the *border gateway protocol* (BGP) represent only three of more than 50 routing protocols that have been developed over the past 20 years. The router represents the first line of protection for a network in terms of security. That protection is in the form of access lists created to enable or deny the flow of information through one or more router interfaces.

Cisco Systems routers support two types of access lists, basic and extended. A *basic* access list controls the flow of information based on network addresses. An *extended* access list controls the flow of information by network address *and* the type of data being transferred within a packet. Although access lists represent the first line of protection for a network, as currently implemented they usually do not examine the actual contents of the information fields of packets—nor do they maintain information about the "state" of a connection. In other words, each packet is examined individually without the router attempting to determine whether the packet is part of a legitimate conversation stream.

Over the past 2 years Cisco Systems has significantly enhanced the capability of access lists to include new functions such as the examination of inbound and outbound traffic based upon time of day and day of week, the ability to insert dynamic entries into standard and extended access lists, and the ability to prevent one of the more common methods of hacker attacks from adversely affecting Web servers and other network devices.

We will examine the types and features of Cisco access lists, including *context-based access control lists* (CBAC) and *reflexive access control lists* (reflexive ACLs). CBAC is the heart of the Cisco *firewall feature set* (FFS). The FFS is a specific code revision available for some Cisco router models. Beginning with IOS 12.0T, CBAC is available on the 800, 1600, 1720, 2500, 3600, and 7200 series routers. This feature maintains information about the state of an existing connection, examines application layer information for a limited number of TCP and UDP protocols, and provides a significantly greater level of security than traditional access lists. Reflexive ACLs are a new feature introduced in the 11.3 revision of the Cisco IOS. Reflexive ACLs maintain a degree of "pseudostate" information by creating dynamic entries in traditional ACLs once a legitimate conversation is started. Future packets are evaluated against the dynamic entries in the reflexive ACL to determine if they are part of an existing connection. Once the conversation is ended, the dynamic entries are deleted from the ACL. However, reflexive ACLs do not understand higher-layer protocols and are not suitable for use with some multichannel protocols such as *file transfer protocol* (FTP). CBAC and reflexive ACLs will be covered in detail later.

Access control lists can be used to perform a significant number of functions in addition to security-related tasks, so the examples provided go beyond security. We will illustrate methods to control router table updates, limit the flow of traffic by time and day, and explore other techniques associated with the use of access control lists.

Book Preview

This section provides an overview of the focus of succeeding chapters. You can use the information in this section either by itself or in conjunction with the index to directly locate specific areas of interest. While the authors recommend that persons not familiar with the basics of IOS and use of access lists read the first few chapters in consecutive order, the last five chapters were developed as modular units focused on a single type of access list, so once you become familiar with the initial chapters, you can read the later chapters based on your need for information and examples concerning a particular type of access list.

Router Hardware and Software

The ability to code and apply an access list requires an understanding of Cisco router hardware and software. Knowledge of the hardware enables understanding how a router operates as well as methods to facilitate its configuration. Chapter 2 examines the basic hardware components of a

Cisco router and its software components, including how to configure a router through its EXEC mode of operation.

Basics of Cisco Access Lists

Once an understanding of the hardware and software components of a router is attained, we discuss basic information concerning Cisco access lists. Chapter 3 defines and examines the different types of access lists, their formats, the use of keywords within each access list format, and, through a series of examples, IOS statements required to perform predefined functions through the use of standard and extended access lists.

Dynamic Access Lists

Chapter 4 discusses advanced router packet-filtering techniques and examines the use of dynamic access lists which are also commonly referred to as *lock-and-key security*. Use of dynamic access lists permits coding of IOS statements, resulting in dynamic entries being inserted into standard and extended access lists, with the openings occurring through a user authentication process. By comparison, normal access lists are fixed with respect to their packet-filtering capability, resulting in less flexibility than that obtained with lock-and-key security.

Time-Based Access Lists

One of the problems associated with conventional access lists is that, once applied to an interface, they remain in effect until deleted. Thus, if you want to implement different rules or policies using access lists that varied by the time of day or day of the week, you would have to delete a current access list and apply a new one. This process is probably not very appealing to a router administrator, especially if a new method of filtering was scheduled for 5:00 p.m. on a Friday. Cisco Systems may have recognized this problem, and added time-based access lists to its IOS, so that security policies and other packet-filtering functions could be affected based upon the time of day and/or day or days of the week. Chapter 5 examines the operation of time-based access lists, including several examples for tailoring this access list capability for specific organizational requirements.

Reflexive Access Lists

A reflexive access list, which is a more flexible version of a dynamic access list, is covered in Chapter 6. We will examine how reflexive access lists can be used to create dynamic openings in an access list on an as-needed basis for supporting single-channel applications. As in other chapters, a series of access list configuration examples is included which you can use as is or easily modify to satisfy specific operational requirements.

Context-Based Access Control

Although reflexive access lists are a considerable addition to the capability of access lists, they are limited to supporting single-channel applications. This means you cannot support multichannel applications such as FTP using reflexive access lists.

Chapter 7 reviews context-based access control, which, while similar to reflexive access lists, adds support for multichannel applications and Java blocking and provides a real-time alert and audit trail. In covering CBAC we will also examine the use of a series of time-out commands that govern packet filtering.

TCP Intercept and Network Address Translation

Chapter 8 discusses two relatively new router capabilities—one to prevent a common hacker attack, referred to as SYN flooding, and the second to illustrate how to use a router to translate IP addresses for security or if an organization has more users than valid IP addresses. We first discuss how TCP's three-way handshake can adversely affect the capability of a Web server by overloading it, preventing the server from responding to legitimate service requests. Once we have an understanding of how SYN flooding literally "eats" up computer resources, we examine the role of TCP intercept, including its intercept and watch modes, the steps required to configure each mode, and IOS statements required to put this feature into effect. The second part of Chapter 8 examines *network address translation* (NAT), including an understanding of the statements used to convert internal IP addresses in an organization to IP addresses that are routable via the Internet.

IPSec

Chapter 9 examines a topic of considerable interest to anyone wishing to implement a Cisco router-based *virtual private network* (VPN). *IP Security* (IPSec) is a collection of technologies for the creation of encrypted tunnels over any IP-based network, regardless of the underlying physical topology. IPSec allows creation of encrypted tunnels between user workstations running Windows 95/98, NT, or even Linux. Examples of configurations for creating IPsec tunnels on Cisco routers that allow router-to-router communication are provided.

Traffic Shaping

The final chapter examines the various methods available on a Cisco router to manipulate the flow of packets, including the ability to throttle the amount of traffic that can transit an interface and selectively drop packets based on traffic classification. These technologies are collectively referred to as "traffic shaping," and they are the focus of Chapter 10.

CHAPTER 2

Router Hardware
and
Software Overview

This chapter provides an overview of Cisco router hardware and software. We will first turn our attention to the basic hardware components of a Cisco router. An examination of basic router software modules follows. Then we will look at router operational modes, and describe, discuss, and illustrate the use of different router functions.

We hope in this discussion to acquaint you with the general operation of Cisco routers and the manner by which they are configured. A number of examples of the use of EXEC commands have been included, enabling the chapter to be used as a review for readers who have familiarity with Cisco products, as well as providing necessary information concerning the configuration of the vendor's routers for persons who may lack prior Cisco experience. In addition, when appropriate, certain guidelines and hints are included that are based upon the authors' years of experience in configuring and operating Cisco routers. Hopefully these hints and guidelines will save you hours of puzzlement and make your router experience more pleasurable.

Basic Hardware Components

Cisco Systems manufactures a wide range of router products. Although those products differ considerably in terms of their processing power and the number of interfaces they support, all use a core set of hardware components. Figure 2-1 illustrates a generic schematic that indicates the key components of a Cisco Systems' router. While the CPU or microprocessor, amount of ROM and RAM, and the number and manner by which I/O

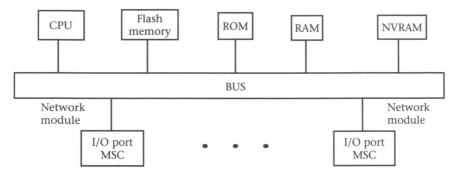

Figure 2-1 Key components of a Cisco Systems' router. CPU = central processing unit; MSC = media-specific converter; NVRAM = nonvolatile RAM; RAM = random-access memory; ROM = read-only memory.

ports and media converters are used can differ from one product to another, each router will have the components shown in Figure 2-1. By examining the function of each hardware component we will obtain an appreciation of how the sum of a router's parts come together to provide its functionality.

Central Processing Unit (CPU)

The *central processing unit* (CPU), or microprocessor, executes instructions that make up the router's operating system, as well as user commands entered via the console or via a Telnet connection. Thus, the processing power of the CPU is directly related to the processing capability of the router.

Flash Memory

Flash memory is an erasable, reprogrammable type of ROM memory. On many routers flash memory is an option that can be used to retain an image of the operating system and the router's microcode. Because flash memory can be updated without having to remove and replace chips, the cost can easily pay for itself by savings on chip upgrades over a period of time. More than one operating system image can be retained in flash memory, provided enough space is available. This feature is useful for testing new images. The flash memory can also be used when implementing a *trivial file transfer protocol* (tftp) of an *operating system's* (OS) image to another router and to store copies of the router's configuration file, which can be useful when a tftp server is unavailable or in emergency recovery procedures.

Read-Only Memory (ROM)

Read-only memory (ROM) contains code that performs power-on diagnostics similar to the power-on self-test (POST) many PCs perform. In addition, a bootstrap program in ROM is used to load operating system software. Although many routers require that software upgrades be performed by removing and replacing ROM chips on the router's system board, other routers may use different types of storage to hold the operating system.

Random-Access Memory (RAM)

Random-access memory (RAM) holds routing tables, performs packet buffering, furnishes an area for the queuing of packets when they cannot be directly output due to too much traffic routed to a common interface, and provides memory for the router's configuration file when the device is operational. In addition, RAM provides space for caching address resolution protocol (ARP) information that reduces ARP traffic and enhances the transmission capability of LANs connected to the router. When the router is powered off, the contents of RAM are cleared.

Nonvolatile RAM (NVRAM)

Nonvolatile RAM (NVRAM) retains its contents when a router is powered off. By storing a copy of its configuration file in NVRAM, the router can quickly recover from a power failure. The use of NVRAM eliminates the need to maintain a hard disk or floppy for the configuration file. As a result, a Cisco router has no moving parts, which means components last much longer. Most hardware failures in computer systems are due to the wear and tear on moving components such as hard drives.

Since Cisco routers do not have hard or floppy disks, a common practice is to store configuration files on a PC, where the files can be easily modified using a text editor. A configuration file can be directly loaded into NVRAM using tftp via the network.

When using the network for entering a router's configuration, the router functions as a client and the PC where the file resides functions as the server. This means you must obtain tftp server software to operate on your PC in order to move files to and from your computer. Later in this chapter, we will also discuss tftp server software.

Input/Output (I/O) Ports and Media-Specific Converters

The *input/output* (I/O) port is the connection through which packets enter and exit a router. Each I/O port is connected to a *media-specific converter*

(MSC) which provides the physical interface to a specific type of media, such as an Ethernet, token-ring LAN, or an RS-232 or V.35 WAN interface.

In Cisco terminology an access list is applied to an interface. However, an interface, in effect, represents an I/O port configured through an *interface* command. Since the fabrication of I/O ports can vary within a router, as well as between routers, it is important to understand how ports are referenced.

If a port is built into a router, it is referenced directly by its number. For example, serial port 0 is referenced in an interface command as follows:

```
interface serial0
```

If a group of ports is fabricated on a common adapter card for insertion into a slot within a router, the reference to a port requires both the slot and port number. Thus, on Cisco 7200 or Cisco 7500 series routers you would use the following format to specify a particular serial port:

```
interface serial slot #/port #
```

A variation of this format occurs on Cisco 7200 series equipment where multiple ports can be fabricated on a port-adapter card and multiple port adapters can reside in a slot. In this situation the following command format would be used to reference a specific serial port:

```
interface serial slot #/port adapter/port #
```

In terms of the flow of data within a router, as packets are received from a LAN, the layer 2 headers are removed as the packet is moved into RAM. When this occurs, the CPU examines its routing table to determine the port where the packet should be output and how the packet should be encapsulated.

The process just described is called the *process switching mode*. Each packet is processed by the CPU which consults the routing table and determines where to send the packet. Cisco routers also have a switching mode called *fast switching*. In fast switching mode the router maintains a memory cache containing information about destination IP addresses and next hop interfaces.

The router builds this cache by saving information previously obtained from the routing table. When the first packet arrives at a particular destination, the CPU consults the routing table. However, once information is obtained about the next hop interface for that particular destination, this information is inserted into the fast switching cache. The routing table is not consulted for new packets sent to this destination, resulting in the router switching packets at a much faster rate and a substantial reduction in the load on the router's CPU.

Variations on fast switching use special hardware architectures included in some higher-end models like the 7200 and 7500 series. However, the principle is essentially the same for all switching modes: a cache that contains destination address to interface mappings. The one exception to this is a switching mode called *netflow switching* which caches not only the destination IP address but also the source IP address and the upper-layer TCP or UDP ports. Prior to IOS version 12.0, this switching mode was available only on higher-end router platforms. Beginning in 12.0T, Cisco introduced this switching mode for low-end platforms such as the 2600.

A few specific points should be noted about fast switching. First, any change to the routing table or the ARP cache forces a purge of the fast switching cache so that, during a topology change, the fast switching cache will be rebuilt. Additionally, the entries in the fast switching cache will vary depending on the contents of the routing table. The entry in the fast switching cache will match the corresponding entry in the routing table. For example, if the router has a route to the 10.1.1.0/24 network, it will cache the destination 10.1.1.0/24. If the router only has a route to the 10.1.0.0/16 network, it will cache the destination 10.1.0.0/16. If there is no entry in the routing table for the network or subnetwork, the router uses the default route and the default major network mask, so it would cache the destination 10.0.0.0/8.

This pattern is true if there is only one route to a particular destination. If there are multiple, equal cost, nondefault paths, the router will cache the entire 32-bit destination. For example, if the destination IP address were 10.1.1.1 and the router had two routes to the 10.1.1.0/24 network, the router would cache the value 10.1.1.1/32 and match it to the first hop. The next destination on the 10.1.1.0/24 network, say 10.1.1.2/32, would be cached and matched with the second next hop. If there were a third, equal cost path, the next destination on the 10.1.1.0/24 network would be cached with the third next hop and so on. Note that this is true *only* for nondefault routes. If the router must use the default route to send a packet, it only caches the major network number and not the full 32-bit address as described previously.

Essentially, the router uses a round-robin method to cache individual destinations to each successive hop. This means that the router will load-share on a per-destination basis. That is, since the fast cache contains a mapping between an end destination and an interface, once the cache has been populated with an entry, all future packets for that destination will use the interface in the cache. The router will not place multiple interfaces in the fast switching cache for the same destination.

In process switching mode, the router load-shares on a per-packet basis. Since there is no fast switching cache, each packet is sent in a round-robin fashion to each successive interface. While this leads to a more evenly distributed network load if there are multiple paths, it also increases the load on the router CPU and slows down the rate at which the router can move packets. In most cases, it is better to leave fast switching turned on and live with the unequal distribution across multiple network paths.

The Router Initialization Process

When you power on a router, it performs a sequence of predefined operations. Additional operations performed by the router depend upon whether or not you previously configured the device. For an appreciation of the router initialization process, let's examine the major events that occur when you power on the device.

Figure 2-2 is a flowchart of the major functions performed during the router initialization process. When you apply power to the router, it initially performs a series of diagnostic tests which verify the operation of its processor, memory, and interface circuitry. Because this test is performed upon power up, it is commonly referred to as a power- on self-test (POST).

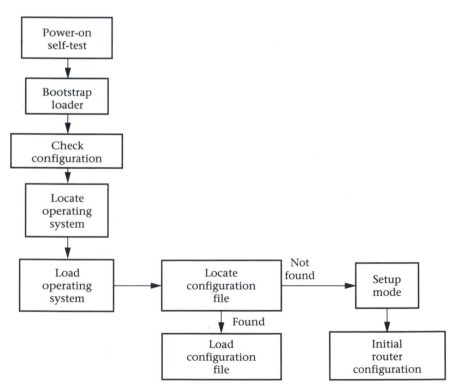

Figure 2-2 The router initialization process.

Once POST is completed, the bootstrap loader executes. The primary function of the loader is to initialize or place a copy of the operating system image into main memory. However, to do so it must first determine where the image of the operating system is located since the image could be located on flash memory, ROM, or even on the network.

The bootstrap loader checks the router's configuration register to determine the location of the operating system's image. The configuration register's values can be set either by hardware jumpers or via software, depending upon the router model. The settings of the register indicate the location of the operating system and define other device functions such as how the router reacts to the entry of a break key on the console keyboard and whether or not diagnostic messages are displayed on the console terminal.

The configuration register in most current model routers is a 16-bit value stored in NVRAM. It is not a physical entity. In older model routers, such as the MGS and AGS+, the configuration register was a physical jumper with 16 pins. This is the origination of the term *register*. The last 4 bits (pins in the case of the hardware register) on both the software and the hardware configuration registers indicate the boot field. The boot field tells the router where to locate its configuration file. The software register is displayed as a 4-digit hexadecimal number, for example, 0×2102. You can display the configuration register with the command show version. Each hexadecimal number represents 4 bits, so the first number reading from right to left is the boot field. The boot field can range in value from 0 to 15. In the previous example, the boot field is 2. Table 2-1 indicates how the router interprets the number in the boot field.

In most cases, the boot register will be set to 2, which means the router will look in the configuration file for boot commands. If none is found, the router will load the first image found in flash memory. If there is no

Table 2-1   The Meaning of the Boot Field Settings

Boot Field Value	Router Interpretation
0	RXBOOT mode. The router must be manually booted using the b command.
1	Automatically boots from ROM.
2-F	Examines the contents of the configuration file in NVRAM for *boot system* commands.

valid IOS image in flash memory or flash memory cannot be found, the router attempts to load an image from a tftp server by sending a tftp request to the broadcast address requesting an IOS image.

Once the configuration register is checked, the bootstrap loader knows the location from which to load the operating system image into the router's RAM and proceeds to load it. After the operating system is loaded, it looks for a previously created and saved configuration file in NVRAM. If the file is found, it will be loaded into memory and executed on a line-by-line basis, so that the router becomes operational and works according to a predefined networking environment. If a previously created NVRAM file does not exist, the operating system executes a predefined sequence of question-driven configuration displays referred to as a *setup dialog*. Once the operator completes the setup dialog, the configuration information will be stored in NVRAM and will be loaded as the default at the next initialization process. The router can be instructed to ignore the contents of NVRAM by setting the configuration register. If the second hexadecimal value from the right is set to 4, 0×2142, the router will ignore the contents of NVRAM. This feature is used during password recovery on the router so that an administrator can bypass the contents of the configuration file.

Figure 2-3 illustrates the initial display generated by a Cisco 4500 router as power is applied, the bootstrap is invoked, and a previously defined configuration is loaded into memory. Note the prompt at the end of the display; it can easily scroll off a screen and, upon occasion, result in a novice waiting a considerable period of time for something to happen without realizing the need to press the RETURN key to begin to access the system.

Now that we have an understanding of the basic hardware components of a router and its initialization process, let's look at router software for an understanding of the two key software components of a router and the relationship of router commands to the software components.

Basic Software Components

As briefly discussed in the prior section, there are two key router software components—the operating system image and the configuration file.

Operating System Image

The operating system image is located by the bootstrap loader, based on the setting of the configuration register. Once the image is located, it is loaded into the low-addressed portion of memory. The operating system image consists of a series of routines that supports the transfer of data through the device, manages buffer space, supports different network functions, updates routing tables, and executes user commands.

```
System Bootstrap, Version 5.2(7b) [mkamson 7b], RELEASE SOFTWARE
(fc1)
Copyright (c) 1995 by cisco Systems, Inc.
C4500 processor with 8192 Kbytes of main memory
program load complete, entrypt: 0x80008000, size: 0x231afc
Self decompressing the image :
#################################################
############################################################
  ########
######################################################### [OK]
                 Restricted Rights Legend
Use, duplication, or disclosure by the Government is
subject to restrictions as set forth in subparagraph
(c) of the Commercial Computer Software - Restricted
Rights clause at FAR sec. 52.227-19 and subparagraph
(c) (1) (ii) of the Rights in Technical Data and Computer
Software clause at DFARS sec. 252.227-7013.


           cisco Systems, Inc.
           170 West Tasman Drive
           San Jose, California 95134-1706

Cisco Internetwork Operating System Software
IOS (tm) 4500 Software (C4500-INR-M), Version 10.3(8), RELEASE
SOFTWARE (fc2)
Copyright (c) 1986-1995 by cisco Systems, Inc.
Compiled Thu 14-Dec-95 22:10 by mkamson
Image text-base: 0x600087E0, data-base: 0x6043C000

cisco 4500 (R4K) processor (revision B) with 8192K/4096K bytes of
memory.
Processor board serial number 73160394
R4600 processor, Implementation 32, Revision 2.0
G.703/E1 software, Version 1.0.
Bridging software.
X.25 software, Version 2.0, NET2, BFE and GOSIP compliant.
2 Ethernet/IEEE 802.3 interfaces.
1 Token Ring/IEEE 802.5 interface.
2 Serial network interfaces.
128K bytes of non-volatile configuration memory.
4096K bytes of processor board System flash (Read/Write)
4096K bytes of processor board Boot flash (Read/Write)

Press RETURN to get started!
```

Figure 2-3   Initial display of a Cisco 4500 router.

Configuration File

The second major router software component is the configuration file. This file is created by the router administrator and contains statements interpreted by the operating system that tell it how to perform different functions built into the OS. For example, the configuration file can include statements that define one or more access lists and tell the operating system to apply different access lists to different interfaces to provide a degree of control over the flow of packets through the router. Although the configuration file defines how to perform functions that affect the operation of the router, it is the operating system that actually does the work since it interprets and acts upon the statements in the configuration file.

The statements in the configuration file are stored in ASCII. As such, the contents can be displayed on the router console terminal or on a remote terminal. It is important to note and remember this if you create or modify a configuration file on a PC attached to a network and use tftp to load the file into your router because the use of a text editor or word processor will normally result in embedded control characters in a saved file that the router will not be able to digest. Thus, when using a text editor or word processor to create or manipulate a configuration file, save the file as an ASCII text (.txt) file. Once the configuration file is saved, it is stored in the NVRAM and loaded into upper-addressed memory each time the router is initialized. Figure 2-4 illustrates the relationship between the two key router software components and router RAM.

Data Flow

The importance of configuration information can be demonstrated by examining the flow of data within a router. Figure 2-5 illustrates the general flow of data within a router.

At the media interface the previously entered configuration commands inform the operating system on the type of frames to be processed. For

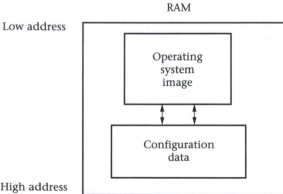

Figure 2-4   Relationship of the two key router software components with respect to router RAM.

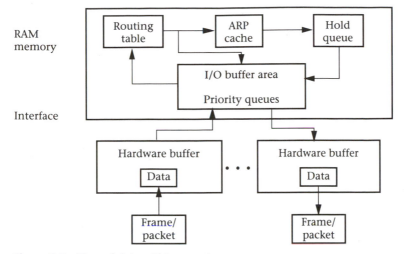

Figure 2-5   Flow of data within a router.

example, the interface could be Ethernet, Token Ring, (*fiber-distributed data interface* (FDDI), or even a serial wide area network port such as an X.25 or frame-relay interface. In defining the interface you may need to provide one or more operating rates and other parameters to fully define the interface.

Once the router knows the type of interface it must support, it can verify the frame format of arriving data as well as correctly form frames for output via that interface or a different interface. In addition, the router can check data integrity on received frames because once it knows the interface, it can use an appropriate *cyclic redundancy check* (CRC). Similarly, the router can compute and append an appropriate CRC to frames placed on the media.

Configuration commands are used within main memory to control the method by which routing table entries occur. If you configure static routing entries, the router will not exchange routing table entries with other routers. The ARP cache represents an area within memory which stores associations between IP addresses and their corresponding MAC layer 2 addresses. As data are received or prepared for transmission, the data may flow into one or more priority queues where low-priority traffic is temporarily delayed while the router processes higher-priority traffic. If your router supports traffic prioritization, configuration statements inform the router's operating system how to perform its prioritization tasks.

As data flow into the router, the location and status are tracked by a hold queue. Entries in the routing table denote the destination interface through which the packet will be routed. If the destination is a LAN and address resolution is required, the router will attempt to use the ARP cache to determine the MAC delivery address as well as the manner in which the outgoing frame should be formed. If an appropriate address is not in cache, the router will form and issue an ARP packet to determine the necessary layer 2 address. Once the destination address and method of encapsulation are determined, the packet is ready for delivery to an outgoing interface port. Again, it may be placed into a priority queue prior to being delivered into the transmit buffer of the interface for delivery to the connected media. Now that we understand the two key router software components, let's discuss how we can develop the router configuration file.

The Router Configuration Process

The first time you take a router out of the box and power it on, or after you add one or more hardware components, you must use the `setup` command. The `setup` command is automatically invoked for either of the previously defined situations or can be used later at the router's command interpreter prompt level, referred to as the EXEC. However, prior to running `setup` or issuing EXEC commands, it is important to determine the cabling needed to connect a terminal device to the router's system console port.

Cabling Considerations

The system console port on a router is configured as a *data terminal equipment* (DTE) port. Since the RS-232 port on PCs and ASCII terminal devices are also configured as DTEs, you cannot directly cable the two together using a common straight-through cable because both the router's port and the terminal device transmit on pin 2 of the interface and receive data on pin 3. A *crossover cable* is needed, where pin 2 at one end is crossed to pin 3 on the other end and vice versa, in order for the two to interface properly. The crossover cable also ties certain control signals together, so it actually functions more than the reversal of pins 2 and 3. However, it is an easily available cable to obtain. Simply specify the term "crossover." Once you install the correct cable, configure your terminal device to operate at 9600 Bd, 8 data bits, no parity, and 1 stop bit.

Console Access

A variety of communications programs are available for accessing the router via its console port. Since Windows95 and Windows98 include the HyperTerminal communications program, we will briefly explore its use for configuring a router.

Figure 2-6 illustrates the use of HyperTerminal for the creation of a new

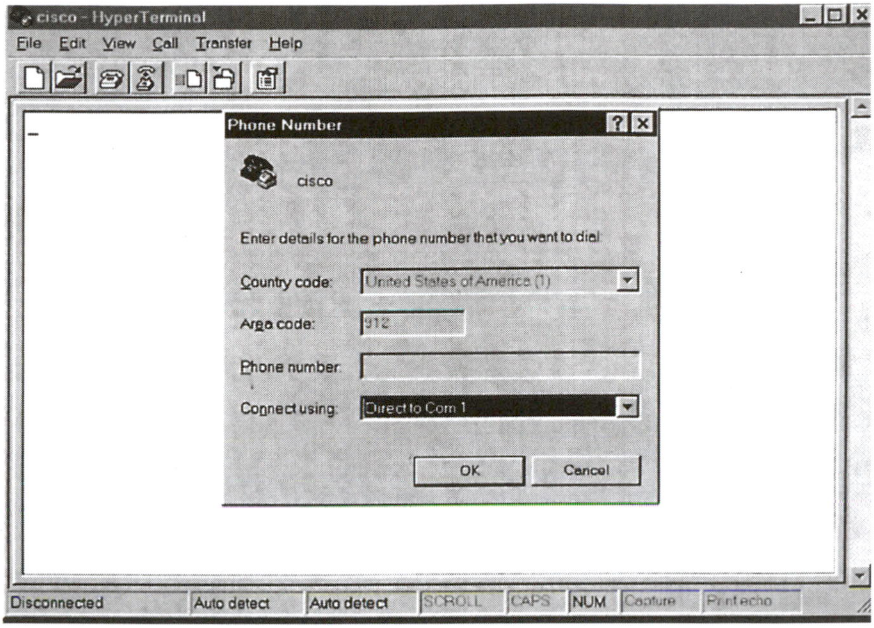

Figure 2-6   Set the connection type to direct when cabling a PC directly to the router console port.

connection appropriately labeled Cisco by the authors. Since you will directly cable your computer to the Cisco console port, you need to configure the phone number entry for a direct com port. In Figure 2-6, com port 1 is shown selected.

Once you select the appropriate direct connect com port and click on the OK button, HyperTerminal will display a dialog box called Port Settings. Figure 2-7 illustrates the Port Settings dialog box for the com 1 port previously configured for the connection we wish to establish to the router.

In Figure 2-7 the Port Settings dialog box allows you to define the communications settings to be used between your PC and the router port. The router console port's default is 9600 bits/s, 8 data bits, no parity, and 1 stop bit, and the configuration in Figure 2-7 is set accordingly.

Setup Considerations

To facilitate the use of the setup facility you should prepare for the use of the router by making a list of the protocols you plan to route, determining the types of interfaces installed, and determining if you plan to use bridging. In addition, because setup prompts you to enter a variety of specific parameters for each protocol and interface, it is highly recom-

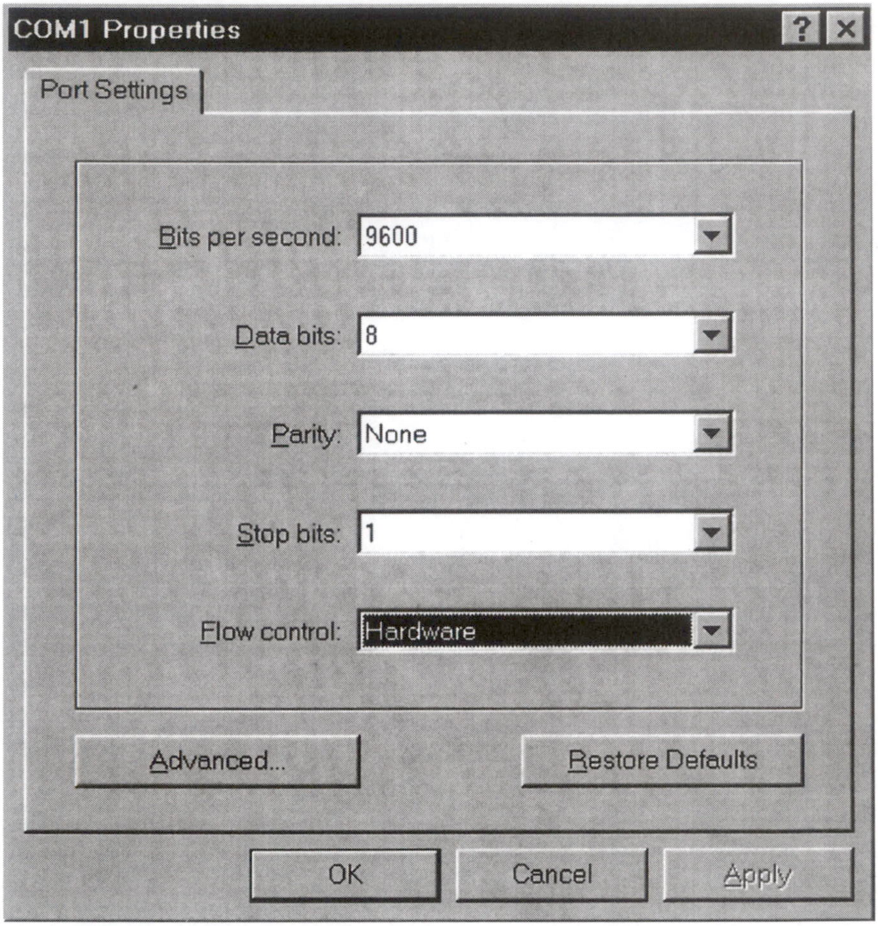

Figure 2-7 The Port Settings dialog box lets you configure the communications parameters to be used by your computer to match those used by the router console.

mended that you consult the appropriate Cisco Systems router manuals to determine these parameters correctly. The setup facility allows you to assign a name to the router and assign both a direct connect and virtual terminal password. Once you complete the setup, you will be prompted to accept the configuration. When the initial setup process is complete, you are ready to use the router's command interpreters.

Figure 2-8 illustrates the use of the router setup command to review and, if desired, modify one or more previously established configuration entries. The name of the router assigned during a previous setup process was CISCO4000, and that name is displayed prior to a prompt character. The prompt character is a pound sign (#) that indicates we are in the

Figure 2-8 An example of the setup command to view an existing router configuration.

```
CISCO4000#setup

            —- System Configuration Dialog —-

At any point you may enter a question mark '?' for help.
Refer to the 'Getting Started' Guide for additional help.
Use ctrl-c to abort configuration dialog at any prompt.
Default settings are in square brackets '[]'.

Continue with configuration dialog? [yes]:

First, would you like to see the current interface summary?
[yes]:

Interface    IP-Address     OK?  Method  Status      Protocol
Ethernet0    192.72.46.3    YES  NVRAM   up          down
Serial0      4.0.136.74     YES  NVRAM   down        down
Serial1      4.0.136.90     YES  NVRAM   down        down
TokenRing0   192.131.174.2  YES  NVRAM   initializing down
Configuring global parameters:

  Enter host name [CISCO4000]:

The enable secret is a one-way cryptographic secret used
instead of the enable password when it exists.

  Enter enable secret [Use current secret]:

The enable password is used when there is no enable secret
and when using older software and some boot images.

  Enter enable password [abadabado]:
  Enter virtual terminal password [gobirds]:
  Configure SNMP Network Management? [yes]:
    Community string [public]:
  Configure IPX? [yes]:
  Configure bridging? [no]:
  Configure IP? [yes]:
    Configure IGRP routing? [no]:
    Configure RIP routing? [yes]:

Configuring interface parameters:

Configuring interface Ethernet0:
  Is this interface in use? [yes]:
  Configure IP on this interface? [yes]:
    IP address for this interface [192.72.46.3]:
    Number of bits in subnet field [0]:
    Class C network is 192.72.46.0, 0 subnet bits; mask is
255.255.255.0
  Configure IPX on this interface? [yes]:
    IPX network number [110]:
```

(Continued)

Figure 2-8 *(Continued)*

```
Configuring interface Serial0:
  Is this interface in use? [yes]:
  Configure IP on this interface? [yes]:
  Configure IP unnumbered on this interface? [no]:
    IP address for this interface [4.0.136.74]:
    Number of bits in subnet field [22]:
    Class A network is 4.0.0.0, 22 subnet bits; mask is
255.255.255.252
  Configure IPX on this interface? [no]:

.  .  .  .   .   .   .
.   .   .   .   .   .   .

The following configuration command script was created:

hostname CISCO4000
enable secret 5 $1$soiv$pyh65G.wUNxX9LK90w7yc.
enable password abadabado
line vty 0 4
password gobirds
snmp-server community public
!
ipx routing
no bridge 1
ip routing
!
! Turn off IPX to prevent network conflicts.
interface Ethernet0
no ipx network
interface Serial0
no ipx network
interface Serial1
no ipx network
interface TokenRing0
no ipx network
!
interface Ethernet0
ip address 192.78.46.1 255.255.255.0
ipx network 110

.   .   .   .   .
.   .   .   .   .
router rip
network 192.78.46.0
network 200.1.2.0
network 4.0.0.0
network 192.131.174.0
!
end

Use this configuration? [yes/no]:
```

router's privileged mode of operation, which we will review shortly. Note the enabled password is shown as "abadabado." That password must be specified after a person gains access to the router console port and enters the command `enable` to obtain access to privileged EXEC commands that alter a router's operating environment. In addition to the enable password, an administrator may also configure an enable secret password. The enable secret password serves the same purpose as the standard enable password, except that the enable secret password is encrypted in the configuration file using MD5. When the configuration is displayed, only the encrypted version of the enable secret password is visible to prevent anyone from determining what the enable secret password is by obtaining a copy of the router configuration. The regular enable password may also be encrypted by using the command `service password-encryption`.

This command will also encrypt the passwords used for the vty and auxiliary and console ports. However, the encryption used is much weaker than that used for the enable secret and many free programs are available on the Internet that crack passwords encrypted this way in a few seconds. The authors recommend always using the enable secret password. If both the enable secret and the standard enable password are set, the enable secret password takes precedence.

To save on space, a portion of the router's setup configuration was eliminated from Figure 2-8 where the double rows of dots are shown. Note that you can use the question mark at each line entry level to obtain online assistance. Also note that once the configuration is completed, a command script is created by the router. This command script represents the latest configuration changes. You are then prompted to accept or reject the entire configuration.

Since the command interpreter is the key to entering router commands that control how the operating system changes router functionality, including applying access lists to interfaces, let's discuss this facility.

The Command Interpreter

The command interpreter, as its name implies, interprets the router commands entered. Referred to as the EXEC, the command interpreter checks each command and, assuming they are correctly entered, performs the operation requested.

If an administrator entered a password during the setup process, you must log into the router using the correct password before you can enter an EXEC command. In actuality two passwords can be required to use EXEC commands as there are two EXEC command levels—user and privileged. By logging into the router, you access user EXEC commands that allow you to connect to another host, provide a name to a logical connection, change the parameters of a terminal, display open connections, and perform similar operations that are not considered critical operations by Cisco Systems. If you use the EXEC enable command to access the use of privileged commands, you can enter configuration information, turn privileged commands on or off, lock the terminal, and perform other critical functions. To use the EXEC enable command you may have to enter another password if one was previously set with the enable-password or enable secret configuration commands.

USER MODE OPERATIONS

When you log into the router, you are in the user command mode where the system prompt appears as an angle bracket (>). If you previously entered a name for the router, that name will prefix the angle bracket. Otherwise the default term router will prefix the angle bracket. Once in the user mode, typing the question mark (?) command results in the display of a list of user-level EXEC commands supported by the router you are using. Figure 2-9 illustrates the use of the ? command at the user level. Note that the command line entry in Figure 2-9 CISCO4000>? indicates that the name CISCO4000 was assigned to the router during the setup process.

Figure 2-9   List of user level EXEC commands.

```
CISCO4000>?
Exec commands:
  atmsig           Execute Atm Signaling Commands
  connect          Open a terminal connection
  disable          Turn off privileged commands
  disconnect       Disconnect an existing network connection
  enable           Turn on privileged commands
  exit             Exit from the EXEC
  help             Description of the interactive help system
  lock             Lock the terminal
  login            Log in as a particular user
  logout           Exit from the EXEC
  name-connection  Name an existing network connection
  pad              Open a X.29 PAD connection
  ping             Send echo messages
  ppp              Start IETF Point-to-Point Protocol (PPP)
  resume           Resume an active network connection
  show             Show running system information
  slip             Start Serial-line IP (SLIP)
  systat           Display information about terminal lines
  telnet           Open a telnet connection
  terminal         Set terminal line parameters
  traceroute       Trace route to destination
  tunnel           Open a tunnel connection
  where            List active connections
  x3               Set X.3 parameters on PAD
```

PRIVILEGED MODE OPERATION

Since you can only configure a router through its privileged EXEC mode of operation, you can assign a password to this mode of operation. As previously noted, the `enable-password` configuration command is used, which means that you first enter the privileged mode without password protection to set password protection.

To enter the privileged EXEC mode, you enter the command `enable` at the > prompt. You are then prompted to enter a password, after which the prompt changes to a pound sign (#), which indicates that you are in the privileged EXEC mode of operation.

Figure 2-10 illustrates the use of the ? command at the privileged command level to display a list of commands supported. The entries in Figure 2-10 show that the privileged mode command set includes all user EXEC commands previously listed in Figure 2-9. In addition, it includes the `configure` command which allows you to apply configuration parameters that affect the router on a global basis.

Figure 2-10   Using the `enable` command to obtain a list of privileged commands.

```
CISC04000#configure
Configuring from terminal, memory, or network [terminal]?
Enter configuration commands, one per line.  End with CNTL/Z.
CISC04000(config)#?
Configure commands:
  aaa                          Authentication, Authorization and
                               Accounting.
  access-list                  Add an access list entry
  alias                        Create command alias
  arp                          Set a static ARP entry
  async-bootp                  Modify system bootp parameters
  autonomous-system            Specify local AS number to which we belong
  banner                       Define a login banner
  boot                         Modify system boot parameters
  bridge                       Bridging Group.
  buffers                      Adjust system buffer pool parameters
  cdp                          Global CDP configuration subcommands
  chat-script                  Define a modem chat script
  clock                        Configure time-of-day clock
  config-register              Define the configuration register
  default-value                Default character-bits values
  dialer-list                  Create a dialer list entry
  dlsw                         Data Link Switching global configuration
                               commands
  dnsix-dmdp                   Provide DMDP service for DNSIX
  dnsix-nat                    Provide DNSIX service for audit trails
  downward-compatible-config   Generate a configuration compatible with
                               older software

 —More—
```

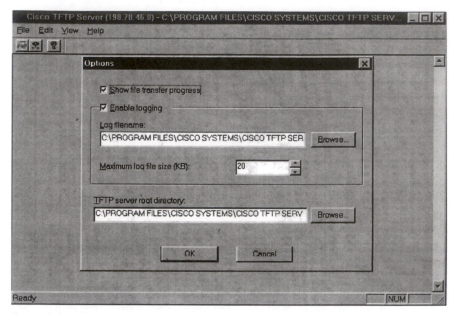

Figure 2-11 Cisco tftp server software allows you to enable or disable logging as well as specify a server root directory.

Examination of the router's response to the entry of the `configure` command shows you can configure the device from a terminal, memory, or via the network. Since a router has neither a hard nor a floppy disk, administrators often store configuration files, including access lists, on a network. When you store the files on the network, you need to create a configuration file using a word processor or text editor and save the file in ASCII text (.txt) mode. Then use tftp to transfer the file to the router. You must install a tftp server program on your computer and indicate the location where the tftp server's root directory resides. Figure 2-11 illustrates a screen display of Cisco tftp server software running on one of the author's PCs. If your organization has an appropriate account with Cisco Systems, you can download the software from the Cisco Web site.

Table 2-2 summarizes the configuration command entry methods and their operational results. Table 2-2 also summarizes the relationship between the use of different command entry methods and the use of different types of storage for both accessing and storing configuration commands. Cisco changed the format of these commands beginning with Version 10.3 of the router operating system. Both forms of the commands are still accepted by the router in the most current releases, although at

Table 2-2 Configuration Command Entry Methods

Command	Operational Result
Configure terminal	**To configure the router manually from the console.**
Configure memory	**To load a previously created configuration from NVRAM.**
Copy startup-config	
Running-config	
Configure network	**To load a previously created configuration from a network server via tftp.**
Copy tftp running-config	
Write terminal	**Display the current configuration in RAM.**
Show running-config	
Write network	**Share the current configuration in RAM onto a network server via tftp.**
Copy running-config tftp	
Show configuration	**Display the previously saved configuration in NVRAM.**
Show startup-config	
Write erase	**Erase the contents of NVRAM.**
Erase startup-config	
Reload	**Loads the contents of NVRAM into RAM. Occurs automatically on power-on.**

some point the older version of the commands will probably be phased out. The newer versions of the commands are shown in italics.

Configuration Command Categories

Configuration commands can be categorized into four general categories: (1) global, which defines systemwide parameters; (2) interface, which defines WAN or LAN interfaces; (3) line, which defines the characteristics

Figure 2-12 Obtaining online help about router access lists.

```
CISCO4000(config)# access-list ?
  <1-99>        IP standard access list
  <100-199>     IP extended access list
  <1000-1099>   IPX SAP access list
  <1100-1199>   Extended 48-bit MAC address access list
  <200-299>     Protocol type-code access list
  <700-799>     48-bit MAC address access list
  <800-899>     IPX standard access list
  <900-999>     IPX extended access lis
```

of a serial terminal line; and (4) router subcommands, which are used to configure a routing protocol.

GLOBAL CONFIGURATION COMMANDS

Global configuration commands are used to define systemwide parameters, including access lists. Figure 2-10, which shows the use of the configure command, also illustrates a list of global commands used by the authors.

As you have probably surmised by now, help information about a specific command is available by entering the command followed by the question mark (?). Figure 2-12 illustrates the use of ? to obtain information about the access list command.

In Figure 2-12 the online help for access lists is a general review of the number range for different access lists supported by the router. In Chapter 3 and later chapters we will examine access lists in considerable detail. At this point, we will simply note they are numbered and used to enable or disable the flow of packets across a router's interface.

INTERFACE COMMANDS

The second category of router commands is interface commands, which define the characteristics of a LAN or WAN interface and are preceded by an interface command. Figure 2-13 illustrates the use of the interface serial0 command followed by the ? command to display a partial list of interface configuration commands that can be applied to the serial0 interface.

The interface command allows you to assign a network to a particular port as well as configure one or more specific parameters required for the interface. For example, interface ethernet0 informs the router that port 0 is connected to an Ethernet network.

The configuration script command in the lower portion of Figure 2-8 contains several occurrences of the interface command. The interface

Figure 2-13 Use of the `interface serial0` command followed by the `?` command to display a list of interface configuration commands.

```
CISCO4000(config)#interface serial0
CISCO4000(config-if)#?
Interface configuration commands:
  access-expression        Build a bridge boolean access expression
  arp                      Set arp type (arpa, probe, snap) or
                           timeout
  backup                   Modify dial-backup parameters
  bandwidth                Set bandwidth informational parameter
  bridge-group             Transparent bridging interface parameters
  carrier-delay            Specify delay for interface transitions
  cdp                      CDP interface subcommands
  clock                    Configure serial interface clock
  compress                 Set serial interface for compression
  custom-queue-list        Assign a custom queue list to an interface
  dce-terminal-timing-enable Enable DCE terminal timing
  delay                    Specify interface throughput delay
  description              Interface specific description
  dialer                   Dial-on-demand routing (DDR) commands
  dialer-group             Assign interface to dialer-list
  down-when-looped         Force looped serial interface down
  dte-invert-txc           Invert transmit clock
  dxi                      ATM-DXI configuration commands
  encapsulation            Set encapsulation type for an interface
  exit                     Exit from interface configuration mode
  frame-relay              Set frame relay parameters
—More—
```

ethernet0 command shows that an Ethernet connection will be defined as port 0. Since the router used for demonstrating the `setup` command has two serial ports, the commands `interface serial0` and `interface serial 1` define two serial interfaces numbered 0 and 1, respectively. The authors' router also has a token-ring adapter, which provides connectivity to a token-ring network. In the prior example the interface command `interface tokenring0` was used to define the first token-ring interface, interface number 0, on the router.

The most common format of the interface command is

```
interface type number
```

where `type` defines the type of interface to be configured. Table 2-3 lists 10 keywords used to define different types of router interfaces.

LINE COMMANDS

Line commands modify the operation of a serial terminal line. Figure 2-14 illustrates the use of the `line` command followed by the `?` command to display a list of lines that can be configured.

Table 2-3 Keywords That Define the Type of Router Interface

Keyword	Interface Type
async	Port line used as an asynchronous interface
atm	Asynchronous transfer mode interface
bri	Integrated services digital network (ISDN) Basic rate interface (BRI)
ethernet	Ethernet 10-Mbit/s interface
fastethernet	Fast Ethernet 100-Mbit/s interface
fddi	Fiber-distributed data interface
hssi	High-speed serial interface
serial	Serial interface
tokenring	Token-ring interface
vg-anylan	100-Mbit/s VG-AnyLAN port adapter

Figure 2-14 List of the serial terminal lines that can be configured.

```
CISCO4000(config)#line ?
  <0-6>   First Line number
  aux     Auxiliary line
  console Primary terminal line
  vty     Virtual terminal
```

ROUTER COMMANDS

The fourth category of privileged commands is router subcommands, which are used to configure IP routing protocol parameters and follow the use of the router command. The top portion of Figure 2-15 illustrates the use of the router command followed by the ? command to display a list of router subcommands supported by the router currently in use.

You can "drill down" to obtain information about a particular router command by entering that command and then entering the ? command, as illustrated in the lower portion of Figure 2-15.

ABBREVIATING COMMANDS

It is often not necessary to type the entire word for the router to accept a command. Generally, three or four letters of the command are enough for

Figure 2-15 List of router commands and specific information on RIP subcommands.

```
CISCO4000(config)#router ?
  bgp       Border Gateway Protocol (BGP)
  egp       Exterior Gateway Protocol (EGP)
  eigrp     Enhanced Interior Gateway Routing Protocol (EIGRP)
  igrp      Interior Gateway Routing Protocol (IGRP)
  isis      ISO IS-IS
  iso-igrp  IGRP for OSI networks
  mobile    Mobile routes
  ospf      Open Shortest Path First (OSPF)
  rip       Routing Information Protocol (RIP)
  static    Static routes

CISCO4000(config)#router rip
CISCO4000(config-router)#?
Router configuration commands:
  default-metric          Set metric of redistributed routes
  distance                Define an administrative distance
  distribute-list         Filter networks in routing updates
  exit                    Exit from routing protocol configuration mode
  help                    Description of the interactive help system
  maximum-paths           Forward packets over multiple paths
  neighbor                Specify a neighbor router
  network                 Enable routing on an IP network
  no                      Negate or set default values of a command
  offset-list             Add or subtract offset from IGRP or RIP
metrics
  passive-interface       Suppress routing updates on an interface
  redistribute            Redistribute information from another routing
                          protocol
  timers                  Adjust routing timers
  validate-update-source  Perform sanity checks against source address
                          of routing updates
```

the router to discern what command is being requested and perform the desired action. For example, the following command:

```
Router# show interface serial0
```

could be abbreviated as

```
Router# sh int s0
```

which is certainly much easier to type. When in doubt, try abbreviating the command using the first three letters. If the first three letters are not enough for the router to determine the command being requested, an "ambiguous command" error will appear at the router prompt. Then use the router's context-sensitive help by typing the first three letters with a question mark at the end. The router will display all of the commands that match the first three letters. You can then add as many characters as necessary to distinguish the command you want.

Table 2-4 Router Shortcut Commands

Shortcut Command	Operational Effect
\<CTL> + \<P> or UP arrow key	Recall the previous command
\<CTL> + \<A>	Move to the beginning of the line
\<CTL> + \<E>	Move to the end of the line
\<ESC> + \<B>	Move back one word
\<CTL> + \<F>	Move forward one character
\<CTL> + \<B>	Move back one character
\<ESC> + \<F>	Move forward one word
Show history	Show recently used commands

Remember, the ? is your friend. By using the built-in context-sensitive help, even a Cisco novice can determine the correct syntax of a command. Table 2-4 lists a few other shortcuts which can greatly assist an administrator when entering configuration commands.

Now that we have a general understanding of the basic hardware and software components of a router and its EXEC command modes, we'll conclude this chapter by focusing on router security management issues.

Security Management Considerations

Regardless of how a router is used, several key security-related areas must be considered, including establishing passwords to secure access to your router and the development of appropriate access lists to govern the flow of acceptable data through the router.

Password Management

Control of access to your router, access to the use of privileged EXEC commands, and even access to individual lines can be managed through the use of passwords. The commands listed in Table 2-5 will help to accomplish access control.

Figure 2-16 illustrates the use of the `configure` line and password commands to change a previously established password which controls access from the console terminal. The new password contains a numeric

Table 2-5 Security Management Commands

Command	Operational Effect
`line console 0`	Establishes a password on the console terminal.
`line vty 0 4`	Establishes a password for Telnet connections.
`enable-password`	Establishes a password for access to the privileged EXEC mode.
`Enable secret`	Establish an enable secret password using MD5 encryption.
`service password-encryption`	Protects the display of passwords from the use of the `show running-config` command.

Figure 2-16 Changing a previously established password for virtual terminal access so that it consists of alphanumerics.

```
CISCO4000#configure
Configuring from terminal, memory, or network [terminal]?
Enter configuration commands, one per line. End with CNTL/Z.
CISCO4000(config)#line vty 0 4
CISCO4000(config-line)#login
CISCO4000(config-line)#password bad4you
CISCO4000(config-line)#exit
CISCO4000(config)#exit
```

character which is used to separate two conventional alphabetic portions of a password. In general, use of a mixture of alphanumerics in your passwords is highly recommended to minimize the risk of a hacker employing a successful dictionary attack.

Access Lists

Another area of security management involves controlling the flow of packets through the router by configuring one or more access lists and applying those lists to one or more router interfaces. Later chapters will provide the details associated with this important topic.

CHAPTER 3

Basics of
Cisco Access Lists

R eaders of a book are similar to students in a class because they represent a diverse mixture of experience. In order to make this book as practical as possible, as well as to take into consideration the mix of readers' backgrounds and different levels of experience, this chapter provides a foundation on the operation and utilization of Cisco access lists. It begins with the definition of an access list, and gives sufficient information so that readers will understand the operation and utilization of access lists equally well.

This chapter presents an overview of the different types of access lists, their general formats, the use of different keywords within an access list, and an understanding of how access lists are applied to an interface. Thus, the information presented serves both as a tutorial on Cisco access lists and a quick reference for persons already familiar with their use but who may want to refresh themselves on operation and utilization before proceeding to subsequent chapters focused on specific types of access list.

Overview

An *access list* is an ordered set of statements that permits or denies the flow of packets across an interface based on matching criteria of access list parameters and information contained in packets. This definition does not mention anything about security or that an access list can be used to establish a security policy or implement the flow of data based upon certain parameters within a packet.

Purpose

While access lists can perform each of the previously mentioned functions and more, it is important to remember that their primary purpose is to permit or deny the flow of packets, based on criteria already established. Thus, packet filtering criteria will result in an access list that implements a certain type of policy even though it does not normally represent a policy. For example, assume you create an access list to prohibit employees on a LAN connected to the Internet from being able to surf the Web during business hours. Such an access list would incorporate certain parameters which, when applied to a router's interface, enable implementation of this organizational policy.

Application

In terms of router interfaces, an access list must be both created and applied to an interface for it to be in effect. Since the flow of data across an interface is bidirectional, an access list can be applied to a specific direction on an interface, either inbound or outbound. Here the term *inbound* refers to the flow of data toward a router while *outbound* refers to the flow of data in a direction away from a router.

Figure 3-1 shows a router with one serial and two Ethernet ports. In this sample network schematic, which we will reference several times in this

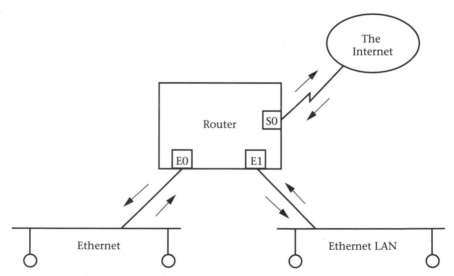

Figure 3-1 Access lists applied to an interface in outbound (arrows point away from the router) and inbound (arrows point toward the router) direction. E0 = Ethernet 0; E1 = Ethernet 1; and S0 = Serial 0 interfaces.

chapter, the serial port provides a connection to the Internet while ports E0 and E1 provide connectivity for two Ethernet LANs.

Note the dual arrows associated with each interface in Figure 3-1. Arrows pointed inbound toward the router indicate the inbound direction on an interface, while arrows pointing away from a router indicate the outbound direction associated with each router interface.

Types of Access Lists

Two types of access lists are supported by Cisco routers—standard and extended. A *standard access list* is limited in functionality because it only allows filtering based upon source address. In comparison, an *extended access list*, as its name implies, extends packet filtering, enabling you to filter packets based upon both source and destination address and upper-layer application data. In this section we will examine both types of access lists, with special attention to *Internet protocol* (IP) access lists since IP is the only protocol supported for transmission on the Internet.

Standard IP Access Lists

The format of a standard IP access list is shown here:

```
access-list[list number][permit|deny][source address][wildcard-mask][log]
```

Note that, in the previous list, the horizontal bar (|) between two items is used as an identifier that indicates the need to select one of the choices on each side of the bar.

Certain items in the standard IP access list require some explanation. First, the term *access-list* requires a hyphen between the two words. Second, the list number is a numeric between 1 and 99 for IP which identifies the access-list statements belonging to a common access list. In addition, any number between 1 and 99 informs the IOS that the access list is associated with the IP protocol. Thus, the list number has a dual function; it defines the protocol that the access list operates on and informs the IOS to treat all access-list statements with the same list number as an entity.

In actuality, Cisco supports a reference to protocols in an access list both by name and by number. Table 3-1 contains a list of protocols supported by name and number. Because the primary focus of this book is upon IP-related access lists, a majority of our coverage of access lists will be oriented toward those with list number ranges 1 to 99 and 100 to 199.

KEYWORDS

Use of the keyword `permit` or the keyword `deny` is what specifies whether or not packets that match an access-list entry are allowed to flow through

Table 3-1 Protocols with Access Lists Specified by Names and Numbers

Protocols with Access List Specified by Name	
Apollo Domain	
IP	
IPX	
ISO CLNS	
NetBIOS IPX	
Source-routing bridging NetBIOS	
Protocols with Access List Specified by Numbers	
IP	1–99
Extended IP	100–199
Ethernet type code	200–299
Ethernet address	700–799
Transparent bridging (protocol type)	200–299
Transparent bridging (vendor code)	700–799
Extended transparent bridging	1100–1199
DECnet and extended DECnet	300–399
XNS	400–499
Extended XNS	500–599
AppleTalk	600–699
Source-route bridging (protocol type)	200–299
Source-route bridging (vendor code)	700–799
IPX	800–899
Extended IPX	900–999
IPX SAP	1000–1099
IPX SAP SPX	1000–1099
Standard VINES	1–100
Extended VINES	101–200
Simple VINES	201–300

an interface or are filtered. The keyword permit allows packets to flow through the interface, while the keyword deny results in packets matching the specified source address within a standard IP access list being sent to the great bit bucket in the sky.

SOURCE ADDRESS

For a standard IP access list the source address is the IP address of a host or group of hosts specified using dotted decimal notation. In actuality, the specification of a group of hosts is based upon the use of the wildcard-mask. Thus, let's briefly examine the wildcard-mask's composition, and look at several examples associated with specifying a range of IP addresses.

THE WILDCARD-MASK

The wildcard-mask supported by Cisco access lists functions in a reverse manner to a subnet mask. That is, the access-list mask uses a binary 0 to represent a match and a binary 1 to represent a "don't care" condition.

To illustrate the operation of a wildcard-mask, let's assume your organization has the class C network address 198.78.46.0. Assuming you did not employ subnets, when you configure each station on that network you would enter a subnet mask of 255.255.255.0. In this situation a 1 bit represents a match, while a 0 bit represents a "don't care" condition. Thus, if you specify 255 in each of the first three positions of the four-position subnet mask field, the result will be a *transport control protocol/internet protocol* (TCP/IP) protocol stack that matches the network address in each packet and does not care about the host address. Since the Cisco wildcard-mask is the opposite of a subnet mask, the following standard IP access-list statement is for all packets with a source network address of 198.78.46.0:

```
access-list 1 permit 198.78.46.0 0.0.0.255
```

In the preceding access-list statement note that the wildcard-mask of 0.0.0.255 is the compliment of the subnet mask. Thus, another technique to specify an access-list wildcard-mask is to determine the subnet mask and take its inverse.

OTHER KEYWORDS

Although most access-list keywords are only applicable to extended access lists, three are applicable to standard IP access lists and they warrant consideration. Those keywords are host, any, and log. The first two keywords, host and any, are alternative methods for specifying an IP address and host mask as a single entity and are not included in the previously presented access format.

Host

Host signifies an exact match and represents the wildcard-mask of 0.0.0.0. For example, assume you want to permit packets from source address 198.78.46.8. You could code the following access-list statement:

```
access-list 1 permit 198.78.46.8 0.0.0.0
```

Since the keyword host signifies an exact match, the previous access-list statement can be recoded as follows:

```
access-list 1 permit host 198.78.46.8
```

Thus, host is an abbreviation for a wildcard-mask of 0.0.0.0.

Any

In a standard access list the keyword any is used as an abbreviation for a source address and wildcard-mask of 0.0.0.0 255.255.255.255. For example, assume you wish to deny packets from source address 198.78.46.8 and permit packets from all other addresses. The standard access-list statements to accomplish this would be as follows:

```
access-list 1 deny host 198.78.46.8
access-list 1 permit any
```

Note the order of the two statements. Access-list statements are processed in a top-down order. If we reversed the order and placed the permit statement before the deny statement, we would not be able to bar or filter packets from host address 198.78.46.8 because the permit statement would allow all packets. Thus, unlike a classroom where a lack of order may be disruptive, in an access list the order of statements can be dangerous because use of the improper order of statements can create security loopholes in a network or allow users to avoid compliance with organizational policies.

Log

The keyword log is applicable to IOS Version 11.3. When included in an access list, this keyword results in the logging of packets that match permit and deny statements in the access list. Thus, another term for an access list that contains the keyword log is a *logged access list*.

When you apply a logged access list to an interface, the first packet that triggers the access list causes an immediate logging message. Subsequent packets examined over 5-min periods are then displayed on the console or logged to memory, with the manner by which messages are logged controlled by the IOS logging console command.

Logged messages include the access-list number, whether the packet was permitted or denied, the source IP address, and the number of packets matched during 5-min intervals after the first match is displayed. For example, assume the following standard IP access list:

```
access-list 1 permit 198.78.46.0 0.0.0.0 log
```

Now let's assume the preceding access list resulted in 10 packets being matched over a 5-min period. When the first match occurs, the following display would occur:

```
list 1 permit 198.78.46.1 1 packet
```

Then, 5 min later, the following display would occur:

```
list 1 permit 198.78.46.8 9 packets
```

The use of the keyword `log` to effect console logging provides both a testing and alert capability. You can use logging to test the development of different access lists by observing the resulting match of packets as different activities are attempted. When used as an alert facility, you would scan the display to locate repeated attempts to perform an activity an access-list statement was developed to deny. Repeated attempts to perform an activity an access-list statement is configured to deny would more than likely indicate a potential hacker attack.

Extended IP Access Lists

An extended IP access list, as its name implies, extends the ability to filter packets. An extended IP access list allows you to filter packets based upon source and destination address, protocol, source and destination port, and a variety of options that permit comparison of specific bits in certain packet fields. The general format of an extended IP access list is shown here:

```
access-list[list number][permit|deny][protocol|protocol keyword][source
    address source-wildcard][source port][destination
    address][destination-wildcard][destination port][log][options]
```

FIELD OVERVIEW

In this section we will briefly examine each field in an extended IP access list to obtain an overview of the use of each field and some of the options supported by this type of access list.

List Number

Similar to a standard IP access list, the list number identifies an extended IP access list. Numbers 100–199 can be used to define 100 unique extended IP access lists.

Permit/Deny

The use of either `permit` or `deny` specifies whether or not packets that match an access-list statement are allowed to flow through an interface or are filtered. Again, this option provides the same function as in a standard IP access list.

Protocol

The protocol entry defines the protocol to be filtered, such as IP, TCP, UDP, ICMP, and so on. The entry of a protocol is important because of the relationship of protocols within the TCP/IP protocol suite that forms datagrams. That is, an IP header is used to transport ICMP, TCP, UDP, and various routing protocols so that if you specify IP as the protocol to be filtered, all matches against other fields will cause the packet to be permitted or denied regardless of whether the packet represents an application transported by TCP, UDP, or an ICMP message. Thus, if you wish to filter based on a specific protocol, you should specify that protocol. In addition, you should place more specific entries ahead of less specific entries. For example, if you code a statement permitting IP for a specific address, followed by denying TCP for that address, the second statement would never take effect. However, by reversing the order you could bar TCP to the address, while permitting all other protocols to that address.

Source Address and Wildcard-Mask

The source address and wildcard-mask function the same as for a standard IP access list. Thus, you can use the term host, followed by a specific IP address, to specify a specific host; the term any to represent a source address and wildcard-mask of 0.0.0.0 255.255.255.255, or an IP address and wildcard-mask to specify a network range. Remember that the wildcard-mask supported by Cisco access lists functions in a reverse manner to a subnet mask, with a binary 0 used to represent a match and a binary 1 used to represent a "don't care" condition.

When you configure an access list and subsequently use the IOS show command to view the list, it is easy to become confused about your prior entry because when a wildcard-mask bit is set to 1 (don't care) IOS converts the bit in the IP address portion of the access list entry to a binary zero. For example, consider the following series of IOS commands that create an extended IP access list and display the contents of the list:

```
router # config terminal
router (config) # access-list 101 permit IP 198.78.46.20 0.0.0.255 host
   205.131.172.1
router (config) # exit
router # show access-list 101
Extended IP access list 101
permit IP 198.78.46.0 0.0.0.255 host 205.131.175.1
```

In this example, station 20 on network 198.78.46.0 is automatically converted to the network address since the wildcard-mask in the host portion of the class C address was set to all 1s (255).

Although not shown, it is important to note that each access list has an implicit "deny all" built into the bottom of the list, so the previously constructed access list has the following statement internally added to the end of the list.

```
access-list 101 deny 0.0.0.0 255.255.255.255
```

Source Port Number

The source port number can be specified in several ways. It can be specified explicitly, either as a numeric or as a recognized mnemonic. For example, you could use either 80 or http to specify the Web's hypertext transmission protocol. For TCP and UDP you can use the keyword operators < (less than), > (greater than), = (equal), and ≠ (not equal).

Destination Address and Wildcard-Mask

The destination address and wildcard-mask have the same structure as the source address and wildcard-mask. This also means you can use such keywords as any and host to specify any destination address and a specific address without having to specify a mask.

Destination Port Number

The destination port can be specified the same as for a source port. That is, you can specify a number, mnemonic, or use an operator with a number or mnemonic to specify a range. The following examples illustrate the use of operators in access-list statements:

```
access-list 101 permit tcp any host 198.78.46.8 eq smtp
access-list 101 permit tcp any host 198.78.46.3 eq www
```

The first statement permits TCP from any host to the specific host 198.78.46.8 as long as the packet conveys SMTP data. The second statement permits TCP packets from any host to the specific host 198.78.46.3 as long as the destination port is Web traffic. In this example the mnemonic www is the same as http and equals the number 80.

Options

A wide range of options is supported by an extended IP access list. One commonly used option is log, which was described earlier when we discussed standard IP access lists. A second commonly used option is established. This option is only applicable to the TCP protocol and is employed to restrict TCP traffic in one direction as a response to sessions initiated in the opposite direction. To accomplish this, an access list statement with the established option examines each TCP packet to determine if its ACK or RST bit is set. If it is set, the packet is part of a previously established conversation. For example, consider the following extended IP access-list statement:

```
access-list 101 permit tcp any host 198.78.46.8 established
```

This access-list statement allows any TCP packet from any source address to flow to the specific host 198.78.46.8 only if the packet's ACK or RST bit is set. This means that the host 198.78.46.8 must have previously initiated the TCP session. Later we will examine the use of various options, including filtering on the type of service (TOS) and IP precedence fields in an IP datagram.

Keywords

Table 3-2 lists commonly used access-list keywords and a brief description of their use. Keywords, such as any, established, host, precedence, remark,

Table 3-2 Access List Keywords

Keyword	Utilization
any	Used as an abbreviation for an address and wildcard-mask value of 0.0.0.0 255.255.255.255. Applicable to source and destination fields.
established	Filters if ACK or RST bits are set (TCP only).
host	Used as an abbreviation for a wildcard-mask of 0.0.0.0. Applicable to both source and destination.
icmp-type	Used for filtering by ICMP message type. You can also specify the ICMP message code (0–255).
port	Used to define the decimal number or name of a TCP or UDP port.
protocol	Used to define the protocol for filtering. Can include one of the keywords eigrp, gre, icmp, igmp, igrp, ip, ipinip, nos, ospf, tcp, or udp, or an integer between 0 and 255 representing an IP protocol.
precedence/precedence	Used for filtering by the precedence level name or number (0–7).
remark	Used for adding text comments to an access list.
TOS/tos	Used for filtering by service level specified by a number (01–5) or name.

and `tos`, are directly placed in an access list. The other keywords represent fields within an access list where a numeric or mnemonic is substituted for the keyword. Although we will examine the use of each keyword in this book, one deserves special mention at this time since its use facilitates including remarks about entries in an access list. That keyword is `remark`.

Commented IP Access-List Entries

Beginning in Version 12.0, the use of the `remark` keyword applies to both standard and extended IP access lists. The keyword `remark` is placed after the access-list number in a separate access-list statement and is then followed by the comment or remark to be entered. The statement with the remark can be placed before or after the actual `permit` or `deny` statement to be described; however, for legibility be consistent with respect to the location of remarks. The following example illustrates the use of two remarks within a common access list:

```
access-list 101 remark allow traffic to Gil's PC
access-list 101 permit ip any host 198.78.46.8
access-list 101 remark allow only Web traffic to Web server
access list 101 permit tcp any host 198.78.46.12 eq 80
```

Creating and Applying an Access List

You can create an access list directly from the console or with a word processor or text editor, first storing the file in ASCII text. In order to store the ASCII file, the PC on which the file is sorted is the server, requiring the installation of a tftp program on the computer, as discussed earlier. Once that is accomplished, the router acts as a client to retrieve the file.

Since we will initially create relatively small access lists, with a limited number of statements, we will illustrate the entry of statements from the console. However, as access lists become more complex, you will more than likely wish to enter your statements into a file; later in this book we will illustrate the use of tftp.

Three items are required to apply an access list to an interface: (1) access list, (2) an interface to apply the access list to, and (3) a method to define the direction the access list is applied to on the interface. Since we have already discussed standard and extended IP access lists, let's go on to the interface and interface direction the access list is applied on.

Specifying an Interface

The `interface` command is used to specify an interface. For example, to apply an access list to serial port 0, you would first have to define the interface with the following command:

```
interface serial0
```

Similarly, to apply an access list to a router port connected to an Ethernet LAN, you would first define the port with the following command, assuming the port was ethernet0:

```
interface ethernet0
```

Since you can abbreviate many keywords in a command, you could also specify the following command:

```
interface e0
```

Using the IP Access-Group Command

The third step in the three-step process is to define the direction of the interface that the access list is applied to by using the `ip access-group` command whose format is shown here:

```
ip access-group[list number][in|out]
```

The list number identifies the access list, while the keyword `in` or `out` identifies the direction in which the access list will be applied. The direction indicates whether packets are examined as they arrive (in) or leave (out) a router interface.

The following example puts all three steps together.

```
interface serial0
ip access-group 107 in
access-list 107 remark allow traffic to Gil's PC
access-list 107 ip any host 198.78.46.8
access-list 107 remark allow only Web traffic to Web server
access-list 107 tcp any host 198.78.46.12 eq 80
access-list 107 remark block everything else
access-list 107 deny ip any any
```

In this example we first used the `interface` command to define serial port 0. Next, we used the `ip access-group` command to apply the access-list statements we will enter as access-list number 107 in the inbound direction on the serial interface. Finally, we entered six access-list statements that form the access list, with three statements using the keyword `remark` so we can provide comments about subsequent statements in the list. Note that the last statement in the access list is only for a doubting Thomas because it represents the implicit `deny all` setting associated with every access list and does not appear unless needlessly explicitly typed. If you wanted to enter the commands and statements previously described directly from a terminal connected to the router's console port, you would first use the privileged `EXEC` command. An example of such a terminal session is shown here:

```
router # config terminal
Enter configuration commands, one per line. End with CTRL/Z.
interface serial0
router (config-if) # ip access-group 107 in
router (config) # access-list 107 remark allow traffic to Gil's PC
router (config) # access-list 107 ip any host 197.78.46.8
router (config) # access-list 107 remark allow only web traffic to web server
router (config) # access-list 107 tcp any host 197.78.46.12 eq 80
router (config) # access-list 107 remark block everything else
router (config) # access-list 107 deny ip any any
router (config) # exit
router # write terminal
```

Named Access Lists

When using a numbered access list with an enterprise router it is possible, although probably unlikely, to run out of numbers. Another limitation of numbered access lists is the fact that although the number informs you of the type of list, until you read the statements in the list it is difficult, if not impossible, to differentiate between the general function of the lists. Cisco may have recognized this, and introduced named access lists in IOS Version 11.2.

Overview

A named access list allows creation of an access list referred to by a name instead of a number. Named access lists apply to both standard and extended lists. The name used is case-sensitive and must begin with an alphabetic character. Within the name you can use just about any alphanumeric character including [,], {, }, _, -, +, /, \, ., &, $, #, @, !, and ?. Although the authors have successfully used names up to 100 characters in length, from a practical standpoint, 20 to 25 characters should be more than sufficient for creating a meaningful access-list designation.

Standard Named IP Access Lists

The format for a standard named IP access list is shown here:

```
ip access-list standard name
```

where name represents the name you assigned to the standard named IP access list. That statement is followed by one or more permit and deny statements, as illustrated by the following example where packets are allowed from three specific hosts, perhaps in the accounting department, since that is the name assigned to the access list:

```
ip access-list standard accounting
permit 198.78.46.8 0.0.0.0
permit 198.78.46.12 0.0.0.0
permit 198.78.46.30 0.0.0.0
```

Application

Since we have not yet applied the named access list to an interface, we do not know if packets are allowed to or from hosts with the three IP addresses listed in the previous example. To apply a named access list, we need to specify an interface as well as use the ip access-group command to define the direction of packet filtering with respect to the router's interface. The format of the ip access-group command, when used in conjunction with both standard and extended named IP access lists, is shown here:

```
ip access-group name [in|out]
```

where name represents the name of the named access list. Assuming we want to apply the previously created accounting access list to the serial0 interface to filter outbound packets, the statements would be as follows:

```
interface serial0
ip access-group accounting out
ip access-list standard accounting
permit 198.78.46.8 0.0.0.0
permit 198.78.46.12 0.0.0.0
permit 198.78.46.30 0.0.0.0
```

Now that we understand standard named IP access lists, let's look at extended named IP access lists.

Extended Named IP Access Lists

Similar to a standard named IP address list, the extended version uses extended followed by the name of the list to identify the access list. The format of the extended ip access-list command is shown here:

```
ip access-list extended name
```

where name represents the name of the extended IP access list.

Application

An extended named IP access list is applied in the same manner as a standard IP named access list. That is, you must use the interface command to define the interface and an ip access-group command with the name of the access list and the direction of packet filtering to be applied to the list.

The following example illustrates the commands required to apply an extended named IP access list called server-security to a router's E1 port in the outbound direction. In this example we will assume the server is located on the class C network 198.78.46.0 and has the host address of .20. We will also assume that because the Web server supports public access,

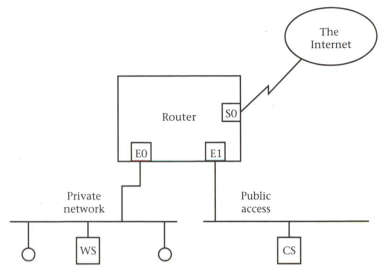

Figure 3-2   Using a router to control access to public and private networks operated by an organization. WS = Web server with address 198.78.46.20; CS = corporate server.

your organization placed the server on a segment by itself, as illustrated in Figure 3-2.

Based on this, the extended IP access list would be applied as follows:

```
interface ethernet1
ip access-group server-security out
ip access-list extended server-security
ip permit tcp any host 198.78.46.20 eq 80
```

In this example we used an extended named IP access list to restrict packets flowing out of the Ethernet 1 port to those transporting Web traffic to the host whose address is 198.78.46.20. Note that we did not apply the access list to the serial interface because if we did, it would, in effect, bar all Internet traffic flowing into the router other than Web traffic to the specified server IP address. Also note that the direction the access list was applied to is out, as filtering is required to occur on packets flowing out of the router onto the 198.78.46.0 network. Finally, note that both standard named IP access lists and extended named IP access lists follow the same construction rules as numbered access lists, with the numbers replaced by the name of the list in both the access list and ip access-group commands.

Editing

Until now we concentrated on the format and construction of named access lists and briefly mentioned a few reasons for the use of this type of access list. However, when you edit a named access list, there is another advantage. That advantage is specific entries in the access list can be deleted. In comparison, you cannot delete specific entries in a numbered access list. Although you can add entries to the bottom of a numbered access list, if you need to revise one or more entries, you must first create a new list, delete the existing list, and then apply the new list. This action is alleviated when working with a named access list since you can simply enter the no version of an access list statement to remove the statement from the list. However, named access lists are similar to numbered access lists in that neither supports the selective addition of statements. To add statements to a named access list, you must delete an existing list and reapply a new or modified list with appropriate entries.

The following console operation illustrates the ability to selectively remove statements from a named access list in which the show command is first used to display the named extended IP access list called server-security. Note that after we listed the extended IP access list, we used the configure terminal command to define the named access list to modify, and then entered the no version of the command to remove it from the access list.

```
router # show access-list server-security
Extended IP access-list server-security
permit tcp any host 198.78.46.20 eq 80
permit icmp any host 198.78.46.20 echo-reply
router # configure terminal
router (config) * ip access-list extended server-security
router (config-int) # no permit icmp any host 198.78.46.20 echo-reply
router (config-int) # exit
router (config) # exit
router # show access-list server-security
Extended IP access-list server-security
permit icmp any host 198.78.46.20 eq 80
```

In the preceding listing, note that we used the no version of the second permit statement to remove it from the access list named server-security. The removed statement, permit icmp any host 198.78.46.20 echo-reply, was placed in the list to enable responses to pings from the server to flow back to the server. *Internet control message protocol* (ICMP) allows specification of an ICMP message type either by numeric or by mnemonic. Table 3-3 provides a summary of ICMP message type codes and the corresponding name of the message.

Many organizations block pings at the router because unsophisticated hackers often use computer laboratories on a Friday evening and initiate pings with the program's continuous option to attack a target. To block such hacker attempts you can use a deny statement that specifically prohibits ICMP echo-request messages similar to the following statement:

```
deny icmp any any echo-request
```

or

```
deny icmp any any eq 8
```

Table 3-3   ICMP Type Numbers

Type	Name
0	Echo reply
1	Unassigned
2	Unassigned
3	Destination unreachable
4	Source quench
5	Redirect
6	Alternate host address
7	Unassigned
8	Echo
9	Router advertisement
10	Router selection
11	Time exceeded
12	Parameter problem
13	Timestamp
14	Timestamp reply
15	Information request
16	Information reply
17	Address mask request
18	Address mask reply
19	Reserved (for security)
20-29	Reserved (for robustness experiment)
30	Traceroute
31	Datagram conversion error
32	Mobile host redirect
33	IPv6 where-are-you

(Continued)

Table 3-3 *(Continued)*

Type	Name
34	IPv6 I-am-here
35	Mobile registration request
36	Mobile registration reply
37	Domain name request
38	Domain name reply
39	SKIP
40	Photuris
41-255	Reserved

The first deny statement uses the name of the ICMP message, while the second example shows the message type number. The reason for including a specific deny icmp statement in your access list is because ICMP is transported via IP. Thus, if you wanted to allow IP traffic, but exclude echo-request packets, you would first deny icmp echo requests prior to permitting IP.

Facilitating the Editing Process

Cisco routers support the tftp protocol as a client, enabling you to create configuration files on a PC operating as a tftp server and download applicable files to the router. As indicated earlier, you should save any configuration file you create using a word processor or text editor as ASCII text.

To illustrate the use of tftp to download a configuration into a router, we need a configuration file. Thus, let's assume you created the following short access-list configuration file, which we will appropriately name acl.txt.

```
acl.txt
interface serial0
IP access-group 101 in
access-list 107 permit tcp any host 198.78.46.20 eq 80
access-list 107 permit tcp any any established
access-list 107 permit icmp any any echo-reply
```

The first statement in this access list allows Web traffic to the specified host. The second statement permits TCP packets that have RST or ACK bits set, which means the packet is a response to a session initiated on the trusted side of the router. Finally, the third statement permits ICMP echo-reply packets from any host outside the network to flow to any host on our network.

To load the previously created file, let's assume it was stored on the host 198.78.46.12. The communications at the router console would be as follows:

```
router # configure net
Host on network configuration file[host]?host
Address of remote host[255.255.255.255]?198.78.46.12
Name of configuration file[router-config]?acl.txt
Confirm using acl.txt from 198.78.46.12?[confirm]
Loading acl.txt from 198.78.46.12 [via e0]:
[ok - xxx bytes]
router #
```

Rules to Consider

In concluding this chapter we will discuss rules for success. These rules are a mixture of fact and suggestion. The factual portion of a rule is based upon the manner in which access-list processing occurs, while the suggestion is the opinion of the authors, based on the processing of access lists.

Top-Down Processing

Access-list entries are evaluated from the top down sequentially, commencing with the first entry in the list. This means you must carefully consider the order in which you place statements in an access list.

Adding Entries

New entries are added to the bottom of an access list, which means it may not be possible to change the functionality of an existing access list, requiring you to create a new list, delete the existing list, and apply the new list to an interface.

Standard List Filtering

Standard IP access lists are limited to filtering on source address so you may need to use an extended IP access list to satisfy specific organizational requirements.

Access-List Placement

Consider placing extended access lists as close as possible to the source being filtered so that you can create filters that do not adversely affect the data flow on other interfaces. Also, consider placing standard access lists as close as possible to the destination. Since a standard access list only uses source addresses, placing the list too close to the source can block the flow of packets to other ports.

Statement Placement

Since IP includes ICMP, TCP, and UDP, you should place more specific entries in an access list before less specific entries to ensure that one statement ahead of another does not negate the effect of a statement appearing later in the list.

List Application

Apply an access list via an `access-group` command. Remember, until the access list is applied to an interface, no filtering will occur.

Filtering Direction

The filtering direction defines whether inbound or outbound packets are examined. Always double-check the filtering direction because it defines which packets are examined.

Router-Generated Packets

Packets generated by a router, such as routing table updates, are not subject to being operated on by an outbound access list. Thus, you can only control router table updates and other router-generated packets via inbound access lists.

CHAPTER 4

Dynamic
Access Lists

This chapter focuses on dynamic access lists, the first kind of enhanced access list we examine. Dynamic access lists are exactly what you would think: access lists that create dynamic entries. Traditional standard and extended access lists cannot create dynamic access-list entries. Once an entry is placed in a traditional access list, it remains there until you delete it manually. With dynamic access lists, you can create specific, temporary openings in an access list in response to a user authentication procedure.

A user opens a telnet session to the router to authenticate him- or herself, normally by providing a userid and password. It is also possible to configure the router to request only a password, but this is not recommended. Once the user is authenticated, the router closes the telnet session and places a dynamic entry in an access list that permits packets with a source IP address of the authenticating user's workstation. This allows you to configure an access list at a security perimeter that would only allow inbound packets from a workstation after the user on that workstation has completed the user authentication phase.

The benefits of this feature are obvious. With traditional access lists, if users on the untrusted side of a router needed access to internal resources, it would be necessary to open up permanent holes in the access list to allow packets from those users' workstations to enter the trusted network. Permanent holes in an access list create the opportunity for an attacker to send packets through your security perimeter and reach the inside network. This problem can be mitigated to a certain degree by only allowing inbound access to certain trusted source IP addresses. However, suppose the users don't have static IP addresses? This would be the case, for example, if the users were dialed up to an *Internet service provider* (ISP). Typically, home users get a different IP address every time they dial their ISP, so it is exceedingly difficult to create access-list entries that permit packets from these users without simultaneously creating large holes in your security perimeter that could be exploited by an attacker. The use of dynamic access lists in this situation, provides a significantly higher degree of security than traditional IP access lists.

> **NOTE**
> Even if you could limit the entries in a traditional extended access list to trusted source IP addresses, these entries could still be exploited by an attacker using IP spoofing. IP spoofing is the procedure whereby an attacker changes the source IP address of packets sent to an IP address believed trusted by the network the attacker is attempting to breach. This danger is always present. It is nearly impossible to determine if the packets which arrive at your security perimeter are from the *real* host. Dynamic access lists only mitigate this problem by creating openings that are very temporary, lowering the probability that an attacker can determine the trusted source IP addresses in time to exploit the openings. We will see later that you can use IPSec to establish the identity of devices sending packets to your network.

Overview

We stated earlier that dynamic access lists are a new type of access list. This is true, but the syntax of dynamic access lists is very similar to the format of traditional access lists, which were covered in earlier chapters. The syntax of a dynamic access-list entry is shown here:

```
access-list <access-list number> dynamic <name> [timeout n]
  [permit|deny] <protocol> any <destination IP> <destination mask>
```

The first entry `<access-list number>` follows the same format as a traditional extended access list and is a number between 100 and 199. The second parameter, `<name>`, is an alphanumeric string that designates the name of the dynamic access list. The `[timeout]` parameter is optional. If specified, it designates an absolute time-out for dynamic entries. The `<protocol>` parameter can be any traditional TCP/IP protocol such as IP, TCP, UDP, ICMP, etc. The source IP address is always replaced by the IP address of the authenticating host, so you should use the keyword `any` for the source IP address of your dynamic entries. The destination IP and mask are the same format used with traditional extended access lists. It is safest to specify a single subnet for the destination IP address, if possible, or even to a specific host. Since you cannot specify more than one dynamic access-list entry per access list, it is typical to specify IP or TCP as the protocol.

NOTE

In actuality, you can specify more than one entry, but additional dynamic entries do not create additional dynamic openings, so specifying multiple dynamic entries is meaningless. Interested readers are encouraged to experiment to see what happens when you place multiple dynamic entries in an access list. The router will accept the commands, but if you examine the results of show access-list, you will see interesting results, as indicated by the following example.

```
access-list 100 permit tcp any host 160.50.1.1 eq telnet
access-list 100 dynamic test permit tcp any any
access-list 100 dynamic test permit udp any any
!
!
Router# show access-list
Extended IP access list 100
   permit tcp any host 160.50.1.1 eq telnet (332 matches)
   Dynamic test permit tcp any any
    permit tcp host 10.1.1.50 any idle-time 5 min.
   Dynamic test permit udp any any
    permit tcp host 10.1.1.50 any idle-time 5 min.
```

Pay close attention to the entries in bold. The dynamic access-list entry is part of a traditional extended access list. The dynamic access-list entry is added at the desired place in your access list, the remaining traditional access-list entries are specified, and then the access list is applied to an interface. The dynamic access-list entry will appear near the beginning of the access list, typically after any antispoofing entries. You will also need to at least allow incoming telnet to the router for the user authentication procedure. If you do not allow incoming telnet connections, users will not be able to create dynamic entries in your access list. It is not necessary to create the telnet entry prior to the dynamic entry. As long as you explicitly allow inbound telnet connections to the router, the dynamic entries will be created as needed.

In addition to creating a dynamic access-list entry, one additional step is needed to allow creation of dynamic entries. The autocommand parameter must be used beneath the vty lines as indicated here:

```
Line vty 0 2
   login local
   autocommand access-enable host timeout 5
```

Notice the use of the `host` parameter when using `autocommand`. Without the `host` parameter, the dynamic entries would not substitute the source IP address of the authenticating host in the dynamic entries, which would allow any host through the dynamic entries, thus eliminating the purpose for using dynamic access lists in the first place. It is very important that you not forget the `host` parameter when configuring the `autocommand` entry.

The time-out value is optional and specifies an idle time-out. It is recommended that either the absolute or idle timer value be configured, otherwise the dynamic entries will not be removed until the router is rebooted. If both the absolute and idle timers are used, the idle timer should be less than the absolute timer.

One additional point worth noting is that if additional steps are not taken, all incoming telnet sessions will be treated by the router as an attempt to open a dynamic access-list entry. Since the telnet session is closed immediately after authentication, this would prevent administrators from managing their routers via telnet. The way around this is to specify the `rotary 1` command beneath some of the vty ports. The `rotary 1` command enables normal telnet access to the router on port 3001. An administrator needs to specify the use of port 3001 when attempting to access the router via a telnet session by specifying the port number immediately after the destination IP address:

```
telnet 160.100.1.1 3001
```

The commands to enable this feature are

```
Line vty 3 4
  Login local
  Rotary 1
```

Notice that only vty lines 3 and 4 are specified and that `autocommand` does not appear. Make sure that your vty lines look like this *before* you save your configuration. If your vty lines are not configured properly, you could completely disable the ability to telnet to the router for management purposes. If the router is remote and you don't have remote access via the auxiliary port, you could find yourself on a long trip to visit your router. As a side note, it's always a good idea to test access lists before saving new additions to a configuration. If your access lists do not perform as expected and you accidentally lock yourself out of the router, a simple reboot is all that is necessary.

Here is a complete sample configuration for reference; only relevant parts of the configuration are shown. The remaining sections of this chapter will show several additional examples of dynamic access-list use.

```
Username test password cisco
!
interface serial0
  remark description to the Internet
  ip address 160.50.1.1 255.255.255.0
  ip access-group 100 in
!
access-list 100 permit tcp any host 160.50.1.1 eq telnet
access-list 100 dynamic test 10 permit ip any any
!
line vty 0 2
  login local
  autocommand access-enable host timeout 5
line vty 3 4
  login local
  rotary 1
```

Notice that the username `test` was created in the router configuration and referenced in the second access-list command. You could specify only the password on the vty lines and not use a username, but this makes it very easy for an intruder to run a password-guessing program against your router, trying successive passwords from a dictionary or password list. Unless you have chosen an exceptionally good password, the chances are high that an attacker would ultimately obtain the correct password. Use of only a password also makes it impossible to track individual user actions, so you would not even know if an attacker had breached your security perimeter because you could not track individual user's actions. Using only a password for authentication is not recommended and we will not show any such examples in this book.

Usage Guidelines

Dynamic access lists are a significant enhancement to IP extended access lists, but this increased functionality also presents additional security concerns. Although dynamic access lists allow restriction of incoming access, based on an external user's ability to provide a userid and password, this information is passed from the user's workstation to the router in cleartext. This means that if anyone were to intercept the packets in transition from the user's workstation to the router by using a packet-sniffing program, he or she could read the username and password combination and duplicate it later to obtain access to your internal resources. This is, obviously, a potentially huge security risk. You would have no way of knowing that a user's authentication information had been captured by an attacker. The attacker could use the captured user information for a long period of time, perhaps indefinitely, before being noticed.

It may seem unlikely that this could happen, however it is very common for an ISP server to be compromised by an attacker and for that attacker to place a packet-sniffing program on the compromised machine. The attacker will then collect a large number of packets and search for keywords such as userid and password. This technique was employed by Kevin Mitnick, perhaps the world's most infamous hacker. The bottom line is that although there is an authentication process for external users to gain access, you should be very careful when deploying dynamic access lists. Here are a few tips to follow when configuring dynamic access lists:

- Do not assign the same name to a dynamic access list that was used with another access list (for example, a named access list).

- Define, at least, the idle time-out or the absolute time-out. If both are defined, the idle time-out should be less than the absolute time-out.

- Limit the dynamic access-list entries, if possible, to particular protocols and particular destination IP addresses.

- Change user passwords frequently. A maximum lifetime of 30 days is recommended; a shorter period is better if your environment permits it.

- Deploy dynamic access lists in conjunction with time-based access lists to limit the periods when users are allowed to create dynamic entries and alert you if someone has captured userid and password information. (For example, repeated attempted logins for a certain user during unauthorized access hours. Only authorized users would be aware of the hours when access is permitted.)

- Deploy logging to the router's buffer or, preferably, to a separate syslog server. Review these logs at least weekly for suspicious activity. Suspicious activity will vary, so you'll have to establish a baseline for what the so-called normal network activity is for your particular site.

Now that we understand dynamic access lists and their capabilities, we will provide several examples.

Dynamic Access-List Application: Example 1

Overview

Assume your organization has a router which connects two Ethernet segments to the Internet, as illustrated in Figure 4-1. The router's connection to the Internet is via serial port 0, while the Ethernet segments are connected via router ports E0 and E1, respectively. Assume you want to allow external users to access the server using IP address 198.78.46.12 on any IP protocol and permit users on the 205.131.175.0 network to access the Internet for Web browsing (http) and FTP.

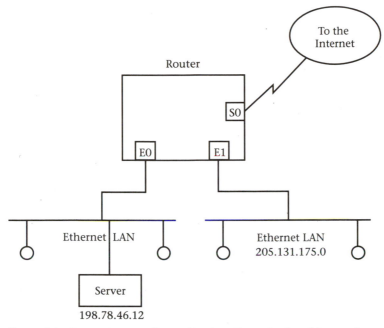

Figure 4-1 Dynamic access-list application: Examples 1 and 2.

Solution

```
Username test password cisco
!
interface serial 0
  ip address 175.10.1.1 255.255.255.0
  ip access-group 100 in
!
access-list 100 permit tcp any host 175.10.1.1 eq telnet
access-list 100 permit udp any eq 53 205.131.175.0 0.0.0.255 gt 1023
access-list 100 permit tcp any eq www 205.131.175.0 0.0.0.255 gt 1023
  established
access-list 100 permit tcp any eq 21 205.131.175.0 0.0.0.255 gt 1023
  established
access-list 100 permit tcp any eq 20 205.131.175.0 0.0.0.255 gt 1023
access-list 100 dynamic test timeout 180 permit ip any host 198.78.46.12
  log
!
logging buffered 64000
!
line vty 0 2
  login local
  autocommand access-enable host timeout 10
line vty 3 4
  login local
  rotary 1
```

Explanation

First, notice that the access list has been applied to the serial port. It is good practice to apply an extended access list as close as possible to the source being filtered. In this case, we are filtering hosts on the Internet, so the serial port is the closest port on the router to the hosts being filtered. The access list is applied *in*, since the packets from the Internet to our serial interface will be inbound from the router's perspective. If we had applied the access list *out*, we would be filtering packets as they left the serial interface toward the Internet, which is not what we wanted. Also, we have created a username "test" which will be used to access the router. In practice, you would create username and password combinations for each user accessing the router. Now, let's examine each of the access-list entries.

The first entry permits incoming packets from any source IP address to host 175.10.1.1 if the destination port is telnet (23). This allows inbound telnet connections to the router's serial interface. We could have allowed incoming telnet connections to other IP addresses on the router, but it is good practice to only allow incoming access to the router's serial interface. The second entry allows incoming packets from any source IP address if the source port is *domain name system* (DNS) (UDP 53) and the destination is on the 205.131.175.0/24 network and the destination port is greater than 1023. This allows DNS replies to hosts on our 205.131.175.0/24 network. All valid DNS requests should be originated from a source port of 1024 or higher, so that all valid DNS replies are sent to a destination port of 1024 or higher. If we did not specify that the destination port is greater than 1023, an attacker could send UDP packets from source port 53 and attempt a denial-of-service (DoS) attack against internal servers. The vast majority of server ports are in the reserved range below 1024, so by blocking packets with a destination port lower than 1024, we close a potential security hole.

The third and fourth entries permit incoming packets from any source IP address if the source port is WWW (TCP 80) or FTP (TCP 21), the destination is on the 205.131.175.0/24 network, the destination port is greater than 1023, and the ACK or RST bit is set in the TCP header. These entries allow return packets that are part of a WWW or FTP conversation initiated by our internal hosts. The reason for specifying the source and destination ports is the same as for the second entry. The use of `established` means that only packets with the acknowledgment (ACK) bit or the reset (RST) bit set will be matched and allowed by this entry. Only packets which are part of an established TCP conversation should have these bits set, which gives an added layer of security to the access list. Note that it is very easy for an attacker to manually set these bits in inbound packets, so this check is by no means foolproof. However, if our internal hosts implement their

TCP/IP stacks correctly, they should ignore inbound packets with an ACK or RST bit set that is not part of a legitimate TCP conversation on that host, which is why the established keyword is important. Note that this check is not possible with UDP packets, which explains why it was not present in access-list entry number 2.

The fifth entry allows incoming packets from any host from source port 20 to any host on network 205.131.175.0/24 if the destination port is greater than 1023 to allow the packets that are part of an FTP data channel connection into the internal hosts. The standard implementation of the FTP protocol requires that the FTP server initiate a connection back to the originating FTP client. The initial packet in the connection would not have the ACK or RST bit set, so we cannot use the established keyword in this entry. There is a version of FTP called *passive mode*, or simply PASV, that does not require the server to initiate a connection to the originating FTP client. In this mode the client initiates a second connection to the FTP server on a port other than 20. The port will be a randomly chosen port greater than 1023. If internal clients use passive mode FTP, we can change our fifth entry to the following:

```
Access-list 100 permit tcp any gt 1023 network 205.131.175.0 gt 1023
   established
```

We have to allow all incoming TCP ports greater than 1023 because we won't know in advance what ports the FTP servers will select (the FTP server data port with passive mode is not 20 as with normal mode FTP). Although we cannot make the entry as specific as we might like, established keywords make this entry a little more secure than allowing sessions to be initiated into an internal network.

Our sixth and final entry is the dynamic access-list entry, which permits access from IP packets from authenticated hosts to server 198.78.46.12. We have defined an absolute time-out of 3 h (180 min) and we are logging these entries (we have also enabled logging to the router's buffer). By logging the packets that match our dynamic entries, we can keep track of our users' activity and establish a normal baseline. We will then be in a position to notice unusual activity that might be an attacker at work. We have also determined the dynamic access-list idle timer as 10 min by defining a time-out with the `autocommand` beneath the vty line configuration. It is best to specify both time-out values to minimize the amount of time dynamic entries will be active and minimize the amount of time an attacker will have to exploit dynamic entries.

The idle timer is reset every time a packet matches the dynamic access-list entry. However, the absolute timer is *not* reset. Even if a session is still active, if the absolute time-out is reached, the dynamic entry will be removed and the user will have to go through the authentication process again. If they have active sessions through the router, those sessions will be dropped. As a result of this, it is recommended that you configure the absolute time-out to a fairly high value, probably on the order of an hour or more. You should, however, keep the idle time-out value low, around 10 min or perhaps even less. We recommend 30 min as a maximum value for the idle timer.

Dynamic Access-List Application: Example 2

Overview

In Example 2, we continue to use the three-port router from Example 1 (see Figure 4-1). We now assume, though, that we wish to restrict when we allow external users to connect to our server at IP address 198.78.46.12. We will also assume that we wish to allow our internal users on the 205.131.175.0/24 network access to the Internet for additional services other than WWW and FTP. We assume that our users will use their Web browsers to access FTP sites, so we will use passive-mode FTP exclusively. We also assume that we want to block access from E0 to E1, just in case our server at IP address 198.78.46.12 is compromised.

Solution

```
Username test password cisco
!
interface ethernet0
  ip address 198.78.46.1 255.255.255.0
  ip access-group 101 in
!
interface serial0
  ip address 175.10.1.1 255.255.255.0
  ip access-group 100 in
!
access-list 100 permit tcp any host 175.10.1.1 eq telnet
access-list 100 permit udp any eq 53 205.131.175.0 0.0.0.255 gt 1023
access-list 100 permit tcp any 205.131.175.0 0.0.0.255 gt 1023
  established
access-list 100 dynamic test timeout 180 permit ip any host 198.78.46.12
  time-range my-time log
!
access-list 101 deny ip any 205.131.175.0 0.0.0.255
access-list 101 permit tcp any any established
!
time-range my-time
  periodic weekdays 8:00 to 18:00
!
logging buffered 64000
!
line vty 0 2
  login local
  autocommand access-enable host timeout 10
line vty 3 4
  login local
  rotary 1
```

Explanation

In this example, two access lists are applied on separate interfaces; we will examine access list 100 first. The first entry in access list 100 is the same as in Example 1; it is needed to allow inbound telnet to the router. The second entry is also the same as in Example 1, and is used to allow inbound DNS replies. The third entry is a variation of the entries we used in Example 1, and uses the established keyword. In this instance, we are not attempting to match on a particular source TCP port; we are only matching the destination network and port and checking for the presence of the ACK or RST bit.

The fourth entry is our dynamic access-list entry, and is very similar to that in Example 1, with one major difference; it specifies a particular time period when this entry will be available. Time ranges will be covered in Chapter 5, so the syntax may be unfamiliar right now, but the example is straightforward. There is a time range called my-time that specifies weekdays (that is, Monday through Friday) from 8:00 a.m. to 6:00 p.m. (18:00). The dynamic entries that are created are valid only during that time. Even if a user successfully completes the authentication procedure, if the time is not within the specified range, for example, if it is a Saturday, access will be denied. A time range is demonstrated here to show how different access-list features can be combined to create powerful and secure access lists.

Dynamic Access-List Application: Example 3

Overview

In this example (Figure 4-2), we continue to use our three-port router, but now we have two servers on interface E0. We assume that we need to allow inbound access from external users to our two servers for telnet and FTP access. We also want our internal users on segment E1 to be able to access resources on the Internet and are unsure what applications they will be using, but we know they will use at least WWW and FTP.

Solution

```
Username test password cisco
!
interface ethernet0
  ip address 198.78.46.1 255.255.255.0
  ip access-group 101 in
!
interface serial0
  ip address 175.10.1.1 255.255.255.0
  ip access-group 100 in
!
access-list 100 permit tcp any host 175.10.1.1 eq telnet
access-list 100 permit udp any eq 53 205.131.175.0 0.0.0.255 gt 1023
```

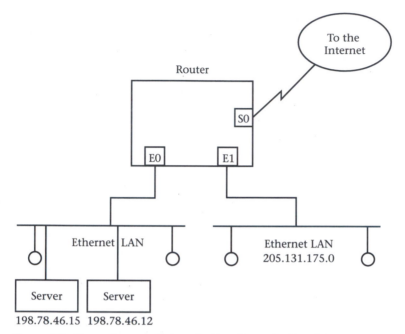

Figure 4-2 Dynamic access-list application: Examples 3 and 4.

```
access-list 100 permit tcp any 205.131.175.0 0.0.0.255 gt 1023
  established
access-list 100 dynamic test timeout 180 permit tcp any 198.78.46.0
  0.0.0.255 log
!
access-list 101 deny ip any 205.131.175.0 0.0.0.255
access-list 101 permit tcp any any established
access-list 101 permit tcp any eq 20 any gt 1023
!
logging buffered 64000
!
line vty 0 2
  login local
  autocommand access-enable host timeout 10
line vty 3 4
  login local
  rotary 1
```

Explanation

In this example, as in Example 2, we use two access lists. Again, the second access list prevents access from the servers on E0 to the users on E1. This is an added security feature in case the servers on interface E0 were compromised; they could not be used to further attack our internal resources on E1. The first access list, 100, is very similar to that in

Example 2, with one modification. The fourth entry, our dynamic entry, has been changed to allow inbound packets from authenticated workstations access to the entire 198.78.46.0/24 subnet to accommodate the introduction of the new server on that subnet. We stated that we only needed inbound WWW and FTP to these servers, so we are allowing TCP only instead of all IP. Since we can only create a single dynamic entry, this is as specific as we can make our dynamic entry and still have the desired functionality.

The second access list, 101, is also very similar to that in Example 2, but a third entry has been added. Since outside users needed FTP access to these servers, we need to allow the servers to initiate the FTP data connection from port 20 to the external users' workstations on a port greater than 1023. If we knew that the external users were always going to use passive-mode FTP, we would not need this entry. We have added it here since we are unsure if external users are using passive-mode or standard-mode FTP.

Dynamic Access-List Application: Example 4

Overview

In our fourth example, we show the use of dynamic access lists by authenticating to a TACACS server instead of a local user database. We return to our standard three-port router with a single server on interface E0 (see Figure 4-2). We wish to allow inbound WWW only to our server. We also want to allow our internal users to surf the Web and utilize FTP servers and nothing else. We also want to allow our internal users to reach our internal server for WWW services.

Solution

```
Aaa new-model
Aaa authentication login default tacacs+ local
Aaa authorization exec tacacs+
!
Username test password cisco
!
interface ethernet0
  ip address 198.78.46.1 255.255.255.0
  ip access-group 101 in
!
interface serial0
  ip address 175.10.1.1 255.255.255.0
  ip access-group 100 in
!
access-list 100 permit tcp any host 175.10.1.1 eq telnet
access-list 100 permit udp any eq 53 205.131.175.0 0.0.0.255 gt 1023
access-list 100 permit tcp any eq www 205.131.175.0 0.0.0.255 gt 1023
  established
```

```
access-list 100 permit tcp any eq 21 205.131.175.0 0.0.0.255 gt 1023
   established
access-list 100 dynamic test timeout 180 permit tcp any host
198.78.46.12 eq www log
!
access-list 101 permit tcp 198.78.46.12 eq www any established
!
tacacs-server host 205.131.175.100
tacacs-server key mykey
!
logging buffered 64000
!
line vty 0 2
   login authentication default
line vty 3 4
   login local
   rotary 1
```

Explanation

The first new commands are those that begin with aaa. The first aaa command enables authentication, authorization, and accounting, hence the term *aaa*. The second aaa command creates the authentication list default and specifies that the TACACS+ server should be consulted for authentication. If the TACACS+ server is unavailable, we will consult the local user database. Note that we only consult the local database if the TACACS+ server cannot be reached. The third aaa command enables checking of the TACACS+ server for EXEC commands. Related to these commands is the login command beneath the vty ports. We reference the authentication list default again beneath the vty ports instead of using the auto-command directly. The TACACS+ server has to be configured correctly for this process to work. Configuring a TACACS+ server is beyond the scope of this book. Consult the Cisco documentation for assistance in configuring your TACACS+ server.

We see that access list 100 contains some familiar entries. The first entry permits telnet sessions to be opened to the router. The second entry permits DNS replies. The third and fourth entries allow return packets for WWW and FTP sessions initiated from our internal users on segment E1, assuming the use of passive-mode FTP. The fifth entry is the dynamic access-list entry and allows only inbound WWW (TCP port 80) to our server at IP address 198.78.46.12.

We have again configured access list 101 on the E0 port to protect internal users in the event the server is compromised. In this example only return connections from our server if the source port is WWW are allowed. This will permit replies to both external and internal users, but prevent connections from being initiated from the server in case it is compromised. This not only protects our internal network on interface E1 but also prevents our server from being used to compromise other sites on the Internet. This is called being a *good Internet citizen* and is highly encouraged.

If you can construct your security perimeter in such a way that it protects not only your internal resources, but also prevents your site from being used by attackers to compromise other sites, it is always advisable to do so. The small extra bit of configuration is always worth it and adds very little overhead to your router. If everyone followed this policy, far fewer attacks would occur. Most attacks come not from the attacker's home machine but from a machine on another victim's network. Attackers are very reluctant to launch sustained attacks from their home machines for fear of being discovered and arrested. So remember, protect yourself and protect others, and to paraphrase a line from Hill Street Blues, let's be careful out there!

CHAPTER 5

Time-Based
Access Lists

This chapter focuses on a relatively new capability of Cisco access lists, the ability to implement access lists based upon a time range which specifies the time of day, day of week, or both. As mentioned in Chapter 1, before IOS Version 12.0 no easy method existed to alter an access list based on the time and day. While you could create multiple access lists and stay late on a Friday evening to remove an existing list and apply an alternate list, that was not an appealing process. Similarly, arriving at the office early every Monday morning to reverse the process was also unappealing. Cisco introduced time-based access lists in IOS Version 12.0 to alleviate this problem. Unlike some other features, time-based access lists are supported on all Cisco IOS platforms.

We first obtain an overview of the rationale of the topic of this chapter and examine several configuration examples. Once this is accomplished, we present a series of examples for construction of time-based access lists.

Rationale

The primary rationale for the use of time-based access lists is the ability to control access to network resources based upon the time of day, day of week, or a combination of the two. Time-based access lists allow network administrators additional control over the flow of data into and out of their networks. The network administrator can define security policies for weekend and after-hours periods that might differ from those during the workday period. In addition, this implementation of data-flow filtering based on time allows the network administrator to be more responsive to organizational policies and procedures. For example, some organizations may wish to allow all, or certain, employees to surf the Web after normal business hours. Time-based access lists make it very easy to satisfy such organizational requirements. Another example of time-based access lists is altering the flow of data via the *type of service* (TOS) field value during different times. You can also use time-based access lists to control logging messages, so that traffic logging occurs at certain times of the day, and allowing or denying data flow to or from different applications during different periods of time. Thus, time-based access lists provide a mechanism for altering filtering of packets to satisfy a variety of organizational requirements.

Overview

Time-based access lists are applicable to both numbered and named access lists. The basic procedure for implementing a time-based access list is a relatively simple two-step procedure. First, you define a time range. Once that is accomplished, you reference the time range in your access list through the keyword `time-range`.

Defining a Time Range

The procedure for defining a time range is also a two-step procedure. In this procedure you first use the `time-range` command to identify the time range appropriately. Next, you use an `absolute` or one or more `periodic` statements to define when the named time range is to occur. The format associated with each IOS command is shown here:

```
time-range time-range-name
absolute [start time date][end time date]
periodic days-of-the week hh:mm to [days-of-the-week]hh:mm
```

where:

`time-range-name`	the name to identify the time range for reference in an access list
`time`	the time entered with respect to a 24-h clock followed by minutes (hh:mm)
`date`	the date expressed in the format day/month/year
`days-of-the-week`	the day or days the time range is to be in effect; arguments can be a single day (that is, Monday), multiple days (Monday, Friday), or daily, weekdays, or weekend

To better understand the time-range command and the use of different variables in the absolute and periodic statements, let's examine the command and each statement in detail.

The time-range command

The time-range command is used to associate a name to the time range created using one absolute or one or more periodic statements. If you wanted to name your time range allow-http, you would use the time-range command as follows:

```
time-range allow-http
```

Once you use the time-range command and assign a name to identify the range, you would then use an absolute and/or periodic statement to define the time range associated with the name. Now, let's focus on each of those statements.

The absolute Statement

The absolute statement specifies an absolute time when the time range is in effect. As previously noted, the keyword absolute is followed by the keyword start and the keyword end. Both start and end, in turn, are followed by the starting and ending time when you want associated permit or deny statements in the access list to go into effect. Remember that time is specified in a 24-h format, while the date is expressed in the format day/month/year. It is easy to enter the incorrect date since North Americans are used to the format month/day/year. Thus, it is important to enter the date in the correct format. Also, if you elect to eliminate either a start or end date, the permit or deny statement associated with the time-based access list will either go into effect immediately if no start date is specified or will result in an indefinite time period if no end date is specified. These situations may not be as intended, which illustrates the importance of carefully considering the format of each statement and the manner in which variables are entered.

To illustrate the use of the absolute command, let's assume you only want to allow HTTP traffic from 5:00 p.m. until 7:00 a.m. You would assign that time range with the following absolute statement:

```
absolute start 17:00 end 07:00
```

In this example the time range is from 5:00 p.m. to 7:00 a.m. each day, with no specified termination. Thus, this time range will remain in effect until it is manually removed.

Now let's assume that, instead of the time range being in effect until the statement is manually altered, you are planning to go on vacation and want to automatically remove its effect at 7:00 a.m. on July 19 rather than return to the office to do so. If today is June 1 and you want the statement to go into effect at 5:00 p.m. this evening, the absolute statement would become

```
absolute start 17:00 1 June 2000 end 07:00 19 July 2000
```

Rules

Like any IOS statement, certain rules associated with the use of absolute start and end variables must be obeyed. One is the previously mentioned omission of a start or end keyword and associated time and date. A second is the times and dates specified for starting and stopping the time range. As you might logically expect, the end time and date must be specified as being after the start time and date.

As an additional example, let's assume you want to allow HTTP traffic commencing on June 1, but do not wish to specify a termination for the time range. The following absolute statement illustrates how you would code a time range that begins at 5:00 p.m. on June 1 and continues indefinitely:

```
absolute start 17:00 1 June 2000
```

Now that we understand the absolute statement, let's look at the periodic statement.

The periodic Statement

Although you can only have one absolute statement associated with a time range, you can have multiple periodic statements. In addition, unlike the absolute statement which allows only start and end times and dates, the periodic statement permits the entry of various arguments, ranging from a single day of the week to a combination of days, or the use of the keywords daily, weekdays, and weekend. Table 5-1 lists the possi-

Table 5-1 Possible periodic Statement Days-of-the-Week Arguments

Argument	Meaning
Monday, Tuesday, Wednesday, Thursday, Friday, Saturday, Sunday	A specific day or combination of days
Daily	Monday through Sunday
Weekdays	Monday through Friday
Weekends	Saturday and Sunday

ble arguments that can be entered for the days-of-the-week variable setting in the previous `periodic` statement format.

Examples

Since the proof of the pudding is in the eating, let's examine a few examples of the `periodic` statement. First, let's assume we want to restrict Web access to weekends, from Saturday at 7:00 a.m. until Sunday at 7:00 p.m. Perhaps your organization allows employees to bring in family members on weekends to surf the Web and use a high-speed T1 access line instead of low-speed access via modem dial-up from home. The `periodic` statement required to accomplish this would be as follows:

```
periodic weekend 07:00 to 19:00
```

Note that because the keyword `weekend` denotes Saturday and Sunday, only the starting and ending times have to be specified; IOS is smart enough to associate the beginning time with Saturday and the ending time with Sunday.

As a second example of the `periodic` statement, let's assume you want to specify the time range of 8:00 a.m. to 5:00 p.m. Monday through Friday. Table 5-1 shows the keyword `weekday` is used to reference the period Monday through Friday. Thus, the following periodic statement would be used:

```
periodic weekday 8:00 to 17:00
```

As a third example of the `periodic` statement, let's assume you want to specify the period of time from 7:00 a.m. to 5:00 p.m. each day of the week. In this situation you would use the keyword `daily` in the periodic statement, as shown here:

```
periodic daily 7:00 to 17:00
```

For a fourth example, let's consider a situation where we want the time range to commence at 5:00 p.m. on Saturday but terminate at 7:00 a.m. on Monday morning. Note that this time period does not fall into daily, weekdays, or weekend. Thus, we could use two `periodic` statements to create the required time range. The first `periodic` statement could use the `weekend` keyword to establish the period from 5:00 p.m. on Saturday until midnight on Sunday, while the second `periodic` statement would use Monday as the argument, as indicated here:

```
periodic weekend 17:00 to 24:00
periodic Monday 00:00 to Monday 7:00
```

As an alternative to the use of two `periodic` statements, we could use a single statement, commencing with the argument Saturday and ending with the argument Monday, as indicated here:

```
periodic Saturday 17:00 to Monday 7:00
```

Although you can use a single `periodic` statement as a substitute for multiple statements, this is only possible when there is a contiguous time period. For example, suppose you want to block access to a Web server every weekday from 11:00 p.m. to midnight and on weekends from 7:00 a.m. on Saturday until 8:00 p.m. on Sunday. In this situation you would have to use multiple `periodic` statements.

Usage Guidelines

Now that we understand the `time-range` command and the `absolute` and `periodic` statements, let's consider a few usage guidelines prior to turning to a series of application examples. Since the use of a time-range access list is dependent upon the router's system clock, it is important to ensure that the clock is set properly. You can accomplish this via the use of NTP or the hardware calendar. A second guideline that warrants attention is the use of `absolute` and `periodic` statements within a `time-range` command. When this situation occurs, `periodic` statement values are evaluated only after the absolute start time is reached. In addition, `periodic` statement values are not further evaluated once the absolute statement end time is reached. To illustrate this concept, let's assume you want to specify a time range of weekends from 8:00 a.m. on Saturday until 5:00 p.m. Sunday, from June 1, 2000 until December 31, 2000. To create this time range you would first use an `absolute` statement to define the starting and ending dates. Next, you would use a `periodic` statement to define the weekend period previously mentioned. Thus, your `time-range` command and `absolute` and `periodic` statements would be as follows:

```
time-range allow-http
absolute start 8:00 1 June 2000 end 17:00 31 December 2000
periodic weekends 8:00 to 17:00
```

Now that we understand how to combine `absolute` and `periodic` statements within a time range, let's look at a series of application examples.

Time-Range Application: Example 1

Overview

Assume your organization has a router which connects two Ethernet segments to the Internet, as illustrated in Figure 5-1. As indicated in the diagram, the router's connection to the Internet is via serial port 0, while the Ethernet segments are connected via router ports E0 and E1, respectively. Assume you want to restrict Web surfing from the 198.78.46.0 network to the period 7:00 a.m. Saturday to 5:00 p.m. Sunday from June 1, 2000 through December 31, 2000.

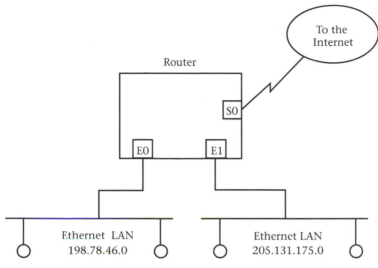

Figure 5-1   Time-range application: Example 1.

Solution

```
interface ethernet0
 ip access-group 101 in
Time-range allow-http
  absolute start 7:00 1 June 2000 end 17:00 31 December 2000
  periodic weekends 7:00 to 17:00
  !
 ip access-list 101 permit tcp any any eq 80 time-range allow-http
```

Explanation

Although we could apply the access list to the serial port, it is good practice to apply the list as close as possible to affected devices. Thus, since we
want to restrict Web surfing from the 198.78.46.0 network, we will use the
Ethernet0 interface for applying the access list.

Since we want to prohibit Web surfing from the 198.78.46.0 network,
we apply the access list created in the inbound direction so that users on
the network have to first transmit packets into the router to surf the Web.
Thus, the `ip access-group` command is shown with the variable *in* in
the command line.

The actual `time-range` command and statements set up the time range
for use in the access list. The `absolute` statement defines the period from
7:00 a.m. on June 1 through 5:00 p.m. on December 31, while the `peri-
odic` statement, which is evaluated within the absolute period, further
limits the time range to weekends from 7:00 a.m. on Saturday through
5:00 p.m. on Sunday.

The last statement in the solution applies the time range named allow-http to the extended IP access list. Note that that access-list statement permits TCP packets whose port number is 80 to flow to any destination when the time-range conditions are satisfied.

Time-Range Application: Example 2

Overview

Let's assume our organization continues to use a three-port router, with two Ethernet segments and one serial port connection to the Internet, as illustrated in Figure 5-2. Let's now assume that we wish to restrict access to a corporate Web server on the 198.78.46.0 network whose host address is 198.78.46.12.

Let's further assume that the server access restrictions include blocking Web access from the Internet on weekends from 7:00 a.m. Saturday until 7:00 a.m. Monday, as well as blocking access to the server from users on the 205.131.175.0 network between the hours of 8:00 a.m. and noon, Monday through Friday. In addition, let's assume that we want the time range to be in effect from June 1 through the end of the year 2000.

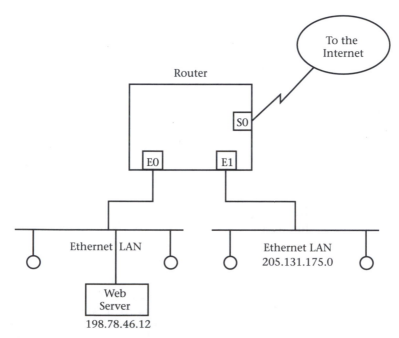

Figure 5-2   Time-range application: Example 2.

Solution

```
interface serial0
ip access-group 101 in
!
time-range block-http1
  absolute start 7:00 1 June 2000 end 1900 31 December 2000
  periodic weekend 7:00 to 24:00
  periodic Monday 0:00 to 7:00
!
interface ethernet1
ip access-group 102 in
time-range block-http2
  absolute start 7:00 1 June 2000 end 19:00 31 December 2000
  periodic weekday 8:00 to 12:00
!
ip access-list 101 deny tcp any host 198.78.46.12 any block-http1
!
ip access-list 102 deny tcp any host 198.78.46.12 eq 80 clock-http2
```

Explanation

In this example we need to establish two different time ranges that correspond to the periods when we wish to block traffic to the Web server from the Internet and from the 205.131.175.0 network. In this solution we labeled one time range as block-http1, while the second time range was labeled block-http2.

The time range for blocking access from the Internet to the Web server was purposely made a bit more complex by extending the blocking period from the weekend through 7:00 a.m. on Monday morning. One absolute statement is required to satisfy this new time range for the period June 1, 2000 through December 31, 2000. As previously noted, you can use either one or two periodic statements to cover a contiguous time period which extends from one argument to another. In this example we elected to use two periodic statements.

The absolute statement defines the overall period for the time range, while the two periodic statements narrow the time range to the period from 7:00 a.m. Saturday through 7:00 a.m. Monday. Since we want to block access during this time range from the Internet to the Web server, we applied the time range named block-http1 to the serial port in the inbound direction via the use of access-list number 101 and the access-group statement with that number. Note that because it is recommended that an access list should be applied as close as possible to the interface where packets originate, we applied access list 101 to the serial interface of the router.

To block users on the 205.131.175.0 network from accessing the Web server during a different time period, we created a second time range which was appropriately labeled block-http2. Since we only want to block Web server access between 8:00 a.m. and noon, Monday through Friday, during the June through December period, we only required one absolute and one periodic statement. Since we want to preclude users on the 205.131.175.0 network from accessing the Web server during the second time period, we applied access list 102 with the time range labeled block-http2 to the Ethernet1 interface in the inbound direction.

Time-Range Application: Example 3
Overview

In this example we assume our organization operates two Web servers, each located on a separate Ethernet segment, as indicated in Figure 5-3. Let's assume that we want to allow access from the Internet to the Web server whose IP address is 198.78.46.12 until 11:00 p.m. on December 31, 2000. During that time period we want to block access from the Internet to the Web server whose IP address is 205.131.175.22. After 11:00 p.m. on New Year's Eve we want to allow access from the Internet to the second Web server. Since we will use the previously discussed time-based access lists, we can party New Year's Eve instead of returning to the office at 11:00 p.m. to modify and reapply existing access lists.

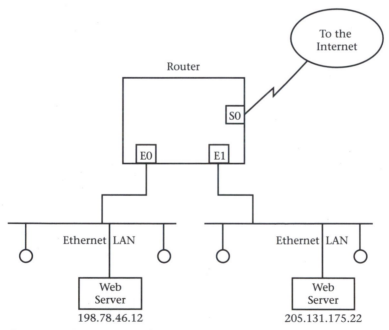

Figure 5-3 Time-range application: Example 3.

Solution

```
interface serial0
 ip access-group internet in
 !
time-range http
 absolute end 23:00 31 December 2000
 !
ip access-list extended internet
 permit tcp any host 198.78.46.12 eq 80 time-range http
 deny tcp any host 205.131.175.22 eq 80 time-range http
 permit tcp any host 205.131.175.22 eq 80
```

Explanation

In the solution to this application, we created an extended named ip access list appropriately labeled *internet*. We once again applied the access list to the port closest to the data source to be filtered, which, in this example, is serial port 0.

Since access to one Web server stops at the point in time when access to a second Web server is to be permitted, we can use one time range. After the time-range command that we named http, we used an absolute statement without the start keyword, which results in the time range starting immediately and lasting until the specified end time.

Within the ip access list named internet we included three statements. The permit statement allows TCP from any host on the Internet to the Web server whose IP address is 198.78.46.12 when the port value is 80 and the time is within the time range. Thus, this statement allows access to the Web server until 11:00 p.m. on New Year's Eve. The second statement in the access list blocks access to the other Web server until the end of the time period. Because the default operation of an access list blocks everything unless specifically permitted, the third statement in the access list is required. Note that the second statement is only in effect until 11:00 p.m. on New Year's Eve. Thus, the third statement permits access to the second Web server once the time-range period expires.

Time-Range Application: Example 4

Overview

In our last time-range application examples we examine the use of the command within an access list developed to perform a specific type of ICMP filtering. We again assume the use of a router with two Ethernet ports and one serial port, with the serial port connected to the Internet (Figure 5-4). As in Example 3, we assume a Web server is located on each Ethernet segment.

Let's assume you want to block access to the server whose IP address is 198.78.46.12 from 11:00 p.m. to midnight on a daily basis from now until

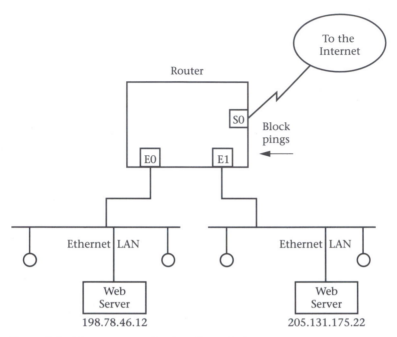

Figure 5-4 Time-range application: Example 4.

the end of the year 2000. Let's further assume you want to restrict pings to the trusted side of the network, which means you want to filter inbound echo requests flowing into the router via the Internet. As a safety mechanism for the server whose IP address is 205.131.175.22, you want to restrict TCP segments flowing to the 205.131.175.0 network to either HTTP flowing directly to the server or tcp traffic that represents a response to a session initiated on the 205.131.175.0 network. Last but not least, you want to block all traffic to the 205.131.175.0 network from the Internet and the 198.78.46.0 network from 5:00 p.m. on Friday until 6:00 a.m. Monday morning from now on.

Solution

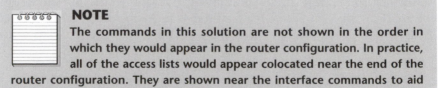

NOTE
The commands in this solution are not shown in the order in which they would appear in the router configuration. In practice, all of the access lists would appear colocated near the end of the router configuration. They are shown near the interface commands to aid discussion only.

```
interface serial0
ip access-group 101 in
access-list 101 deny icmp echo-request any any
access-list 101 permit ip any any
!
interface ethernet1
ip access-group 102 out
time-range block-http
 absolute end 24:00 31 December 2000
 periodic daily 23:00 to 24:00
access-list 102 deny tcp any host 198.78.46.12 eq 80 block-http
!
interface ethernet0
ip access-group 103 out
time-range block-traffic
 absolute
 periodic Friday 17:00 to Monday 6:00
access-list 103 deny ip any any block-traffic
access-list 103 permit ip 198.78.46.0 0.0.0.255 any
access-list 103 permit tcp any host 205.131.175.20 eq 80
access-list 103 permit tcp any any established
```

Explanation

This example includes operations that are well-suited for applying to the serial port and to each Ethernet port. Thus, three access lists are shown in the solution.

The first access list, which is applied to the serial port, blocks all pings entering the router while permitting all other packets. In performing the latter operation we then have to create access lists for each Ethernet port. While we could create one complex access list, in certain situations it is better to follow the "division of labor" rule and apply applicable access lists to each interface to both reduce the complexity of a common list and minimize the potential for error. In this example, since blocking pings is common to both Ethernet interfaces, we associated the applicable deny statement to block echo requests with the access list configured for the serial port.

The first range, which is labeled block-http, uses an absolute and a periodic statement to create the period during which we want to block access to the Web server whose IP address is 198.78.46.12. Note that the time range labeled block-http is associated with the Ethernet 1 interface. Also note that after using a deny statement in the access list to block Web traffic during the set time period, we allow all other IP traffic to flow out of the router toward the Ethernet segment.

Since we want to block all traffic to the 205.131.175.0 network from the Internet from the present time forward, without an expiration date, we used an absolute statement without any arguments in the time range labeled block-traffic. Then, the periodic statement sets the time period of 5:00 p.m. on Friday through 7:00 a.m. on Monday. The first statement in access list 103 blocks all traffic from the Internet and the other Ethernet segment during the predefined time interval associated with the time range labeled block-traffic. The second statement in the access list permits all traffic originating from the other Ethernet segment. Thus, the third statement in the access list that permits HTTP to the Web server is only applicable to traffic originating from the Internet. Similarly, the fourth statement that only allows sessions originating on the 205.131.175.0 network is also only applicable to traffic from the Internet since the second statement allows all traffic from the other segment.

CHAPTER 6

Reflexive
Access Lists

Chapter 4 examined the first enhanced access-list capability added to Cisco routers, dynamic access lists or lock-and-key security. Although dynamic access lists are a significant enhancement for traditional IP access lists, they have several limitations, including the opening of access from the untrusted side of a router without control from the trusted side and the inability of the router administrator to provide different users with different kinds of access. As a result, Cisco introduced reflexive access lists in IOS Version 11.3, and that topic is the focus of this chapter.

We will first discuss the operation and utilization of reflexive access lists and then examine the use of reflexive access lists to satisfy a series of applications.

Overview

Reflexive access lists create dynamic openings for IP traffic on one side of a router based on sessions originating from a different side of the router. In normal mode of operation, a reflexive access list is configured and applied to create openings from the untrusted side of a router such as its serial port connection to the Internet. These openings are created based on sessions originating from the trusted side of the device such as from Ethernet or Token Ring users connected to a segment or ring which, in turn, is connected to a port on the router. In this process, the access list performs what can be referred to as *reflexive filtering*, which results in the name assigned to this type of access list. Reflexive access lists were introduced in IOS Version 11.3 and are available on all router platforms.

Operation

Although the authors follow Cisco Systems' method of referring to reflexive access lists as a separate type of access list, in actuality it is important to note that reflexive access lists are a feature or functional capability added to extended IP named access lists because reflexive access lists are restricted to use within a named IP access list by nesting reflexive entries under the named access list.

Term Origination

Each statement in a reflexive access list results in the creation of a *mirror image* or reflected entry in an existing access list when the conditions in a statement are satisfied. For example, assume a user initiated an outbound telnet session from IP address 198.78.46.8 to IP address 205.131.175.12 using source TCP port number 1045. The originating outbound packet would have the following characteristics:

Source IP address: 198.78.46.8

Source TCP port: 1045

Destination IP address: 205.131.175.12

Destination TCP port: 23 (telnet)

A reflected access list entry is created by using a reflexive access-list statement, enabling inbound return traffic. That entry would be as follows:

```
permit tcp 205.131.175.12 eq 23 198.78.46.8 eq 1045
```

Note that this reflected entry is a mirror image of the outbound packet. The source and destination IP addresses and the source and destination port numbers have been exchanged. Thus, this entry is the reverse image of the original outgoing packet, just as if the original packet were viewed in the reflection of a mirror. This is the rationale for the name of this Cisco access list.

Characteristics

Similar to other types of access lists, certain characteristics are associated with reflexive access lists. Table 6-1 lists the major characteristics of the temporary entries created by reflexive access lists.

In examining the characteristics of the entries listed in Table 6-1, a few

Table 6-1 Characteristics of Reflexive Access-List Temporary Entries

The entry is always a permit entry.

The entry specifies the same protocol as the original outbound packet such as TCP, UDP, ICMP, or IP.

The new entry swaps the source and destination IP addresses.

The new entry swaps the source and destination upper-layer port numbers (for ICMP, certain type numbers are used).

The entry exists until either the session is closed or an idle time-out value is reached.

The entry expires when the last packet of the session flows through the interface.

words concerning the capabilities of reflexive access lists are in order. First, the use of a time-out value is critical for protocols other than TCP because while the FIN bit setting of TCP conversations can be monitored to detect the termination of a session, UDP and other protocols do not have this capability. The effect is that non-TCP sessions cannot be closed without looking further into a packet to read and interpret its contents, a task not commonly performed or associated with routers, resulting in the dependence of a time-out condition governing session inactivity. As noted later in this chapter, you can assign individual time-out values to dynamic openings (holes) created by different types of sessions or you can use a global time-out value of 300 s (5 min). Even the global time-out value can be altered to reduce the duration of dynamic openings (holes) through which responses flow to sessions originated from the opposite side of a router.

Data Flow

Figure 6-1 is an example of the data flow in a reflexive access list. The Ethernet segment resides on the internal or trusted side of the router, while the serial port connection to the Internet represents the external or untrusted side of the router.

In normal mode of operation a reflexive access list is created which examines traffic from the Ethernet segment flowing to the Internet to enable creation of dynamic, temporary openings that permit traffic to flow through the router if the traffic was part of the session that originated on the trusted side of the router. While this sounds similar to the

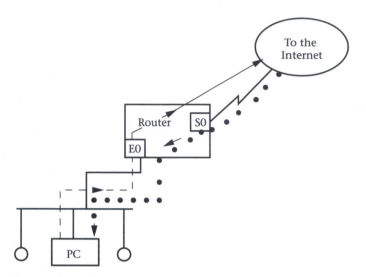

Figure 6-1   Reflexive access-list data flow.

use of the keyword `established` in an extended IP access list which enables TCP datagrams that are part of a session to flow through a router, it is important to note that `established` is applicable only for TCP. Additionally, the `established` keyword checks only for the presence of an ACK or RST bit in the packet, and this bit is easily spoofed by an attacker.

In comparison, reflexive access lists are applicable to all IP protocols supported by Cisco extended IP named access lists, including UDP, TCP, and ICMP. It is also important to note that unlike a conventional access list whose entries can be considered permanent until deleted or modified by a new list, a reflexive access list is restricted to creating temporary openings. Such openings are automatically created when a new IP session begins and are removed either when the session ends or when a time-out value is reached.

Access-List Creation

As previously mentioned, a reflexive access list is actually a feature or capability added to extended IP named access lists in IOS Version 11.3. Thus, you create an extended IP named access list with a `permit` statement for all protocols for which you want to create reflected entries. In doing so you would use the keyword `reflect` in each `permit` statement to indicate that a reflexive opening should occur in the access list.

In addition to using the keyword `reflect` in one or more `permit` statements, two related IOS statements must be considered. One is the `evaluate` statement which is added at the end of the list and terminates the reflexive access list. The second is the `ip reflexive-list timeout` command, which is used to change the global time-out value of 300 s for temporary reflexive access-list entries. To better understand the creation and operation of a reflexive access list, let's look at the format of each of the three IOS statements and commands.

The `permit` Statement

As noted earlier in this chapter, a reflexive access list is created through the use of nested `permit` entries in an extended IP named access list. To identify the `permit` statement as a reflexive statement, the keyword `reflect` is added to the statement, as shown here:

```
permit protocol source destination reflect name[timeout seconds]
```

In this format the protocol entry represents any TCP/IP protocol supported by an extended IP named access list. Source and destination represent the source and destination IP addresses, including allowable keywords `any` or `host` and applicable wild-card masks. The keyword `name` represents the name of the extended IP named access list.

To identify the `permit` statement as applicable for creating temporary openings, use the keyword `reflect` in the statement. Because reflexive entries are only applicable to an extended IP named access list, the `permit` statement will include the name of the access list. Finally, you can use the keyword `timeout` to specify a time-out period for individual reflected entries that will differ from the default global time-out value of 300 s or a different value assigned through the `ip reflexive-list timeout` statement, which we will review shortly.

The use of a time-out value is optional and, if not specified, a default value of 300 s is used. However, it is important to note that that default value is not applicable to TCP traffic because a TCP reflexive access-list entry closes immediately after receipt of a packet with the RST bit set and within 5 s of detecting 2 FIN bits. Since UDP and ICMP do not have similar options in their headers, an idle time-out is necessary to determine when entries for these kinds of protocols should be deleted.

To illustrate the `permit` statement, let's assume the Ethernet network in Figure 6-1 has the IP address 198.78.46.0 and you want to allow dynamic openings from the Internet in response to employees that telnet to hosts on the Internet. To accomplish this task, you would code the following statement, where `my-list` represents the name of the extended IP named access list in which the `permit` statement will be entered.

```
permit tcp any any eq telnet reflect my-list
```

As a second example of how to create an appropriate `permit` statement for reflective entries, let's assume your organization uses the host whose IP address is 198.78.46.10 to manage several devices via *simple network management protocol* (SNMP) on a distant network whose IP address is 205.131.175.0. The appropriate `permit` statements to allow reflective entries inbound from the Internet are shown here:

```
permit udp host 198.78.46.10 205.131.175.0 0.0.0.255 eq 161
permit udp host 198.78.46.11 205.131.175.0 0.0.0.255 eq 162
```

The reason two statements were coded reflects the nature of SNMP. UDP port 161 is used for SNMP, while port 162 is used for SNMP traps.

The `evaluate` Statement

The `evaluate` statement terminates an extended IP named access list that includes one or more reflexive entries. The format of this statement is shown here:

```
evaluate name
```

where `name` represents the name of the named access list. For `permit` statements with the keyword `reflect` to work, those statements must be nested beneath the named access-list with the `evaluate` statement terminating the list. As several examples later in this chapter will show, you can mix both reflexive and nonreflexive statements in the access list.

The `ip reflexive-list timeout` Command

As briefly discussed earlier in this section, you can change the global timeout value for temporary reflexive access-list entries from the default of 300 s by using the `ip reflexive list timeout` command whose format is shown here:

```
ip reflexive-list timeout seconds
```

where the only parameter you need to specify is the time-out value in seconds. Now that we understand the IOS statements associated with reflexive access lists, let's learn how to determine an appropriate interface for a reflexive access list.

Interface Selection Procedure

Similar to creating a conventional access list, you must consider the location and direction for a reflexive access list. However, because of how a reflexive access list operates, you will more than likely always define applicable reflex statements in an outbound extended IP named access list since doing so results in temporary openings occurring in the inbound direction. To illustrate why this is the normal way to create reflexive access lists, let's examine a few examples. First, let's assume your organization's router is connected to the Internet as illustrated in Figure 6-1.

In the network configuration in Figure 6-1, the Ethernet segment located behind the router is the trusted side of the router, while the serial port connection to the Internet is the untrusted side of the router. By configuring a reflexive access list for the serial interface in an outbound extended IP named access list, only IP traffic entering the router that is part of a session previously established from the internal trusted network will not be sent to the great bit bucket in the sky. While you could apply a reflexive access list in the opposite manner, unless someone on the Internet queried your internal hosts, those hosts could never access the Internet unless specific nonreflexive entries in the access list permit their transmission. Thus, since most organizations prefer to limit inbound traffic from the Internet to responses to queries issued by employees, reflexive access lists are normally, and perhaps exclusively, applied in an outbound extended IP named access list.

A second common use of reflexive access lists is the situation where your organization operates both public access and private access network segments. For example, an organization's internal network that links several geographically separated locations is considered a private network, while a segment with a Web server, DNS server, FTP server, and other hosts set up for access by anyone with a computer is considered a publicly accessible segment.

Suppose your organization connects both your internal private network and the public access servers located on a separate segment to the Internet via a common router, as illustrated in Figure 6-2. In the network configuration in Figure 6-2, Cisco's current firewall literature refers to the segment containing the publicly accessible servers as a *protected demilitarized zone* (P-DMZ). In some literature the term DMZ is also referred to as a nonpopulated LAN placed between a router and firewall to ensure that all data to or from the router are examined by the firewall. Current firewall literature normally refers to this as the *unprotected DMZ* (U-DMZ) to distinguish it from the P-DMZ. The P-DMZ is also referred to as the *dingy* side of the firewall, while the U-DMZ is referred to as the *dirty* side of the firewall. The inside segments of the firewall are, of course, called the *clean* side. These designations are simply convenient ways of communicating the level of trust conveyed to devices on a particular segment of a firewall.

Use of a reflexive access list configured for the ethernet0 port shown in Figure 6-2 can prevent IP traffic from entering your internal, private network unless such traffic is part of a session previously established from

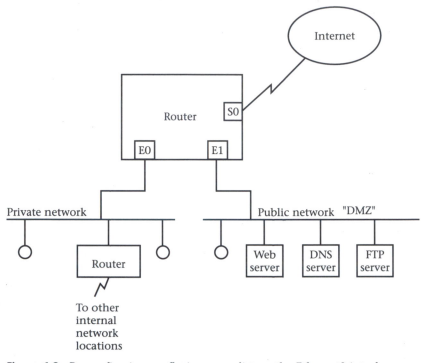

Figure 6-2 By configuring a reflexive access list on the Ethernet0 interface, you control access to the private network to session responses while allowing all IP traffic to flow to your public network.

hosts behind the Ethernet0 interface. Thus, in this situation, placing the reflexive access list on the internal interface permits traffic from the Internet to flow unobstructed to the servers on the public P-DMZ network segment. However, for added security, you should consider permitting only applicable Web, FTP, and DNS traffic via the serial port to the Ethernet 1 segment by creating a conventional access list that would be applied to the serial port in the inbound direction.

Observing Reflexive Lists in Action

For readers from Missouri, the "show me" state, it is often important to see a concept in action. Once you develop a reflexive access list, you can view its effect by using the IOS show command. Let's begin with a simple access list which blocks RFC 1918 addresses in the inbound direction and creates reflective statements for TCP, UDP, and ICMP protocols through their association with an access list applied to a router's serial port in the outbound direction. Through the use of the `show` command we observe the following access list:

```
router # show access-list
extended IP access list infilter
 deny ip 10.0.0.0 0.255.255.255 any
 deny ip 172.16.0.0 0.31.255.255 any
 deny ip 192.168.0.0 0.0.255.255 any
 evaluate my-packets
extended IP access list outfilter
 permit tcp any any reflect my-packets
 permit udp any any reflect my-packets
 permit icmp any any reflect my-packets
```

Now let's assume a user on the trusted side of the network initiates a telnet session with the following characteristics:

Source IP address: 198.78.46.8

Source TCP port: 1045

Destination IP address: 205.131.175.12

Destination TCP port: 23 (Telnet)

If we return to the router console and initiate another `show` command to display the access list, we observe the following:

```
router # show access-list
extended IP access list infilter
 deny ip 10.0.0.0 0.255.255.255 any
 deny ip 172.16.0.0 0.31.255.255 any
 deny ip 192.168.0.0 0.0.255.255 any
 evaluate my-packets
extended IP access list outfilter
 permit tcp any any reflect my-packets
 permit udp any any reflect my-packets
 permit icmp any any reflect my-packets
reflexive IP access list my-packets
permit tcp host 205.131.175.12 eq telnet host 198.78.46.8 eq 1045
(10 matches) (time left 110 seconds)
```

This display not only indicates the temporary openings created in the reflexive access list but also indicates the number of matches that occurred and the remaining time of the opening in the access list.

Limitations

Two key limitations are associated with reflexive access lists. One is similar to other types of access lists in that it involves the order in which entries are placed in the list. The second is associated with the type of application you want to support. In this section we will examine both.

Statement Placement

Similarly to conventional access lists, the order of statements within a reflexive access list is crucial to obtaining your desired goal when developing and applying the list. What makes order placement more interesting is the fact that you can mix reflexive and nonreflexive entries in an access list. Since only packets that reach the reflexive access list entries will be enabled to create reflected entries, you should carefully review placement of statements. For example, consider the following example that includes both reflexive and nonreflexive statements.

```
ip access-list extended outfilter
permit ip any any
permit tcp any any reflect my-packets
permit udp any any reflect my-packets
permit icmp any any reflect my-packets
```

Note that the first statement nested under the ip access list permits all IP packets. Because this entry does not include the keyword `reflect`, it is not a reflexive access-list entry. Because all IP packets would be matched by this entry, none of the remaining reflexive access-list entries would ever be matched, so no reflected entries would ever be created in the corresponding inbound list!

Application Support

Although the introduction of reflexive access lists significantly enhanced network administrators' ability to control data flow based upon session initiation from the trusted side of a router, they are limited with respect to their ability to support single-channel operations such as telnet. In comparison, FTP, which uses one channel for control and a second channel for the actual data transmission, is a multichannel operation that is not supported by reflexive access lists. This statement is true for normal-mode FTP but not for passive-mode FTP. It is FTP's use of an active open from the server to the client that is not supported by reflexive access lists and not its use of multiple client-to-server connections. Passive-mode FTP allows the client to open the second connection to the server and not vice versa, so passive-mode FTP could be handled properly by reflexive access lists. Another limitation of reflexive access lists is the inability to support applications that use port numbers that change during a session. While certain multichannel applications are supported by context-based access control (CBAC), which is covered later in this book, no method is presently available to create dynamic openings to support applications that use port numbers that change during a session using reflexive access lists.

Now that we understand how to determine an appropriate interface and direction for reflexive access lists and their limitations, let's look at several examples that illustrate the use of this type of access list.

Reflexive Access-List Application: Example 1

Overview

Let's assume your organization operates a two-port router—one Ethernet port and one serial port, with the latter providing an Internet connection. Let's further assume that you want to allow users on your internal corporate network to surf the Web, access DNS information, and ping distant hosts while precluding other hosts on the Internet from independently accessing hosts on your organization's network. As indicated in Figure 6-3, we will assume that your organization has the class C network address of 198.78.46.0.

Solution

```
interface serial0
 ip access-group outfilter out
 ip access-group infilter in
 !
ip access-list extended outfilter
 permit tcp any any eq 80 reflect my-packets
 permit udp any any eq 53 reflect my-packets
 permit icmp any any
 !
ip access-list extended infilter
 evaluate my-packets
```

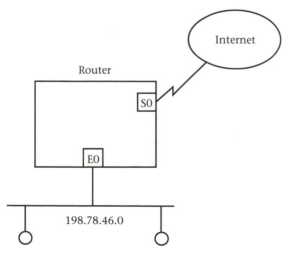

Figure 6-3 Reflexive access-list application: Example 1.

Explanation

In this solution we assigned the name outfilter to our extended IP named access list and associated the list with the serial port in the outbound direction because we want temporary, dynamic openings to occur in the inbound direction in response to network users on the 198.78.46.0 network initiating certain types of sessions. Since we want to provide all users on the internal Ethernet network with the ability to initiate certain types of applications, the keyword any was used with each permit statement for both source and destination IP address fields. Thus, the class C network address, while interesting to note, does not need to be included in our reflexive access list.

Although we specified port 80 for TCP and port 53 for UDP to enable HTTP and DNS temporary openings, we specified all ICMP outbound. ICMP is unique because it does not use port numbers as with TCP and UDP, but instead uses type codes, which may or may not be the same for outbound and inbound traffic. For example, the ping program uses an outbound ICMP message of type echo-request. However, the reply from the remote host is an ICMP message of type *echo-reply*. In our testing, the authors discovered that reflexive access lists can allow the return echo-reply from the remote pinged host, while simultaneously blocking any pings initiated from the remote host. In other words, the reflexive access list allowed echo-replies from the remote host but blocked echo-requests. It should be noted, however, that although the reflexive access lists blocked ICMP echo-requests, it did not block other types of ICMP packets.

For example, the authors were able to successfully send an ICMP source-quench (ICMP type 4) packet through the reflexive access list. Therefore, it appears that reflexive access lists can differentiate some ICMP messages but not all. Care should be taken when using reflexive access lists since after dynamic openings are created by outbound pings, a skilled attacker could create inbound ICMP messages that would be allowed through the dynamic openings. You may want to evaluate whether to use reflexive access lists to filter ICMP at all. Since there are a very limited number of ICMP types that you would want to allow into your network, it is probably more secure to just allow those few types in and filter all other inbound ICMP types. In the remaining examples in this chapter, we do not use reflexive entries to filter ICMP. (For those interested, the authors recommend allowing only echo-response, administratively-prohibited, time-exceeded, and packet-too-big. These ICMP types should cover nearly all needed ICMP services. We specifically do not recommend allowing source-quench messages, since these could be used in a DoS attack and are of limited value in most networks. If you find you need source-quench messages, you can permit them as well.

Reflexive Access-List Application: Example 2

Overview

In this example of a reflexive access list, we assume that our organization decided to promote the company by constructing and operating a publicly accessible Web server. To provide a high level of security it was decided to place the Web server on a separate Ethernet segment, as illustrated in Figure 6-4.

Since we now have two Ethernet segments, we want to allow Web and DNS traffic to the private portion of the network based upon sessions originated by users on the private network. In addition, we want to restrict ICMP packets to echo-response packets to the private portion of the network and only allow Web traffic to the public segment where the Web server resides.

Solution

```
interface serial0
  ip access-group infilter in
  ip access-group outfilter out
!
ip access-list extended outfilter
  permit tcp any any eq 80 reflect my-packets
  permit udp any any eq 53 reflect my-packets
!
```

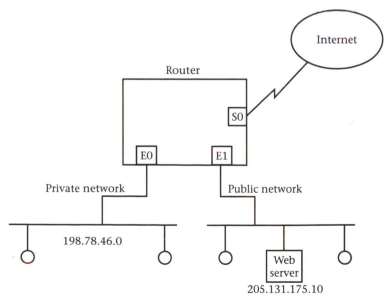

Figure 6-4 Reflexive access-list application: Example 2.

```
ip access-list extended infilter
 permit tcp any host 205.131.175.10 eq 80
 permit icmp any 198.78.46.0 0.0.0.255 echo-response
 evaluate my-packets
```

Explanation

In this example we created two extended IP named access lists, one of which is applied to the serial port in the outbound direction while the second is applied in the inbound direction. Note that the extended access list named outfilter has two reflexive entries, one for HTTP (port 80) and a second for DNS (port 53). Since this reflexive access list is applied to the serial port, it also creates temporary openings (holes) in the router for any HTTP and DNS session initiated by stations on the 205.131.175.0 network, which may not be your intention. Thus, a better solution would be to apply the extended access list named outfilter to the ethernet0 interface as an inbound filter, which better follows the rule of thumb of attempting to apply an access list to the closest source of packets to be filtered. However, if we did this, we would need to leave the inbound filter on the serial interface to ensure that the dynamic openings were created on the correct interface. Note that we could place both filters on the Ethernet interface, but this would allow all inbound packets into the serial interface, which would leave the router itself vulnerable to attack, even though the inside Ethernet interface would be protected.

It is worth reiterating that the inbound and outbound filters do not need to appear on the same interface. You can place the inbound and outbound filters on different interfaces and allow reflexive access lists to create the appropriate openings. As long as both the inbound and outbound filters reference the same reflexive access-list name, the appropriate entries will be created. In our examples, the reflexive access-list name is my-packets.

Returning to our example, we used a common access list named infilter to allow Web traffic to flow to the server on the public network and echo-response packets to flow to stations on the 198.78.46.0 network. Since each access list has an implicit deny all at the end of the list, Web queries to the 198.78.46.0 network and echo-responses to the 205.131.175.0 network are barred. However, because the access list named outfilter creates dynamic openings in the access list named infilter, as previously mentioned, any user on the 205.131.175.10 network can surf the Web and initiate DNS queries.

Reflexive Access-List Application: Example 3

Overview

Until now, we relied on the default value of 300 s for closing openings associated with non-TCP traffic. In this example we assume we wish to be

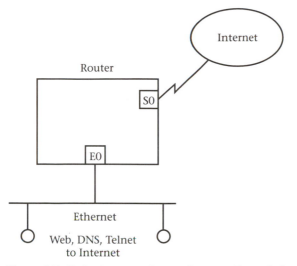

Figure 6-5 Reflexive access-list application: Example 3.

more specific when controlling openings resulting from reflexive access-list statements being executed.

We assume your organization has one Ethernet network segment connected to the Internet via a router's serial port, as indicated in Figure 6-5. Let's further assume you want to restrict reflected openings to Web traffic, DNS, and telnet. Let's also further assume you want to restrict the time-out period for Web traffic to 4 min, DNS traffic to 3 min, and telnet to 1 min.

Solution

```
interface serial0
 ip access-group outfilter out
 ip access-group infilter in
!
ip access-list extended outfilter
 permit tcp any any eq 80 reflect my-packets timeout 240
 permit tcp any any eq 23 reflect my-packets timeout 60
 permit udp any any eq 53 reflect my-packets timeout 180
ip access-list extended infilter
 evaluate my-packets
```

Explanation

In this example we needed to restrict the dynamic openings resulting from sessions originating on the internal Ethernet network. Since we were also restricted to the type of traffic permitted to flow through the router, we could not use a single permit TCP statement. Instead, we used one for

HTTP (port 80) and a second for telnet (port 23). We also used a `permit` UDP statement to allow responses to DNS queries originated on the internal network. In examining the statements in the solution note that an appropriate time-out value was assigned to each statement to satisfy the previously described requirements.

Reflexive Access-list Application: Example 4

Overview

In a fourth example we assume the Ethernet network segment used in Example 3 now has a Web server whose IP address is 198.78.46.8 (Figure 6-6). In addition to restricting traffic from the Internet to responses to Web, DNS, and telnet sessions initiated by workstations on the Ethernet network, we want to allow traffic from elsewhere on the Internet to the Web server.

In configuring our access list, let us further assume that we wish to retain the previously established time-out values of 4 min for Web traffic, 3 min for DNS, and 1 min for telnet.

Solution

```
interface serial0
 ip access-group outfilter out
 ip access-group infilter in
 !
```

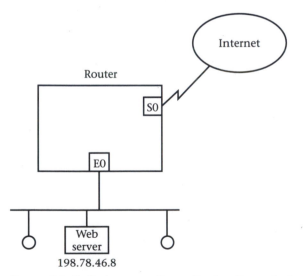

Figure 6-6 Reflexive access-list application: Example 4.

```
ip access-list extended infilter
 permit tcp any host 198.78.46.8 eq 80
 evaluate my-packets
!
ip access-list extended outfilter
 permit tcp any any eq 80 reflect my-packets timeout 240
 permit tcp any any eq 23 reflect my-packets timeout 60
 permit udp any any eq 53 reflect my-packets timeout 180
```

Explanation

This application is a continuation of Example 3, with a requirement to allow Web traffic from the Internet to the corporate Web server. To accomplish this we configured an explicit `permit` TCP statement on the inbound access list. That `permit` statement restricts inbound TCP to Web traffic directed to the Web server's IP address.

Reflexive Access-List Application: Example 5

Overview

In this example (see Figure 6-7) we add a bit of complexity to our application by assuming our organization again operates both public and private network segments connected to the Internet via a common router.

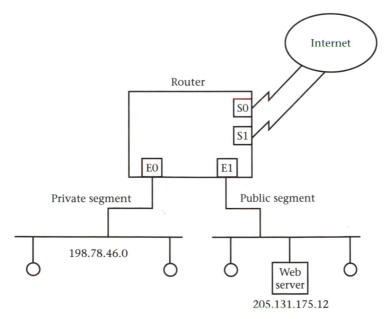

Figure 6-7   Reflexive access-list application: Example 5.

However, in this example we assume that, due to both the level of traffic and security concerns, our router has two serial connections to the Internet. One serial connection (port S0) will be used for providing Internet access to the private network segment with the network address 198.78.46.0, while the second serial port (port S1) will be used to provide Internet connectivity to the public Ethernet segment whose network address is 205.131.175.0 and the Web server on that segment that has the IP address 205.131.175.12.

For the private segment we assume we want to restrict users on that network to telnet, Web, and DNS operations. In addition, we assume we want all sessions to have a global time-out of 3 min and preclude all other IP traffic from the Internet to the private network. For the public network we restrict pings to the Web server, disabling pings to other addresses on that network. In addition, we want to limit HTTP traffic from the Internet to the Web server. However, because it is possible that our organization may decide to add some workstations to the public network segment, we want to allow such stations to access telnet, DNS, and Web servers on the Internet by creating dynamic openings in response to sessions they may initiate.

Solution

```
interface serial0
 ip access-group infilter0 in
 ip access-group outfilter0 out
 !
ip reflexive-list timeout 180
 !
ip access-list extended infilter0
 evaluate my-packets0
 !
ip access-list extended outfilter0
 permit tcp any any eq 23 reflect my-packets0
 permit udp any any eq 53 reflect my-packets0
 permit tcp any any eq 80 reflect my-packets0
 !
interface serial1
 ip access-group infilter1 in
 ip access-group outfilter1 out
 !
ip access-list extended infilter1
 permit icmp any host 205.131.175.12 echo request
 permit tcp any host 205.131.175.12 eq 80
 evaluate my-packets1
 !
ip access-list extended outfilter1
 permit tcp any any eq 23 reflect my-packets1
 permit udp any any eq 53 reflect my-packets1
 permit tcp any any eq 80 reflect my-packets1
```

Explanation

In this solution we created two groups of access lists, one for each of the serial interfaces. To easily distinguish the inbound and outbound access list for each interface we used an elementary naming convention, with either a 0 or 1 added to the terms `infilter`, `outfilter`, and `my-packets` to note the serial interface each extended named access list would be applied to. Also note that a global time-out of 180 s is assigned to all reflexive entries.

The first access list, which is named `infilter0`, will only evaluate entries that match `my-packets0`, that is, replies to outbound packets matching `outfilter0`. Next, an access list named `outfilter0` includes three `permit` statements that result in reflected entries automatically being created in the inbound access list when users on the private network segment initiate telnet, Web, or DNS activity.

For the second serial interface (serial1) we named the access lists `infilter1` and `outfilter1`. The extended access list named `infilter1` contains two `permit` statements, one allowing users on the Internet to ping the organization's public Web server while the second `permit` statement allows HTTP access to the server from the Internet.

CHAPTER 7

Context-Based Access Control

C hapter 6 examined reflexive access lists, which allow creation of dynamic openings in an inbound access-list in response to an outbound data connection. In this context, outbound means that transmission flows from a trusted network to an untrusted network such as from your internal LAN to the Internet. This functionality permits traffic from untrusted networks to our internal network only when the traffic is part of a data session that was initiated from the internal network. While this functionality is a significant enhancement to the "established" keyword with traditional extended access lists, reflexive access lists cannot handle multichannel applications such as FTP, CU-SeeMe, H.323, etc. *Multichannel* applications are those that use one connection for the commands that are sent between the client and server and another, possibly multiple, connections for the data sent between the client and server. Often, the connection for the data channel may be initiated from the server to the client. Without understanding the behavior of these applications, the router would not know whether these data channels from the server to the client should be permitted or denied access.

As discussed previously, reflexive access lists can only securely handle single-channel applications such as telnet and DNS, which makes them of limited value in many enterprise networks. *Context-based access control* (CBAC) addresses this shortcoming and its use allows secure handling of many multichannel applications. CBAC was originally introduced in IOS version 11.2P in a special feature set called the *firewall feature set*, or simply FFS. The original release was available only on the 1600 and 2500 series router platforms. In release 12.0T, FFS is available on the 800, uBR900, 1600, 1700, 2500, 2600, 3600, 7100, and 7200 series platforms. This chapter will focus on the operation and utilization of CBAC. Once this is accomplished, the use of CBAC to satisfy a series of applications will be examined.

Overview

CBAC works similarly to reflexive access lists. Outgoing sessions are inspected, and temporary openings are created to enable the return traffic. The difference between them is that CBAC can examine and securely handle a variety of applications based on upper-layer information. Reflexive access lists like traditional access lists, cannot examine information in the packet higher than layer 4. In other words, they cannot determine anything except the TCP/UDP ports in use and the IP addresses in use. They cannot make any intelligent determination of actions to be taken based on the behavior of the applications used. For example, reflexive access lists would not know to open certain additional ports for FTP and others for CU-SeeMe traffic. Conversely, CBAC *can* open the needed ports for these applications and many more. A list of the applications for which CBAC provides intelligent filtering is shown in Table 7-1.

> **NOTE**
> State information on IP fragments can now be retained so that succeeding IP fragments after the first in a sequence are blocked or allowed based on the upper-layer information contained in the first IP fragment. Prior to 12.0.5T, fragments other than the first were allowed through the router even if the first IP fragment was blocked. Note that this feature can cause problems if IP fragments other than the first arrive at the router interface prior to the first IP fragment. The router would not have any state information for that series of fragments and all fragments arriving at the router prior to the first would be dropped. Some fragments would not arrive at the destination and the entire packet would have to be resent by the originating device.

Characteristics

CBAC functions by examining packets as they enter or leave specified interfaces. The information contained in the packet, such as IP addresses and layer 4 port numbers, is installed in a packet *state information* table. The state table is used by CBAC to create temporary openings in an access list for return traffic. CBAC also tracks the sequence numbers in use dur-

Table 7-1 Applications That CBAC Can Handle Securely

Single-channel TCP (that is, telnet)
Single-channel UDP (that is, DNS)
CU-SeeMe (White Pine version)
FTP
H.323 (NetMeeting, ProShare, etc.)
Java (applets embedded in HTTP)
Microsoft NetShow (new in 12.05T)
Unix r commands (rlogin, rexec, etc.)
RealAudio
RPC (Sun version)
SMTP
SQL*Net
StreamWorks
TFTP
VDOLive
*IP fragments (new in 12.05T).

ing a TCP conversation to ensure that they fall within the expected range. Additionally, CBAC examines application-layer information for certain protocols to ensure that appropriate return traffic is allowed through the router to the internal network. For example, CBAC monitors an outgoing FTP session and permits the resulting data connection to be initiated from the FTP server to the originating client. CBAC is aware of the behavior of the FTP application and can intelligently create the necessary openings in the inbound router access lists. It does this by monitoring the FTP command channel and examining the PORT and PASV commands and evaluating their content for expected values. For example, the IP address contained in the PORT command must be the same IP address as that used in the original FTP request.

CBAC performs similar functions for the other protocols listed in Table 7-1 and examines application-layer command channels to ensure that the application requests are correctly formed. While this feature alone is impressive, CBAC additionally provides:

- Java blocking
- Denial-of-service prevention and detection
- Real-time alerts and audit trails

As you can see, CBAC is much more than just an access-list enhancement; it is a comprehensive set of security tools. Each of these features will be examined in detail in the following sections.

Operation

We will now discuss the operation of CBAC and how it can be used to secure your network.

Process

The process CBAC follows to monitor outbound traffic sessions and create appropriate inbound access-list entries is as follows:

1. An outgoing packet reaches a router interface. The packet is evaluated against an access list applied to the interface. The access list should allow all traffic to be inspected by CBAC. (Traffic denied by the access list will be dropped.)

2. CBAC will examine the packet and record information about it in the state table (this table is viewable with the command `show ip inspect session detail`). The information in the state table includes the source and destination IP addresses and TCP or UDP port numbers.

3. CBAC creates a temporary opening in an access list for the return traffic; these openings will vary depending on the application used. The temporary entries will be placed on the interface that will receive the return traffic.

4. A return packet reaches a router interface. The return packet is permitted by the temporary access-list entries and inspected by CBAC. CBAC will update the state table and modify the temporary access-list entries if necessary. All future packets that are part of this network conversation are inspected similarly to update tables and access-list entries as needed.

5. When the connection is completed, the entries in the state table and the inbound access list are removed. For TCP these entries are removed after a normal FIN exchange between the client and server. For UDP there are configurable inactivity timeouts.

Note that two access lists are needed for CBAC to operate: one that defines which packets are to be inspected by CBAC and one that includes the entries that are actually created. A detailed example of this principle is given later.

However, before discussing the features of CBAC in greater detail, it is important to point out that it does have a few weaknesses despite its obvious advantages:

- CBAC inspects only TCP and UDP packets. Other IP traffic (such as Internet Control Message Protocol, or ICMP) must be filtered with traditional IP access lists.

- Packets with the router as the source or destination address are not inspected by CBAC.

- If both *Cisco encryption technology* (CET) and CBAC are configured, CBAC will not be able to accurately inspect the contents of the CET-encrypted packets. In this case, the only multichannel protocols that CBAC will be able to inspect are StreamWorks and CU-SeeMe. CBAC should be configured to inspect only these applications and generic TCP and UDP sessions if you are using encryption.

- If both IPSec and CBAC are configured, CBAC can inspect the traffic correctly as long as the CBAC router is the end point of the IPSec tunnel. If the router is not the end point of the tunnel, CBAC cannot inspect the packets because the packets will not have a TCP or UDP header.

- CBAC uses approximately 600 bytes of memory per connection to maintain each entry in the state table. In addition, a small amount of additional processing occurs during the inspection process.

These weaknesses are minor compared to the benefits of CBAC, but they are important to remember and will save confusion during the configuration process, discussed in the next section.

Configuration

The following steps must be performed to configure CBAC:

1. Choose an interface where you will configure CBAC.
2. Configure access lists on the interface.
3. Define time-outs and thresholds.
4. Define the inspection rules.
5. Apply the inspection rules.

Each of these topics will be covered in detail.

Step 1—Choose an Interface

The first step is to decide whether to configure CBAC on an *internal* or *external* interface. An *internal interface* is an interface on the router where client sessions originate. This is often called the *trusted* or *clean* side of the router. It will be the interface on the router closest to the devices you are attempting to protect. Normally this will be your internal LAN. An *external interface* is an interface on the router where client sessions exit the router. This is often called the *untrusted* or *dirty* side of the router. It will be the interface closest to the devices you are attempting to filter. Normally this would be the Internet or a connection to an external organization.

If there are more than two interfaces, the extra interfaces are normally used as a *demilitarized zone* (DMZ). A DMZ is a segment that provides services to both the internal and external interfaces. For example, a Web server used by both internal and external clients would be placed on the DMZ. The purpose of the DMZ is to provide services to external clients while still limiting inbound traffic to the internal network so that if a host on the DMZ is compromised, hosts on the internal network are still protected. If a device on the internal side of the router were compromised, the router could not prevent further compromise of internal hosts. The use of the term DMZ should not be confused with an alternate use, that is, a network with only a router and firewall connection that forces all data to and from a public/private network connection through the firewall. A good source for further discussion on the design of secure perimeters is *Building Internet Firewalls* (ITP 1995) by Chapman and Zwicky.

If only an internal and external interface exists, it is most common to configure CBAC on the external interface. This way, any traffic attempting to enter the network will be inspected by CBAC. If there are one or more DMZ segments, CBAC can be configured on either the interface closest to the originating hosts or on the interface closest to the destination hosts. CBAC is intelligent enough to create openings in an access list on an interface other than the interface where inspection is defined. As we will see, if CBAC is configured to inspect traffic arriving at an inside interface, it can create openings in an inbound access list on the outside interface of the router for the return traffic.

If CBAC is configured in two directions, CBAC should be configured for one direction first, and then configured independently for the second direction. When configuring CBAC in complex situations such as this, it is best to configure CBAC on the interface where the traffic originates. CBAC will take care of creating the necessary openings for the return traffic. An example is provided later.

Step 2—Configure Access Lists

Access lists must be configured for both outbound and inbound traffic for CBAC to operate. The outbound access list specifies traffic to be inspected by CBAC. This access list may be either a standard or extended IP access list. The inbound access list is the access list where temporary openings are actually created and managed by CBAC. This access list must be an extended IP access list. Note that, in this context, an access list filtering inbound traffic could be applied either inbound on the untrusted interface of the router or outbound on the trusted interface of the router.

> **NOTE**
> It should be reiterated that CBAC is only useful for dynamically allowing packets that are part of a network connection initiated from the internal network to an external network. It does *not* assist in allowing external devices to initiate network connections through the router. While CBAC can inspect traffic initiated from an external network to an internal network, it can only create openings for return traffic from the internal network to the external network, which is of limited value from a security perspective. The point here is that CBAC cannot protect you from traffic that you explicitly allow external devices to initiate through the router. For example, if you allow inbound HTTP to your Web server, CBAC cannot protect you from HTTP application-layer attacks such as exploitation of cgi scripts. CBAC is not the end point of security, but part of an overall security policy.

Step 3—Define Time-Outs and Thresholds

CBAC uses configurable timers to determine the duration of inactive sessions. Also, as stated earlier, CBAC helps to prevent *denial of service* (DoS) attacks by monitoring the number and frequency of half-open connections. For TCP, a half-open session is one that has not completed the initial three-way handshake. For UDP, it is a session for which the firewall has detected no return traffic. Each of the applicable commands is listed in Table 7-2 along with its default value and a brief description.

Note that CBAC counts both UDP and TCP when determining the number and rate of half-open sessions. Also, half-open sessions are *only* monitored for connections configured for inspection by CBAC. Later in this book a feature called TCP intercept will be discussed that can be used to monitor all TCP connection requests.

Step 4—Define Inspection Rules

The definition of inspection rules is very simple for most protocols. For all protocols, except RPC (remote procedure call) and Java, the format is

```
ip inspect name inspection-name protocol >[alert {on|off}] [audit-trail
   {on|off}] [timeout seconds]
```

Table 7-2 Commands Used to Configure Time-Out Values with CBAC

Command	Default Value	Description
Ip inspect tcp synwait-time *seconds*	30 s	Length of time to wait for TCP session to establish.
Ip inspect tcp finwait-time *seconds*	5 s	Length of time TCP is managed after FIN exchange.
Ip inspect tcp idle-time *seconds*	3600 s	TCP idle time-out.
Ip inspect udp idle-time *seconds*	30 s	UDP idle time-out.
Ip inspect dns-timeout *seconds*	5 s	DNS lookup idle timer.
Ip inspect max-incomplete high *number*	500 sessions	Maximum number of half-open connections before CBAC begins closing connections.
Ip inspect max-incomplete low *number*	400 sessions	Number of half-open connections causing CBAC to stop closing connections.
Ip inspect one-minute high *number*	500 sessions	Rate of half-open sessions per minute before CBAC begins closing connections.
Ip inspect one-minute low *number*	400 sessions	Rate of half-open sessions per minute causing CBAC to stop deleting connections.
Ip inspect tcp max-incomplete host *number* block-time *seconds*	50 sessions	Number of existing half-open sessions with the same destination address before CBAC begins closing sessions.

Example

```
ip inspect name firewall ftp alert on
ip inspect name firewall smtp audit-trail on timeout 60
```

The keyword `alert` allows CBAC to send messages to a syslog server or the routers' buffer when it detects that a violation has occurred in a monitored application. For example, if CBAC is configured to monitor SMTP and an illegal SMTP command is detected, the router sends an `alert` to the syslog server. Each application has its own set of `alert`s that the router issues for different illegal conditions.

The keyword `audit-trail` permits CBAC to track the connections used for a protected application. The router will log information about each connection, including source and destination IP addresses, ports used, and the number of bytes transferred so an administrator can obtain detailed information on the applications' traffic characteristics in their network. If a large amount of traffic is being monitored by CBAC, the amount of logging produced by using the `audit-trail` capability could be significant.

For RPC, the format is slightly different:

```
ip inspect name inspection-name rpc program-number number [wait-time
   minutes] [alert {on|off}] [audit-trail {on|off}] [timeout seconds]
```

Example

```
ip inspect name firewall rpc program-number 10001
ip inspect name firewall rpc program-number 12000 timeout 60
```

For Java blocking, a list of permitted IP addresses must be created using a standard IP access list:

```
access-list 1-99 [permit|deny] source [source-wildcard]
ip inspect name inspection-name http [java-list access-list] [alert
   {on|off}] [audit-trail {on|off}] [timeout seconds]
```

Example

```
access-list 1 permit 175.100.10.0 0.0.0.255
ip inspect name firewall http java-list 1 audit on
```

If you reference an undefined access list in the `java-list` definition, the default behavior denies all java applets. Additionally, CBAC can only block java applets and not ActiveX. If extensive content filtering is desired, Cisco recommends implementing a dedicated content-filtering product.

When both specific application and generic TCP or UDP inspection rules are given, the specific application inspection takes precedence. For example, if both FTP and TCP are configured for inspection, the FTP inspection rule takes precedence, so you can enable both specific TCP applications such as FTP and HTTP and generic TCP. Of course, the converse is true. If you enable only generic TCP for inspection, FTP traffic will not be inspected and CBAC will not be able to create the necessary openings for the FTP data channel connection from the server to the client. This is a good way to enable only those applications that you want your internal users to access. If you don't want your users to be able to use NetShow, don't enable NetShow for inspection by CBAC and it will not work correctly since CBAC will not create the necessary openings for the return data channels from the server to the client.

Step 5—Apply the Inspection Rules

The final step is to apply the created inspection rules to an interface. Inspection rules are applied in the same manner as an access list. The inspection rules should be applied in the direction of the outbound traffic. If you are configuring inspection on an internal interface, the outbound traffic is entering the interface, so the inspection rules should be applied inbound. If you are configuring inspection on an external interface, the outbound traffic is leaving the interface, so the inspection rules should be applied outbound. Of course, if you are applying CBAC to inbound traffic from the external interface, an inspection rule should be applied inbound on the external interface as well. You would normally only configure an inspection rule on an external interface if you are configuring CBAC in two directions.

The syntax to apply an inspection rule is

```
ip inspect inspection-name {in|out}
```

Additional Commands

Several additional commands are also useful for gathering information about CBAC (see Table 7-3). Although a brief explanation and sample output from selected commands is shown in Table 7-3, the reader should consult the Cisco command reference for IOS version 12.0 for additional details.

> **NOTE**
> The authors have found that `debug ip inspect protocol` provides the most useful information when debugging a firewall configuration, although perhaps too much information to examine on a busy router. The use of `show ip inspect sessions detail` is useful as well, but for short-duration network conversations, it may be difficult to see the results as the sessions will appear and disappear very quickly. Logging this information to a syslog server can be helpful for capturing the output produced by the debug commands.

Table 7-3   Useful Commands for Configuring CBAC

Command	Sample Output

show ip inspect config
 	
This command shows all specific portions of a configuration
	2621#sh ip inspect config
	Session audit trail is disabled
	Session alert is enabled
	one-minute (sampling period) thresholds are
	[400:500] connections
	max-incomplete sessions thresholds are [400:500]
	max-incomplete tcp connections per host is 50.
	    Block-time 0 minute.
	tcp synwait-time is 30 sec — tcp finwait-time is
	    5 sec
	tcp idle-time is 3600 sec — udp idle-time is 30
	    sec
	dns-timeout is 5 sec
	Inspection Rule Configuration
	Inspection name firewall
	tcp alert is on audit-trail is off timeout 3600
	udp alert is on audit-trail is off timeout 30
	fragment Maximum 50 In Use 0 alert is on audit-
	    trail is off timeout 1
	smtp alert is on audit-trail is off timeout 3600
	ftp alert is on audit-trail is off timeout 3600

show ip inspect interfaces
 	
This command shows the interfaces where CBAC inspection is configured
	2621#sh ip inspect int
	Interface FastEthernet0/0
	Inbound inspection rule is firewall
	tcp alert is on audit-trail is off timeout 3600
	udp alert is on audit-trail is CBAC off timeout
	    30
	fragment Maximum 50 In Use 0 alert is on audit-
	    trail is off timeout 1
	smtp alert is on audit-trail is off timeout 3600
	ftp alert is on audit-trail is off timeout 3600
	Outgoing inspection rule is not set
	Inbound access list is 110
	Outgoing access list is not set

Table 7-3 *(Continued)*

Command	Sample Output

show ip inspect session [detail]
 	
This command shows information regarding the CBAC state table.
	`2621#sh ip inspect session detail`
	`Established Sessions`
	`Session 8136B8DC (199.0.200.40:1235) =>`
	`   (199.0.200.1:23) tcp SIS_OPEN`
	`Created 00:00:15, Last heard 00:00:13`
	`Bytes sent (initiator:responder) [25:140] acl`
	`   created 1`
	`Inbound access-list 120 applied to interface`
	`   FastEthernet0/1`

show ip inspect name *inspection-name*
 	
This command shows the enabled protocols for CBAC inspection
	`2621#sh ip inspect name firewall`
	`Inspection name firewall`
	`tcp alert is on audit-trail is off timeout 3600`
	`udp alert is on audit-trail is off timeout 30`
	`fragment Maximum 50 In Use 0 alert is on audit-`
	`   trail is off timeout 1`
	`smtp alert is on audit-trail is off timeout 3600`
	`ftp alert is on audit-trail is off timeout 3600`

show ip inspect all
 	
This command shows the output of all the pre-ceding commands
	`debug ip inspect function-trace`
	`debug ip inspect object-creation`
	`debug ip inspect object deletion`
	`debug ip inspect events`
	`debug ip inspect detailed`
	`debug ip inspect timers`
	`debug ip inspect protocol`

To disable CBAC, use the command:

```
no ip inspect
```

This command removes all CBAC configuration entries and should obviously be used with caution. However, if you do accidentally delete your CBAC configuration, just power-cycle the router without committing your changes to NVRAM. If you accidentally save your changes, you can always use tftp to place a saved configuration back on the router. (You have saved router configurations, right?)

Logging

In addition to its traffic inspection capabilities, CBAC can log a wide variety of messages to a syslog server or to the router's log buffer for later examination or to provide up-to-the-minute alerts. To enable the audit trail functionality use the global command:

```
ip inspect audit-trail
```

This will record the source and destination IP addresses and ports in use for each network conversation and the number of bytes transferred. Be aware that this can result in a large amount of logging so you may wish to selectively enable or disable it on a per-application basis. As shown earlier, you can selectively enable or disable audit trails and alerts for each application you define for CBAC inspection with the ip inspect name *list-name protocol* command. Alerts are on for all applications by default, but you can disable them with the global command ip inspect alert-off. If you disable alerts globally, you can selectively enable them on a per-application basis so that application violations, such as illegal SMTP commands or illegal FTP behavior, can be logged.

To configure logging to the routers' log buffer use the command:

```
logging buffered
```

To configure logging to a syslog server use the commands:

```
logging IP-address
logging facility facility-type
logging trap level (optional, the default is informational,
  the highest level)
```

You will probably also want to enable time stamping of syslog messages:

```
service timestamps log datetime
```

Of course, the time stamp on the router will only be useful if you also update the router's clock via NTP. If you intend to use audit trails for event correlation, it is crucial to enable NTP on the router and have the router's clock synchronized to an accurate time source. An example of how to configure NTP on your router follows:

```
clock timezone PST -8
clock summer-time PDT recurring
```

```
ntp update-calendar
ntp server server-ip

interface ethernet0
    ntp broadcast
```

Note that if you listen to an NTP-speaking clock source on the Internet, use NTP authentication. If you don't use NTP authentication, an attacker could send your router incorrect time and it may be very difficult to reconstruct an accurate chronology of an attack. This caveat is also applicable to time-based access lists covered previously.

Additionally, it may be impossible to successfully prosecute a successful attacker if your log information does not have accurate time stamps, even if the evidence they provide is conclusive. An example of how to configure NTP authentication follows:

```
ntp authenticate
ntp authentication-key number md5 value
ntp trusted-key key-number
```

The reader should refer to the Cisco documentation for additional information on the use of these commands.

Now that we understand the procedures for implementing and monitoring CBAC on a router, we will present several examples that fully illustrate the use of these features. Each will contain an overview of an application requirement, a network schematic, the IOS statements, commands required to satisfy the applications needs, and a detailed explanation of the solution presented.

CBAC Examples

CBAC Application: Example 1

In this example, an organization has a two-port router, one Ethernet and one serial. The serial port is connected to an ISP and the Ethernet port is connected to the internal network. This organization needs to permit internal users to access the Internet for Web browsing, FTP, and e-mail. The network administrator has a healthy dose of paranoia, and only wants to allow embedded java applets from the 177.100.0.0/16 network, which is the parent company of this organization.

The administrator would also like to know when java applets have been blocked or permitted and is interested in knowing how much FTP traffic is in use. Additionally, the internal users need to be able to ping and trace route to hosts on the Internet for troubleshooting purposes. There are no internal servers, so all needed services are provided by the ISP.

As indicated in the network schematic (Figure 7-1), assume that your organization has the class C network address of 198.78.46.0.

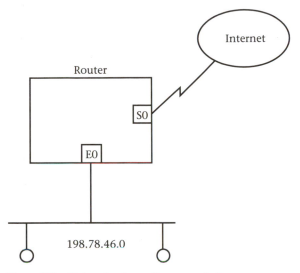

Figure 7-1 Network schematic: example 1.

Solution

```
Ip inspect alert-off
Ip inspect name firewall http java-list 1 alert on
Ip inspect name firewall ftp audit-trail on
Ip inspect name firewall smtp
Ip inspect name firewall udp
Ip inspect name firewall tcp
!
interface ethernet0
 ip address 198.78.46.1 255.255.255.0
 ip access-group 101 in
!
 interface serial0
 IP address 150.100.1.2 255.255.255.252
 ip inspect firewall out
 ip access-group 102 in
!
ip access-list 1 permit 177.100.0.0 0.0.255.255
!
ip access-list 101 permit ip any any
!
ip access-list 102 permit icmp any any echo-reply
ip access-list 102 permit icmp any any time-exceeded
ip access-list 102 permit icmp any any packet-too-big
ip access-list 102 permit icmp any any administratively-prohibited
ip access-list 102 permit icmp any any unreachable
```

Explanation

In this solution, we define the protocols for which we wish to enable
CBAC inspection. We previously stated that we wished to allow Web

browsing, but that we wanted to restrict inbound java so that embedded java applets would only be allowed if they originated from Web sites in the 177.100.0.0/16 network. Notice the `java-list` command specifies that CBAC should use access list 1 to selectively allow java and that we have defined access list 1 so that it only allows the 177.100.0.0/16 network. Also notice that we have specified that alerts are on for HTTP, which was also one of the requirements. The `ip inspect alert-off` command in the configuration disables global alerts, so we have to selectively enable it for HTTP.

Notice that we have also configured inspection for FTP and SMTP. FTP access was a specific requirement and SMTP is needed for sending e-mail. We have defined that audit-trail capabilities are on for FTP so we can track the IP addresses of the FTP sites that are visited and the number of bytes transferred. Additionally, we have defined inspection for generic UDP and TCP. We need generic UDP so that our internal users can perform DNS lookups on the DNS servers at the ISP. We do not have an in-house DNS, so we must use the one provided at our ISP. Since it would seem that we have fulfilled all of our requirements, the question may arise as to why we have enabled inspection for TCP. The reason is to allow the *post office protocol* (POP) so our internal users can retrieve their e-mail from the ISP's mail server. SMTP is normally used only for sending e-mail, while the POP protocol is used to retrieve it. If we did not specify that generic TCP be inspected, our users would be able to send e-mail but not receive it, which obviously would not be very useful.

For the serial interface, the inspection is defined outbound on the interface, which means that all traffic leaving the serial interface toward the Internet will be inspected by CBAC. We could also have applied the inspection inbound on the Ethernet interface since traffic inbound from the Ethernet interface would also be going in the direction of the Internet. Access list 102 is applied inbound on the serial interface to block all incoming traffic, except what is explicitly permitted. Notice that we have allowed several kinds of ICMP traffic. Remember that CBAC only inspects TCP or UDP traffic, so we must explicitly enable any other types of IP traffic to be allowed. We are allowing `echo-reply` so internal users can ping hosts on the Internet. The permission of the `time-exceeded` parameter and the `unreachable` will allow `traceroute` to function from the internal network to the Internet. Both of these functions were part of the original specification for this example. The permission of the `packet-too-big` and `administratively-prohibited` ICMP messages allow for path MTU (maximum transmissible unit) discovery and messages indicating possible access lists on Internet sites we are trying to reach. If we did not permit these ICMP messages, our internal users might experience significant delays when attempting to reach sites they are not able to reach and might not be able to reach some sites at all. No other entries are needed in the access list because CBAC will ensure that the necessary entries are created for return traffic once traffic from the internal network is initiated toward the Internet. There are no permanent holes in the access list that an attacker could use to their advantage.

We have also defined access list 101 which is applied inbound on the Ethernet interface. Since this access list is a permit any, we did not have to use an access list at all. It is placed in this sample configuration because most of the Cisco documentation states that an inbound access list is needed on the router interface where the traffic originates, and we have repeated this statement in this chapter. In reality, this access list is not needed if it is merely a permit any access list. Of course, if we wished to limit the applications that internal users could initiate to the Internet, we would need the access list. An example is shown later in this chapter. For the moment, just understand that the statement that an inbound access list is required on the interface where the outbound traffic is initiated is not completely accurate, although it is good practice.

The configuration is, in most respects, straightforward, although some may doubt that such a simple configuration will work. We assure you that it will. Here is sample output from a debug ip inspect ftp-cmd after initiating an FTP session from the internal network:

```
03:16:08: CBAC FTP sis 8160CEC8 FTP-Server: 220 locutus.com FTP server
          (Version wu-2.5.0(1) Tue Aug 31 16:26:57 BST 1999) ready.~~
03:16:08: CBAC FTP sis 8160CEC8 FTP-Client: USER anonymous~~
03:16:08: CBAC* FTP sis 8160CEC8 FTP-Server: 331 Guest login ok, send
          your complete e-mail address as password.~~
03:16:08: CBAC FTP sis 8160CEC8 FTP-Client: PASS xxxxxxxxxxx
03:16:08: CBAC* FTP sis 8160CEC8 FTP-Server: 230-~~
03:16:08: CBAC* sis 8160CEC8 User authenticated
03:16:08: CBAC* FTP sis 8160CEC8 FTP-Server: 230-~~WelcomesFTP
          site!~~230-~~~ ftp.com~~230-~~~~ ~~230-~~ "Welcom"
03:16:08: CBAC FTP sis 8160CEC8 FTP-Client: feat~~
03:16:08: CBAC* FTP sis 8160CEC8 FTP-Server: 500 'FEAT': command not
          understood.
03:16:08: CBAC FTP sis 8160CEC8 FTP-Client: syst~~
03:16:09: CBAC* FTP sis 8160CEC8 FTP-Server: 215 UNIX Type: L8~~
03:16:09: CBAC FTP sis 8160CEC8 FTP-Client: PWD~~
03:16:09: CBAC* FTP sis 8160CEC8 FTP-Server: 257 "/" is current
          directory.~~
03:16:09: CBAC FTP sis 8160CEC8 FTP-Client: TYPE A~~
03:16:09: CBAC* FTP sis 8160CEC8 FTP-Server: 200 Type set to A.~~
03:16:09: CBAC FTP sis 8160CEC8 FTP-Client: PORT 199,0,200,34,4,54~~
03:16:09: CBAC FTP sis 8160CEC8 Handle PORT command 199.0.200.34:1078
03:16:09: CBAC* FTP sis 8160CEC8 FTP-Server: 200 PORT command
          successful.~~
03:16:09: CBAC FTP sis 8160CEC8 FTP-Client: LIST~~
03:16:10: CBAC* FTP sis 8160CEC8 FTP-Server: 150 Opening ASCII mode data
          connection for /bin/ls.~~
03:16:10: CBAC* FTP sis 8160CEC8 FTP-Server: 226 Transfer complete.~~
```

The output from show ip session detail, in which we captured the DNS request and the initial FTP command channel connection, is as follows:

```
Established Sessions
 Session 8155C76C (199.0.200.34:1079)=>(204.166.61.245:53) udp SIS_OPEN
    Created 00:00:02, Last heard 00:00:02
    Bytes sent (initiator:responder) [30:0] acl created 1
    Inbound access-list 102 applied to interface Serial0
 Session 8160CEC8 (199.0.200.34:1080)=>(198.93.2.50:21) ftp SIS_OPEN
    Created 00:00:02, Last heard 00:00:02
    Bytes sent (initiator:responder) [0:0] acl created 1
    Inbound access-list 102 applied to interface Serial0
```

After a few seconds, the initial opening for the DNS request is closed and only the FTP command channel connection remains. You may not see the FTP data channel connection in the state table; it depends on the amount of data transferred. However, the router allows packets from the server to the client on the data channel and the command channel.

We should also note in this example that we have not changed any of the default settings for TCP or UDP time-outs or thresholds for preventing DoS attacks. Examples where some of these time-outs are changed will be given later. All of the values related to CBAC can be seen with the command show ip inspect config:

```
Session audit trail is disabled
Session alert is disabled
one-minute (sampling period) thresholds are [400:500] connections
max-incomplete sessions thresholds are [400:500]
max-incomplete tcp connections per host is 50. Block-time 0 minute.
tcp synwait-time is 30 sec — tcp finwait-time is 5 sec
tcp idle-time is 3600 sec — udp idle-time is 30 sec
dns-timeout is 5 sec
Inspection Rule Configuration
 Inspection name firewall
 http java-list 1 alert is off audit-trail is off timeout 3600
 ftp alert is off audit-trail is on timeout 3600
 smtp alert is off audit-trail is off timeout 3600
 udp alert is off audit-trail is off timeout 30
 tcp alert is off audit-trail is off timeout 3600
```

This command is very useful because it provides a quick snapshot of all of the parameters available when configuring CBAC. In future examples, the output of these commands will not be shown in the interest of space and to avoid redundancy.

CBAC Application: Example 2

In this example, an organization has a considerably more complex configuration than the one in Example 1. This company has decided to provide services to external users on the Internet such as Web browsing and FTP. For the time being, they are not going to filter java applets imbedded in HTTP. Additionally, the organization has decided to provide and manage its own mail and DNS servers. The organization would like to allow both internal and external users to access the Web and FTP server.

They also want to allow internal users to send and retrieve e-mail, but not allow external users to use their e-mail server for retrieving mail. Additionally, the public DNS will exchange DNS records with a secondary DNS 150.100.5.100 at the ISP, but will not exchange DNS records with a DNS server that is on the private network. The external DNS will only have entries for those servers that are world accessible and not any internal devices. Likewise the internal DNS server will not have records for the external devices but will forward requests to the external DNS for lookups that it cannot resolve. This is referred to as a *split-brain* DNS and is a very common configuration for security-conscious organizations.

Other requirements are that internal users can `ping` and `traceroute` to both the Internet and the DMZ segment. The administrators of this organization also want to ensure that state information about IP fragments is retained since some IP fragment attacks have occurred in the past. Finally, the administrators want to ensure that if one of the machines on their DMZ is compromised, an attacker cannot use that machine to launch further attacks against either their internal LAN or other sites on the Internet. The internal network will use the 198.78.46.0/24 network as in the previous example and the DMZ segment will use the 205.131.175.0/24 network. (See Figure 7-2.)

Solution

```
Ip inspect alert-off
Ip inspect name outbound ftp
Ip inspect name outbound smtp
Ip inspect name outbound udp
Ip inspect name outbound tcp
Ip inspect name outbound fragments alert on
!
ip inspect name inbound ftp audit-trail on
ip inspect name inbound smtp audit-trail on
ip inspect name inbound udp audit-trail on
ip inspect name inbound http audit-trail on
interface ethernet0
 ip address 198.78.46.1 255.255.255.0
 ip access-group 101 in
 ip inspect outbound in
!
interface ethernet1
 ip address 205.131.175.1 255.255.255.0
 ip access-group 103 in
!
interface serial0
 IP address 150.100.1.2 255.255.255.252
 ip access-group 102 in
 ip inspect inbound in
!
ip access-list 101 permit ip 198.78.46.0 0.0.0.255 any
!
ip access-list 102 permit tcp any host 205.131.175.2 eq 80
```

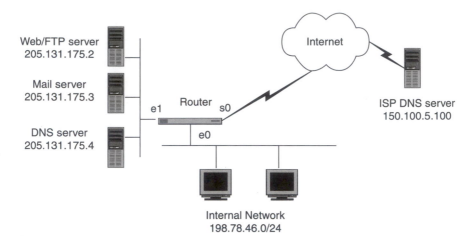

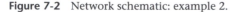

Figure 7-2   Network schematic: example 2.

```
ip access-list 102 permit tcp any host 205.131.175.2 eq 21
ip access-list 102 permit tcp any host 205.131.175.3 eq 25
ip access-list 102 permit tcp host 150.100.5.100 host 205.131.175.4 eq
53
ip access-list 102 permit udp any host 205.131.175.4 eq 53
ip access-list 102 permit icmp any any echo-reply
ip access-list 102 permit icmp any any time-exceeded
ip access-list 102 permit icmp any any packet-too-big
ip access-list 102 permit icmp any any administratively-prohibited
ip access-list 102 permit icmp any any unreachable
!
ip access-list 103 permit icmp any any echo-reply
ip access-list 103 permit icmp any any time-exceeded
ip access-list 103 permit icmp any any packet-too-big
ip access-list 103 permit icmp any any administratively-prohibited
ip access-list 103 permit icmp any any unreachable
ip access-list 103 permit tcp host 205.131.175.3 any eq 25
ip access-list 103 deny ip any any
```

Explanation

This example begins by defining the inspection rules. Two separate sets of
rules have been defined, and they are called *outbound* and *inbound* because
one set of rules inspects traffic as it flows out of our domain and another
inspects traffic as it flows into our domain. The names are a matter of preference and any names could have been chosen. The outbound inspection
rules are applied inbound on the Ethernet0 interface. All traffic leaving
the internal network bound for either the DMZ segment on Ethernet1 or
for the Internet will be inspected by this rule set. The rules specify that
FTP, SMTP, TCP, UDP, and IP fragments should be inspected. This means
that CBAC will create the necessary openings in either access list 102 or
103 to permit the return traffic for sessions initiated from the Ethernet0
interface. CBAC will create the openings to allow the return traffic from

either the DMZ or the Internet as needed. It is not necessary for inspection rules to be applied to the interface where the openings are created.

We are allowing FTP, SMTP, UDP, TCP, and IP fragments to trigger inspection for sessions originated from the inside network on interface Ethernet0. UDP is needed for DNS lookups and TCP is needed for Web browsing and POP3. We have not defined that HTTP should be inspected because we are not filtering any imbedded java applets. We are not auditing any traffic initiated from the inside and we have turned on alerts only for IP fragments. Notice further that we have applied access list 101 inbound on Ethernet0 and are allowing only packets with a source IP address in the range 198.78.46.0/24 to ensure that only packets with legitimate IP addresses are allowed outbound from our internal network. No other IP addresses should be in use on our internal network.

Our second set of inspection rules are named inbound because it inspects packets inbound from the Internet to our DMZ. This set of rules is very similar to the outbound rules, except we are not inspecting IP fragments and have auditing enabled for each application being inspected. We have enabled auditing because we want audit data on who is using the services on our DMZ. Be aware that this could generate a tremendous amount of data for busy sites, so, in practice, you should enable the auditing information to be sent to a syslog server. We discussed how to enable logging to a syslog server earlier in this chapter.

We have enabled inbound inspection of FTP and SMTP so that external users can access our FTP server and so that our SMTP server can respond to mail sent from SMTP servers on the Internet. We have enabled UDP inspection so that external users can query our external DNS and we have enabled HTTP inspection so that external users can browse our Web server. We have not enabled TCP inspection, so even if an external TCP session other than FTP, SMTP, or HTTP were initiated to our DMZ, no openings would be created to allow the return traffic. We should point out, though, that access list 102 applied inbound on serial0 prevents any applications other than FTP, SMTP, HTTP, or DNS from being initiated to our DMZ servers. All other applications will be blocked at the serial0 interface. For access list 102, we are allowing FTP, SMTP, and HTTP to the respective servers on our DMZ. We have two entries for DNS. The first entry permits DNS zone transfers from the secondary DNS server at our ISP to our DNS server on our DMZ. The second entry permits external queries of our DNS server using standard UDP. These entries ensure that only the DNS server at our ISP can transfer our DNS zones, but allows anyone to query our DNS server. As in Example 1, we are permitting certain ICMP types inbound to allow `ping` and `traceroute` to devices on the Internet and other ICMP types for flow control purposes.

The inbound inspection rules are applied inbound on serial0. Any traffic initiated from the Internet will be inspected and the necessary openings will be created in access list 103 which is applied inbound on Ethernet1, our DMZ. We are not allowing any sessions to be initiated from the Internet to our internal network, so all packets initiated from the Internet to our internal network will be dropped. Only packets which are part of a data session originated from our internal network to the Internet will be allowed through the access list applied on serial0. As noted earlier, the necessary openings for the return traffic will be created by the inspection rules outbound applied on Ethernet0.

The final part of this example is access list 103, which is applied inbound on Ethernet1, the DMZ. This access list allows the same ICMP types as access list 102, and allows our SMTP server to initiate connections to other SMTP servers on the Internet to transfer mail. No other sessions can be initiated from the DMZ servers. All necessary openings in access list 103 will be created by either the inspection rules applied on Ethernet0 or the inspection rules applied on serial0. CBAC will ensure that only the necessary openings are created. By preventing any session from being initiated from our DMZ servers, we prevent an attacker from using one of our DMZ servers to attack devices on our internal network or the Internet. Most attacks do not originate from the attacker's machine but from another machine that the attacker has compromised. In the future, companies may be legally liable if their site is used to attack other sites, even if the machine has been compromised by an outside party. For this reason, it is wise to do all you can to prevent attackers from using your devices to commit illegal acts.

This completes Example 2. The important point to note is that although we applied our inspection rules on Ethernet0 and serial0, CBAC creates the necessary return openings on whichever interface is necessary to allow return traffic. In this case, traffic initiated from Ethernet0 causes CBAC to create openings in the access list on either Ethernet1 or serial0, depending on whether the traffic is destined for the DMZ or the Internet. Likewise, traffic from the Internet to the DMZ will be inspected and the necessary openings will be created in the access list on the Ethernet1 interface. As stated earlier, traffic from the Internet cannot be initiated to the Ethernet0 interface, so CBAC does not need to create openings on the access list applied to the Ethernet0 interface. We have applied the inspection rules closest to the interface where the traffic to be inspected originates. Although we could have applied the inspection closest to the interface where the traffic exits the router, we find it conceptually easier to apply our inspection rules in the manner discussed.

CBAC Application: Example 3

Example 3 shows how CBAC can be used to prevent certain DoS attacks and how CBAC can protect your environment when multimedia applications are used. In this scenario, an organization wishes to set up a connection to one of its partners via a direct connection. The partner will be trusted to access some internal resources, but not all, so we need to allow very select access from the partner. This type of a connection is typically referred to as an *extranet* connection to distinguish it from the *intranet* which is entirely internal and the Internet which is entirely external.

The requirements are to allow internal clients to collaborate with our partner through the use of the Microsoft NetMeeting application. Additionally, we will allow our partner to retrieve files from an internal FTP server and to use an internal HTTP server. We are going to change some of the default CBAC session time-out values to prevent our FTP and HTTP server from being overloaded by inbound requests either intentionally or accidentally. We will not require DNS lookups to our partner's DNS server, nor will we allow DNS lookups from our partner. We have configured our DNS so that it is aware of the server it needs to resolve for the NetMeeting application and we assume that our partner has done the same to access our FTP and HTTP server. The final requirement is to allow inbound `ping` from our partner but not `traceroute`. The internal network will use the 198.78.46.0/24 network as in Example 2 and the partner network is 175.50.1.0/24. (See Figure 7-3.)

Solution

```
Ip inspect alert-off
Ip inspect name partner-out h323
Ip inspect name partner-out tcp
!
Ip inspect name partner-in ftp alert on
Ip inspect name partner-in http alert on
!
ip inspect one-minute high 200
ip inspect one-minute low 150
!
interface ethernet0
  ip address 198.78.46.1 255.255.255.0
  ip access-group 101 in
!
```

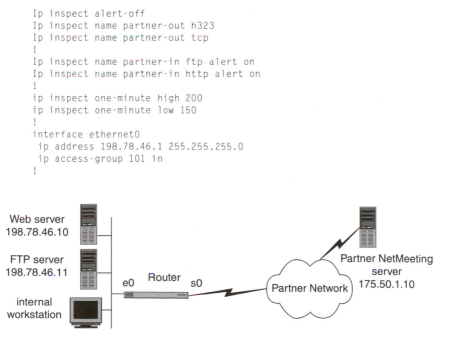

Figure 7-3 Network schematic: example 3.

```
interface serial0
 IP address 170.20.1.1 255.255.255.0
 ip access-group 102 in
 ip inspect partner-in in
 ip inspect partner-out out
 !
 ip access-list 101 permit ip 198.78.46.0 0.0.0.255 any
 ip access-list 101 permit icmp any any echo-reply
 ip access-list 101 permit icmp any any packet-too-big
 ip access-list 101 permit icmp any any administratively-prohibited
 ip access-list 101 permit icmp any any unreachable

 !
 ip access-list 102 permit tcp any host 198.78.46.10 eq 80
 ip access-list 102 permit tcp any host 198.78.46.11 eq 21
 ip access-list 102 permit icmp any any echo-reply
 ip access-list 102 permit icmp any any time-exceeded
 ip access-list 102 permit icmp any any packet-too-big
 ip access-list 102 permit icmp any any administratively-prohibited
 ip access-list 102 permit icmp any any unreachable
```

Explanation

Example 3 begins by defining our inspection rules. In this case, we have two sets of inspection rules. The first is *partner-out*, which defines the traffic that is to be inspected from our internal network to our partner. Note that we have defined the H.323 protocol and TCP in our inspection rule. Although we will not be using any applications other than Microsoft NetMeeting, the additional TCP inspection rule is needed. NetMeeting requires an additional TCP connection in addition to the traditional H.323 channels required by the specification. Our second set of inspection rules is *partner-in*, which defines the traffic to be inspected from our partner's network to our internal network. We have defined both FTP and HTTP for inspection and have enabled alerts for both of these applications. Although we do not anticipate any attackers coming through this connection, if CBAC detects unusual activity from our partner, we wish to be alerted so that we can inform our partner immediately. We have additionally defined the maximum number of incomplete TCP and UDP sessions allowed in 1 min. Once the maximum number of half-open sessions is reached, CBAC will begin deleting half-open connections until the 1-min low number is reached.

We have applied the partner-out inspection rule set outbound on the serial0 interface. CBAC will ensure that the appropriate entries are created in access list 102 which we have applied inbound on the serial interface. We have also applied the partner-in inspection rule set to the serial0 interface in the inbound direction to ensure that the appropriate entries are created in access list 101 which we have applied inbound on the Ethernet interface. Access list 101, which is applied inbound on the Ethernet interface, will allow our internal IP addresses outbound and will permit our partner to ping our internal hosts but will not allow traceroute. Notice that the `time-exceeded` ICMP messages are not allowed in access list 101 as in access list 102. We are also allowing our standard ICMP message types for error conditions and flow control as in our earlier examples. In addition to ICMP messages, access list 102 permits inbound FTP and HTTP to the specified server addresses but nothing else. CBAC will create openings for NetMeeting on an as-needed basis by inspecting the traffic defined by the inspection rule set partner-out. We should note that we could have defined the partner-out inspection "in" on the Ethernet interface and the example would have worked just as well. We have applied the rule set outbound on the serial interface only because it seemed more consistent with the names we chose for our rule sets.

CBAC Application: Example 4

Our fourth example returns to an example that involves a company connecting to the Internet. In this example, a company wants to secure its internal hosts but still provide outside access to servers on its DMZ. In this respect, this example is very similar to Example 2. However, this company wishes to use two routers instead of a single router. The use of two routers provides an additional layer of security. If the Internet-connected router is compromised, the inside router still provides additional security. This is a very common configuration and follows the time-honored firewall principle of *defense in depth*.

The requirements are to allow world access to our DMZ for FTP, Web services, and a RealAudio streaming content server. No connections from the Internet or the DMZ will be allowed to our internal network. Our internal clients will be allowed to connect to the DMZ or the Internet for FTP, HTTP, DNS, and RealAudio. Additionally, we will use CBAC to limit the number of inbound TCP connections to our world-accessible servers, as in Example 3. Finally, we will allow both `ping` and `traceroute` from our internal network to the Internet. The internal network will use the 198.78.46.0/24 network as in the previous examples and the DMZ segment will use the 205.131.175.0/24 network. (See Figure 7-4.)

Solution

```
Router1
    Ip inspect alert-off
    Ip inspect name internet-in RealAudio
    Ip inspect name internet-in ftp
    Ip inspect name internet-in http
    !
    ip inspect name internal-out RealAudio
    Ip inspect name internal-out ftp
    Ip inspect name internal-out http
    Ip inspect name internal-out udp
    !
```

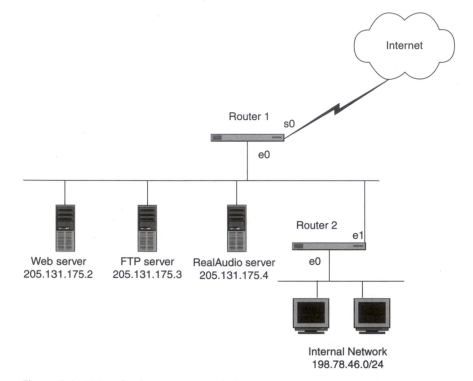

Figure 7-4   Network schematic: example 4.

```
ip inspect one-minute high 300
ip inspect one-minute low 200
!
interface ethernet0
 ip address 205.131.175.1 255.255.255.0
 ip access-group 101 in
 ip inspect internet-out in
!
interface serial0
 IP address 170.20.1.1 255.255.255.0
 ip access-group 102 in
 ip inspect internet-in in
!
ip access-list 101 permit ip 198.78.46.0 0.0.0.255 any
!
ip access-list 102 permit tcp any host 205.131.175.2 eq 80 ip
  access-list 102 permit tcp any host 205.131.175.3 eq 21
ip access-list 102 permit tcp any host 205.131.175.4 eq realaudio
ip access-list 102 permit icmp any any echo-reply
ip access-list 102 permit icmp any any time-exceeded
ip access-list 102 permit icmp any any packet-too-big
ip access-list 102 permit icmp any any administratively-prohibited
ip access-list 102 permit icmp any any unreachable
```

```
Router2
    Ip inspect alert-off
    Ip inspect name internal-out RealAudio
    Ip inspect name internal-out ftp
    Ip inspect name internal-out http
    Ip inspect name internal-out udp
    !
    interface ethernet0
     ip address 198.78.46.1 255.255.255.0
     ip access-group 101 in
    !
    interface ethernet1
     IP address 205.131.175.100 255.255.255.0
     ip access-group 102 in
     ip inspect internal-out out
    !
    ip access-list 101 permit ip 198.78.46.0 0.0.0.255 any
    !
    ip access-list 102 permit icmp any any echo-reply
    ip access-list 102 permit icmp any any time-exceeded
    ip access-list 102 permit icmp any any packet-too-big
    ip access-list 102 permit icmp any any administratively-prohibited
    ip access-list 102 permit icmp any any unreachable
```

Explanation

We will examine the configuration for router 1 first. We begin by defining the CBAC inspection rule sets. In this example, we have defined two rule sets. The first is *internet-in*, which is used to inspect traffic arriving from the Internet to our DMZ segment. This rule set will inspect FTP, HTTP, and RealAudio and will create the necessary openings in access list 101 to allow the return traffic from the servers on our DMZ. Access list 101 permits only IP traffic from our internal network 198.78.46.0/24 to initiate connections to the Internet. The servers on the DMZ cannot initiate connections to the Internet, but may respond to connections initiated to them from the Internet so that if one of our DMZ servers is compromised, it cannot be used to further attack our internal network or other devices on the Internet.

The second rule set is *internet-out*, which is used to inspect traffic initiated from the inside network to the Internet. This rule set will inspect FTP, HTTP, RealAudio, and UDP traffic from our internal segment and will create the necessary openings in access list 102 to allow return traffic from the Internet to our internal network 198.78.46.0/24. Access list 102 is configured to permit inbound connections to our FTP, Web, and RealAudio servers on their respective ports. It also allows the ICMP message types needed for outbound `ping` and `traceroute` and allows for error messages and flow control.

It should be noted that although CBAC creates openings in access list 101 to allow return connections from our DMZ servers, these openings cannot create further openings in access list 102. For example, an inbound connection to our FTP server would cause an access-list entry to be created in access list 101 to allow the packets from the DMZ FTP server back out to the device on the Internet that initiated the connection. Normally, packets that match access list 101 would be inspected by CBAC and would trigger creation of a corresponding access-list entry in access list 102. However, the dynamic entries created by CBAC are inspected by CBAC and will not trigger additional access-list entry creation so a clever attacker cannot initiate an FTP transfer to the FTP server, place a program on the server, and then use that program to create outbound connections on certain ports. Even if the program tried to initiate connections on the same ports specified by the dynamic entries created by CBAC, CBAC would not create additional openings and the return packets would be denied.

Let's now turn our attention to the configuration of router 2. Its configuration is very similar to that of the router in Example 1. We begin by defining our inspection rule set. On router 2, we have only defined a single rule set named *internal-out* and have specified that FTP, HTTP, RealAudio, and UDP are candidates for CBAC inspection. This is the identical inspection rule set defined on router 1. This is no accident. We must maintain consistency between router 1 and router 2 for our outbound traffic to ensure that what is allowed outbound by one router is also allowed outbound by the other router. Similarly, access list 101 is identical to the access list 101 defined on router 1. We are allowing only packets with a source IP address from the 198.78.46.0/24 network to initiate connections outbound through interface Ethernet0. Access list 102 is applied inbound to interface Ethernet1 and is configured only to allow inbound ICMP message types for `ping`, `traceroute`, error messages, and flow control. CBAC inspection will ensure that the necessary openings are created in access list 102 to allow return traffic from either the Internet or the DMZ to our internal network.

Notice that by separating our internal and Internet routers, we have greatly simplified the configuration of our internal router. Since we are, by default, only allowing ICMP messages inbound, it is much more likely that we will block something we want than that we will allow something we wish to block. It is important to remember that if you use a dual-router configuration like the one in this example, you should ensure that your configurations are consistent between your internal and Internet router. If the configurations are not consistent for outbound traffic, you may permit traffic through one router and block it at the next. If your configurations do not produce the desired results, you can use the `debug` and `show` commands discussed earlier to troubleshoot your configuration.

In closing this chapter, it is worth pointing out that we have tried to illustrate the powerful features available with CBAC. CBAC can be used with a variety of applications and provides a significantly higher level of security than traditional IP access lists. While examples of CBAC could fill an entire book of its own, the examples presented here should provide you with the necessary foundation to adapt CBAC for use in your own environment. Remember to use the `debug` and `show` commands when diagnosing problems in your configuration. Initially, you may also want to enable alerts and audit trail functionality so you can obtain baseline information on the traffic patterns in your network.

CHAPTER 8

TCP Intercept
and
Network Address
Translation

This chapter discusses technologies that are not access lists themselves but closely related to them and that provide additional functionality for controlling data traffic in a network. The features discussed allow you to further secure and control the traffic in and out of your network by intelligently acting upon the data, for example, by manipulating the source and/or destination address in an IP packet or by allocating bandwidth to certain kinds of traffic over others. This chapter discusses two features that provide powerful enhancements for controlling data traffic in your network: TCP intercept and *network address translation* (NAT). We begin with an overview of TCP intercept and a discussion of its features and how it can be implemented in a network. We also discuss all of the available commands that allow configuration and troubleshooting a TCP intercept. The section on TCP intercept ends with several examples that use this feature. After discussing TCP intercept, we present an overview of NAT, including an introduction to NAT and a discussion of its features and how they can be implemented in a network. We discuss the commands available for configuring and troubleshooting NAT and provide many detailed examples.

TCP Intercept Overview

TCP intercept was introduced in IOS version 11.3 and is available on all router platforms. It prevents SYN attacks against internal hosts (SYN attacks were briefly discussed in Chap. 7). A SYN flood attack is very simple. The first packet in the TCP three-way handshake sets the SYN bit.

When a device receives this initial packet requesting a provided service, the device responds with a packet setting the SYN and ACK bits and then waits for an ACK from the originator of the conversation. If the originator of the request does not respond to the host, the host times out the connection. However, while the host is waiting for completion of the transaction, the half-open TCP connection consumes CPU and memory resources on the host. The consumption of resources while waiting for the TCP handshake to complete is the essence of the attack.

Thousands of normal looking packets with the SYN bit set are sent to a host to establish a TCP connection on a listening port on the device. However, the source IP address in these packets is forged. The source address of the forged packets is an unreachable address; in most cases it will either be an unregistered address from RFC 1918 (that is, 10.0.0.0/8, 172.16.0.0/15, and 192.168.0.0/16) or a registered address the attacker knows does not exist. Since the return packets from the attacked host to the originating source IP address will never reach an actual host, the attacked host will never receive a response to its request to complete the initial three-way handshake. The attacked host must wait to time out thousands of SYN requests and eventually the attacked hosts' resources are consumed and the host becomes unusable. If sufficient numbers of SYN packets are sent, some operating systems may even crash altogether and require a reboot.

This is a very popular DoS attack and, while in itself it is bad enough, it is also sometimes used as part of a more sophisticated attack. An attacker might know, for example, that one of your servers trusts packets from another server outside your firewall as a result of having compromised another machine outside your firewall and installing a sniffer and watching your network traffic. If the attacker cannot compromise the trusted server outside the firewall and cannot break through the firewall, he or she might attempt to exploit the trust between the two machines.

The first step would be to initiate a SYN flood against the trusted outside host, preventing it from responding to any new network conversations. The attacker would then send packets to the inside server with a source IP address of the outside server. The inside server would respond to the trusted server's IP address, but the outside trusted server would be unable to respond due to the DoS attack. The attacker's machine might not see the packets, but if the attacker can predict the TCP sequence numbers in use by the inside server, he or she could successfully complete the TCP three-way handshake and possibly further compromise the inside server. Depending on the services allowed through the firewall, a machine on the inside could be compromised through a combination of a DoS attack against an outside trusted host and IP spoofing. This attack is illustrated in Figure 8-1.

The central point is that a SYN flood can be dangerous far beyond just taking down a single host and could be used in combination with other attack methods to compromise other hosts on a network.

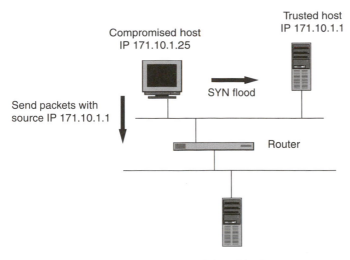

Figure 8-1 DoS attack against outside trusted host. The attack proceeds in two phases: (1) SYN flood legitimate host to "anesthetize" it and prevent it from responding; (2) Send packets to the internal host and spoof the source IP so the internal host believes the packet originated from the trusted host.

TCP intercept prevents this attack by intercepting and validating TCP connection requests before they reach the target host. This feature operates in two modes: intercept and watch. In *intercept mode*, the router intercepts incoming TCP SYN requests and establishes a connection with the client on the servers' behalf and with the server on the clients' behalf. If both connections are successful, the router merges the two connections together transparently. The router has configurable, aggressive time-outs to prevent its own resources from being consumed by a SYN attack. In *watch mode*, the router passively watches half-open connections (that is, those that have not completed the TCP three-way handshake) and will actively close connections on the server after a configurable length of time. Access lists are defined so they specify the source and destination packets that are subject to TCP intercept.

Enabling TCP Intercept

Only two steps are necessary to enable TCP intercept:

1. Configure the access list that permits the hosts' IP addresses to be protected:

```
access-list [100-199] [deny|permit] tcp source source-wildcard
    destination destination-wildcard
```

2. Enable TCP intercept:

```
ip tcp intercept list access-list-number
```

In step 1, you can use an extended IP access list. It is common to specify "any" as the source IP address because you typically want to have TCP intercept examine all inbound connections to vulnerable hosts. In step 2, you actually enable the TCP intercept feature. If the access list in step 2 is not defined, TCP intercept will not examine any inbound connections.

Setting the Mode

TCP intercept works in either intercept or watch mode, with the default being intercept. In intercept mode, the router responds to the incoming SYN request on the servers' behalf with a SYN-ACK response to the originating source IP address and waits for an ACK from the originator of the connection. If an ACK is received, the original SYN packet is sent to the server and the router completes the three-way handshake with the server on behalf of the originating client. This mode places a small additional memory and CPU burden on the router and introduces a small additional delay in completing the initial connection.

In watch mode, the router allows SYN request through to the server. If the session is not established in 30 s (the default), the router sends an RST to the server to clear the connection. The amount of time the router waits is configurable. The TCP intercept mode can be set with the following command:

```
ip tcp intercept mode {intercept|watch}
```

The default mode is `intercept`.

Aggressive Thresholds

When the router believes a protected device is under attack, as defined by its thresholds, it will actively delete connections until the number of half-open connections falls below this threshold. Oldest connections are dropped first, unless the command `ip tcp intercept drop-mode random` is used. When an aggressive threshold is exceeded, the router performs the following actions:

1. Each new connection causes the oldest (or random) connection to be deleted.
2. The initial retransmission time-out is reduced by one-half to 0.5 s.
3. If in watch mode, the time-out is reduced by one-half to 15 s.

Two factors determine aggressive behavior. If either of the thresholds is exceeded, aggressive behavior begins until both values fall below their threshold mark. The parameters and their default values are shown here along with a short description of each parameter:

1. `ip tcp intercept max-incomplete high` *number* 1100. The maximum number of half-open connections that can exist before the router begins dropping connections.

2. `ip tcp intercept max-incomplete low` *number* 900. The maximum number of half-open connections that can exist before the router stops dropping half-open connections.

3. `ip tcp intercept one-minute high` *number* 1100. The maximum rate of half-open connections per minute that can exist before the router begins dropping connections.

4. `ip tcp intercept one-minute low` *number* 900. The minimum rate of half-open connections per minute that can exist before the router stops dropping connections.

The value of the total number of half-open connections and the rate per minute of half-open connections work in conjunction. If either of the maximum values is reached, TCP intercept is triggered to begin dropping half-open connections. Once TCP intercept is triggered, both values must fall below the low setting for TCP intercept to stop dropping connections.

Additional Commands

Additional commands that are useful for examining information about TCP intercept, along with a simple example of TCP intercept, are as follows:

```
show tcp intercept connections
show tcp intercept statistics
ip tcp intercept list 101
!
access-list 101 permit tcp any host 160.10.1.1
```

The next section presents detailed examples of TCP intercept using the format previously outlined.

TCP Intercept Application: Example 1

In this example, an organization uses a router with an Ethernet interface connecting to the internal LAN and a serial interface connecting to an ISP. There is a Web server on the Ethernet interface using IP address 198.50.1.100 that we wish to protect with TCP intercept. The router is a low-end router, so we wish to conserve as many resources as possible while still monitoring incoming TCP connections. (See Figure 8-2.)

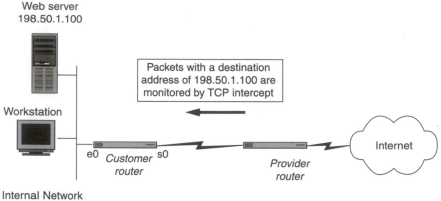

Figure 8-2   Network schematic: example 1.

Solution

```
Ip tcp intercept list 101
Ip tcp intercept mode watch
1
interface ethernet0
 ip address 198.50.1.1 255.255.255.0
!
interface serial0
 IP address 171.100.1.1 255.255.255.0
!
ip access-list 101 permit tcp any host 198.50.1.100
```

Explanation

In this solution, we first define access list 101, which specifies that packets with any source IP address destined to 198.50.1.100 should be matched. We then defined our TCP intercept command and specified that access list 101 is to be used to match packets that will be monitored. We have also defined that TCP intercept should operate in watch mode, which uses less router resources than the default intercept mode. These are all the steps needed to enable TCP intercept to protect our Web server.

TCP Intercept Application: Example 2

In this example, the same organization as in Example 1 uses a router with an Ethernet interface connecting to the internal LAN and a serial interface connecting to an ISP. However, in this case the organization does not simply have a single Web server but an entire Web server farm using IP addresses from 198.50.1.1 to 198.50.100. No other IP addresses are in use on this segment. We want to use TCP intercept to protect all of the Web

```
Packets with a destination
address of 198.50.1.1 through
198.50.1.100 are monitored
      by TCP intercept
```

Figure 8-3   Network schematic: example 2.

servers. Router resources are not a factor as we have selected a higher model router and expect a large number of incoming TCP requests since we have 100 Web servers. (See Figure 8-3.)

Solution

```
Ip tcp intercept list 101
Ip tcp intercept max-incomplete high 3000
Ip tcp intercept max-incomplete low 2500
Ip tcp intercept one-minute high 2000
Ip tcp intercept one-minute low 1500
!
interface ethernet0
 ip address 198.50.1.120 255.255.255.0
!
interface serial0
 IP address 171.100.1.1 255.255.255.0
!
ip access-list 101 permit tcp any 198.50.1.0 0.0.0.128
```

Explanation

In this solution, we define access list 101, which specifies that packets with any source IP address destined to IP addresses in the range 198.50.1.0 to 198.50.1.128 should be matched. Note that this matches more addresses than are actually in use since the Web server IP addresses go only to .100, but this will not cause any problems. We then define our TCP intercept command and specify that access list 101 is to be used to match packets that will be monitored by TCP. We have also changed the TCP intercept default threshold settings since we anticipate having a large number of open SYN requests at any one time due to the large number of servers on our server farm. We have left the default TCP intercept mode of intercept since our router has the resources to manage each TCP connection.

This completes our coverage of TCP intercept. The next section discusses network address translation (NAT).

Network Address Translation Overview

NAT is a feature that dynamically modifies the contents of IP packets flowing through the router so that the source and/or destination IP addresses are altered. Packets leaving the router will have the source or destination address translated to a different IP address so an administrator can hide the IP addresses in use on an internal network behind a router performing NAT. This technique is a requirement for organizations using addresses from the RFC 1918 unregistered address space or using IP addresses that are registered to other organizations.

Characteristics

NAT can be used to alter both the source and destination IP addresses in IP headers and the IP checksum is updated automatically by the NAT process. Some applications imbed the source IP address of hosts in the data portion of the IP packet, so additional modification of the packet is required. For these applications, the NAT process must also modify the data portion of the packet to match the modified source IP address in the IP header. Cisco's version of NAT can handle many applications that place the IP address in the data portion of the packet. Cisco's version also allows load-sharing TCP traffic by permitting TCP requests to a single IP address to be serviced by multiple hosts. These features will be covered later in this chapter.

NAT is most often used at administrative domain boundaries such as the Internet or connections between different organizations. NAT is useful not only for organizations that do not have registered IP addresses, but also for organizations that have a registered IP address range but have more hosts than can be accommodated by the number of addresses. Unregistered addresses may be used internally and registered addresses used only when packets communicate with external networks. The NAT process is transparent to both source and destination hosts for most applications.

Caveats

Although NAT is a very useful tool, it does have some drawbacks. The central difficulty with NAT is that, as mentioned earlier, some applications imbed the original source IP address in the data portion of the IP packet. Therefore, after undergoing NAT, the source IP address of the packet does not match the IP address imbedded in the data portion of the packet. Applications which imbed the IP address in the data portion of the packet function improperly if the source IP address in the IP header does not match the source IP address imbedded in the data portion of the packet. The Cisco implementation can handle most popular applications that include the IP address in the data portion of the packet. One notable exception is NetBios session services. NetBios services are used by Windows NT, so it is very prevalent in many data networks. Cisco is actively working to enhance their NAT offering to include full

Table 8-1   Applications Supported by Cisco NAT

Any TCP/UDP traffic that does not carry the source or destination
IP address in the data portion of the IP packet
ICMP
FTP
NetBios over TCP (except session services)
RealAudio
White Pines CUSeeMe
Streamworks
DNS "A" and "PTR" queries
H.323*
NetMeeting*
VDOLive
Vxtreme

*Support in 12.0.1 and higher IOS versions.

support for all NetBios services. Table 8-1 lists the applications currently supported by Cisco.

The applications in Table 8-2 are not supported by Cisco NAT. If you use these applications, you should be aware that they will most likely function improperly if they transit a router performing NAT.

Table 8-2 Applications Not Supported by Cisco NAT

IP Multicast
Routing table updates
DNS zone transfers
BOOTP
Talk, ntalk
SNMP
NetShow

NAT Terms

Several terms used when discussing Cisco NAT are helpful:

1. Inside local address. IP addresses assigned to hosts on the internal network. These addresses are normally only known by internal hosts.
2. Inside global address. IP addresses assigned to internal hosts by the NAT process; the addresses of internal hosts as seen by external hosts.
3. Outside local addresses. IP addresses assigned to external hosts by the NAT process; the addresses of external hosts as seen by internal hosts.
4. Outside global addresses. IP addresses assigned to hosts on the external network. These addresses are known by external hosts but may not be known by internal hosts.

Inside addresses are used by the internal network and may or may not be translated. Outside addresses are used by external networks and also may or may not be translated. The term *local* refers to addresses as seen by internal hosts. The term *global* refers to addresses as seen by external hosts. Note that outside local and outside global addresses may be the same if outside addresses are not being translated by NAT, that is, the addresses of external hosts may be the same on external networks as on the internal network. In fact, this is usually the case.

The easiest way to remember this terminology is that the first word, inside or outside, reflects the origination of the packet. The terms *inside local* and *inside global address* both indicate that the packet originated from the inside network. The second word, local or global, indicates where the addresses are *seen*. Local addresses are seen locally on the inside network. Global addresses are seen globally on the outside network. As discussed, an inside local address originated from the inside network and that is how the addresses are seen on the inside network. These addresses would not have undergone NAT since they originated on the inside and are being seen by inside devices. Conversely, inside global addresses originated from the inside network but are being viewed on the outside network. These addresses would normally be the NAT translated addresses.

Enabling NAT

Familiarity with several commands is required to enable NAT functionality on the router. First, you need to determine the interfaces on which you will enable NAT and whether they will be an inside or outside interface. Normally, the interface that connects to your internal network will be the NAT inside and any interfaces that connects to external networks, such as the Internet, will be the NAT outside interface. These designations are important because they will be referred to later in the configuration in other NAT commands. The syntax of each interface command is

```
ip nat {inside | outside}
```

Examples

```
Interface ethernet0
  Description internal network
  Ip nat inside
Interface serial0
  Description connection to Internet
Ip nat outside
```

Once you have determined the interfaces where you will enable NAT, you must then determine your inside global addresses. Remember from our definitions that these will be the addresses that are seen on external networks for packets originating from the internal network. These will normally be the translated addresses.

The translated addresses to be used can be dynamic or static. If we don't care which inside local addresses are translated to which inside global addresses, we can allow the router to pick an available address from a pool of addresses. We define this pool of addresses with the `ip nat pool` command:

```
ip nat pool <name> <start-ip> <end-ip> {netmask <netmask> |
  prefix-length <prefix-length>} [type {rotary}]
```

Examples

```
Ip nat pool test 171.100.1.1 171.100.1.50 netmask 255.255.255.0
Ip nat pool test 171.100.1.1 171.100.1.50 prefix-length 24
```

Note that these commands are equivalent. Also note that we have defined host addresses .1 through .50 as the available pool of inside global addresses. Even though we have specified that the mask is for the entire subnet, the `<start-ip>` and `<end-ip>` limit the range of addresses to .1 through .50.

Once we define a NAT pool, the router will pick the first address available from the pool when a new mapping from an inside local address needs to be made to an inside global address. You cannot determine beforehand which address will be chosen from the pool. If you need a predetermined IP address mapping from an inside local address to an inside global address, you will need to use a static mapping. We will provide examples of this later.

In the `ip nat pool` command syntax, the `rotary` keyword is used to have an available pool of inside local IP addresses mapped to the same inside global IP. This is useful, for example, if you have a busy Web site and want to have multiple servers answer incoming Web requests to the same IP address. We will also provide an example later.

Once you have created a pool of available inside global addresses, you need to specify which packets will be allowed to obtain addresses from the pool by using an access list with the `ip nat inside source` command. You can also specify static mappings between inside local and inside global addresses. With either method you use the `ip nat inside source` command as shown here:

```
ip nat inside source {list <acl> pool <name> [overload] | static
  <local-ip> <global-ip>}
```

Examples

```
Ip nat inside source list 101 pool test
Ip nat inside source static 10.1.1.100 171.100.1.1
```

When used with the `list` keyword, this command specifies that packets matching the access list `list` are allowed to obtain addresses from the NAT pool named in `name`. The `overload` keyword specifies that *port address translation* (PAT) is to be enabled. PAT allows translation of many inside local addresses to a single inside global address by maintaining TCP/UDP port information as well as IP address information in the NAT translation table. This feature is useful in situations with a limited number of inside global addresses. The single PAT address can be the same IP address as that of the NAT outside interface, which is useful in companies with only one available address from an ISP. In most configurations, the Internet connected router must itself have a globally routable IP address, so it is useful to use this same address as the PAT address. An alternative syntax can be used in this situation:

```
ip nat inside source list <acl> interface <interface> overload
```

You can also translate outside global addresses to outside local addresses, which is useful when an overlap exists between the addresses used internally and the addresses used by an organization with which you wish to communicate. For example, if both organizations were using over-lapping addresses from RFC1918 such as the 10.0.0.0/24 network, the syntax to translate an outside global address is

```
ip nat outside source {list <acl> pool <name> | static <global-ip>
  <local-ip>}
```

Examples

```
Ip nat outside source list 102 pool outside
Ip nat outside source static 171.50.19.1 10.50.1.1
```

Examples of all of these commands will be provided later.

Additional Commands

When configuring NAT on a router, familiarity with several other commands is useful. First, several time-out values can be configured to conserve addresses and router memory since each NAT translation takes up a small amount of available memory. If port address translation is not used, only one NAT time-out command is applicable:

```
ip nat translation timeout {<0-2147483647> | never}
```

The time-out value is expressed in seconds and the default is 24 h or 36,400 s. In environments with a potentially large number of NAT translations, it is best to adjust this time-out down to 1 to 2 h, perhaps even less if the router does not have a lot of memory. If PAT is in use, several time-out options are available because the router tracks port numbers in addition to IP addresses in its NAT table (note that port numbers are not tracked in the NAT table when PAT is not used). When PAT is enabled, the following timers are available:

```
ip nat translation udp-timeout {<0-2147483647> | never}
ip nat translation tcp-timeout {<0-2147483647> | never}
ip nat translation finrst-timeout {<0-2147483647> | never}
ip nat translation icmp-timeout {<0-2147483647> | never}
ip nat translation port-timeout {<0-2147483647> | never}
ip nat translation syn-timeout {<0-2147483647> | never}
ip nat translation dns-timeout {<0-2147483647> | never}
```

Most of these values are self-explanatory. The `finrst-timeout` refers to the time-out after a FIN or RST TCP packet is seen by the router. The `port-timeout` value applies to both TCP and UDP. The `syn-timeout` value applies when a SYN TCP packet is seen. Most of these time-out values are very low, on the order of a few minutes, and can be left at their default settings. The exception to this rule is TCP, which has a time-out of 24 h. As noted previously, you will most likely want to lower the TCP timeout to 1 to 2 h or less.

Use of PAT results in a significantly shorter time period during which inactive entries remain in the NAT table due to the increased number of timers. For example, even if the TCP time-out is 24 h, if a FIN or RST packet that is part of a NAT translation is seen, entry will be removed in 1 min. Since a normally terminated TCP conversation sees a FIN or RST, only TCP connections which ended abnormally would remain in the NAT table for an extended period of time. This is why it is recommended that you lower the TCP time-out. There is little value in leaving translations in the NAT table for connections that ended abnormally.

In addition to the time-out commands, several other useful commands are shown here with a brief description and sample output from each:

1. Show ip nat translations verbose

```
2621#sh ip nat trans ver
Pro Inside global      Inside local   Outside local   Outside global
tcp 171.0.200.21:1030  10.1.1.2:1030  171.0.200.1:23 171.0.200.1:23
    create 00:00:46, use 00:00:25, left 00:00:34,
    flags:
extended, timing-out, use_count: 0
icmp 171.0.200.21:768  10.1.1.2:768   171.0.200.1:768   71.0.200.1:768
    create 00:00:54, use 00:00:51, left 00:00:08,
    flags:
extended, use_count: 0
```

2. Show ip nat statistics

```
2621#sh ip nat statistics
Total active translations: 2 (0 static, 2 dynamic; 2 extended)
Outside interfaces:
  FastEthernet0/1
Inside interfaces:
  FastEthernet0/0
Hits: 84 Misses: 12
Expired translations: 8
Dynamic mappings:
— Inside Source
access-list 1 pool test refcount 2
  pool test: netmask 255.255.255.0
        start 171.0.200.21 end 171.0.200.24
        type generic, total addresses 4, allocated 1 (25%), misses
```

3. Debug ip nat [<list>] [detailed]

```
2621#debug ip nat detail
IP NAT detailed debugging is on
02:00:24: NAT: installing alias for address 171.0.200.21
02:00:24: NAT: ipnat_allocate_port: wanted 768 got 768
02:00:24: NAT*: o: icmp (171.0.200.1, 768) -> (171.0.200.21, 768)
           [14337]
02:00:25: NAT*: i: icmp (10.1.1.2, 768) -> (171.0.200.1, 768) [14593]
02:00:25: NAT*: o: icmp (171.0.200.1, 768) -> (171.0.200.21, 768)
           [14593]
02:00:26: NAT*: i: icmp (10.1.1.2, 768) -> (171.0.200.1, 768) [14849]
02:00:26: NAT*: o: icmp (171.0.200.1, 768) -> (171.0.200.21, 768)
           [14849]
02:00:27: NAT*: i: icmp (10.1.1.2, 768) -> (171.0.200.1, 768) [15105]
02:00:27: NAT*: o: icmp (171.0.200.1, 768) -> (171.0.200.21, 768)
           [15105]
02:00:30: NAT: i: tcp (10.1.1.2, 1033) -> (171.0.200.1, 23) [15361]
02:00:30: NAT: ipnat_allocate_port: wanted 1033 got 1033
02:00:30: NAT: o: tcp (171.0.200.1, 23) -> (171.0.200.21, 1033) [0]
02:00:30: NAT*: i: tcp (10.1.1.2, 1033) -> (171.0.200.1, 23) [15617]
```

One additional NAT command that can be greatly beneficial is

```
Clear ip nat translation { * | <global-ip> | <global-ip> <local-ip>
  <proto> <global-port> <local-port> }
```

This command can be used to clear translations from the NAT table, which is useful for troubleshooting purposes. In the examples that follow, these commands will not be covered again in the interest of space and avoidance of redundancy, but it is a good idea to familiarize yourself with them and examine the output in your environment. The next section provides several detailed examples of the use of NAT.

NAT Application: Example 1

In this example, an organization uses a router with two Ethernet interfaces. Ethernet0 is connected to the internal network and Ethernet1 is connected to a LAN segment the organization shares with its ISP's router. On the internal network the company is using addresses from the 10.0.0.0/24 address space, which are not routable on the Internet. The company has been provided an IP address range 171.100.1.0/24 for their use. The interface of the company router uses IP address 171.100.1.1 and the interface of the ISP router uses IP address 171.100.1.2, leaving the remaining addresses from 171.100.1.0/24 available for NAT translation. The company wants to place the necessary commands on the router to enable its internal users to access the Internet using valid, globally routable addresses from the address space provided by the ISP. (See Figure 8-4.)

Solution

```
interface ethernet0
 ip address 10.1.1.1 255.255.255.0
 ip nat inside
!
interface ethernet1
 IP address 171.100.1.1 255.255.255.0
 ip nat outside
!
ip access-list 1 permit 10.0.0.0 0.255.255.255
!
ip nat pool internet 171.100.1.3 171.100.1.254 netmask 255.255.255.0
ip nat inside source list 1 pool internet
```

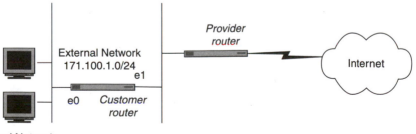

Figure 8-4 NAT application schematic: example 1.

Explanation

In this solution, we define the interfaces that will participate in NAT and whether they are a NAT inside or outside interface by placing the appropriate commands beneath each interface. This is a crucial first step when configuring NAT. If you do not define an interface as a NAT inside or NAT outside interface or define them incorrectly, NAT will not work correctly. If no NAT interfaces are defined, NAT will not work at all and `debug ip nat detail` will not show you anything. If you have defined all of your other NAT commands but NAT does not seem to be functioning, make sure you have the proper NAT commands beneath each interface.

Once we have defined the appropriate NAT commands beneath each interface, we then define the NAT pool from which we will draw our inside global addresses. We have defined the beginning IP as 171.100.1.3 and the ending IP as 171.100.1.254. We excluded the .1 and .2 addresses because those addresses are in use by the customer and ISP router. Since these addresses are part of the same subnet as the Ethernet1 interface on the customer router, the customer router will answer ARP queries from the ISP router with its own MAC address. This allows the ISP router to resolve the IP addresses from the NAT pool and send packets with a destination IP address picked from the NAT pool to the customer router.

Note that the pool of NAT addresses does not have to be from the same subnet as that configured on the customer router interface. The next example shows a similar configuration in which the NAT pool is not part of the address space connected to the router.

NAT Application: Example 2

In this example, an organization uses a router with two interfaces, an Ethernet and a serial. Ethernet0 is connected to the internal network and the serial interface is connected via a point-to-point (PPP) link to the ISP's router. On the internal network the company is using addresses from the 10.0.0.0/24 address space, which are not routable on the Internet. The company has been provided an IP address range 171.100.1.0/24 for their use. The PPP link to the ISP uses addresses from the 198.50.1.0/30 subnet. The company wants to place the necessary commands on the router so its internal users can access the Internet using valid, globally routable addresses from the address space 171.100.1.0/24 provided by the ISP. We are going to exchange OSPF (open shortest page first) updates with the upstream ISP router to receive a default route from that router and inform the ISP router of the subnets that are in use on the company router. (See Figure 8-5.)

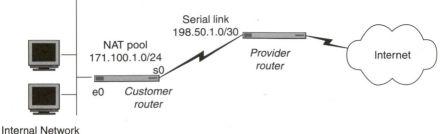

Figure 8-5   NAT application schematic: example 2.

Solution No. 1

```
interface ethernet0
 ip address 10.1.1.1 255.255.255.0
 ip nat inside
!
interface serial0
 IP address 198.50.1.1 255.255.255.252
 ip nat outside
!
ip access-list 1 permit 10.0.0.0 0.255.255.255
!
ip nat pool internet 171.100.1.1 171.100.1.254 netmask 255.255.255.0
ip nat inside source list 1 pool internet
!
ip route 171.100.1.0 255.255.255.0 null0
!
router ospf 1
  network 198.50.1.0 0.0.0.255 area 0
  redistribute static
```

Solution No. 2

```
Interface loopback 0
  Ip address 171.100.1.1 255.255.255.0
  Ip ospf network point-to-point
!
interface ethernet0
  ip address 10.1.1.1 255.255.255.0
  ip nat inside
!
interface serial0
 IP address 198.50.1.1 255.255.255.252
 ip nat outside
!
ip access-list 1 permit 10.0.0.0 0.255.255.255
!
ip nat pool internet 171.100.1.2 171.100.1.254 netmask 255.255.255.0
ip nat inside source list 1 pool internet
!
```

```
router ospf 1
  network 198.50.1.0 0.0.0.255 area 0
  network 171.100.1.0 0.0.0.255 area 0
```

Explanation

In solution no. 1, we begin by defining the interfaces that will participate in NAT and whether they are a NAT inside or outside interface by placing the appropriate commands beneath each interface. Once we have defined the appropriate NAT commands beneath each interface, we then define the NAT pool from which we will draw our inside global addresses. We have defined the beginning IP as 171.100.1.1 and the ending IP as 171.100.1.254. We have not excluded any host IP addresses except .0 and .255 since we are not using any IP addresses from this range on any of the router interfaces. By not using the same IP subnet in the NAT pool as used on the customer router interface, we have gained a few host addresses. However, now we have introduced a new problem.

In our previous example the ISP's router was also directly connected to the subnet from which we allocated our NAT pool. In such a situation, the ISP router would just issue an ARP request for the individual NAT addresses used from the NAT pool and the customer router would respond with its own MAC and the process would work fine. Now, however, the upstream ISP router is not directly connected to the NAT address pool subnet 171.100.1.0/24, so it must be told how to reach that NAT pool subnet through either a routing protocol or a static route. In solution no. 1, we have enabled OSPF and we are redistributing a static route for the 171.100.1.0/24 network into OSPF. The upstream ISP router will receive this route and forward all packets with a destination address of our NAT pool to our router.

Alternatively, the ISP could have installed a static route on its router pointing all packets for the 171.100.1.0/24 network to our router. However, we wanted to illustrate a way to propagate routing information about the NAT pool addresses when the addresses are not pulled from a directly connected subnet. Notice that we have installed a static route for the entire 171.100.1.0/24 subnet to null0. Since we will have more specific entries in the NAT address table than for the entire 171.100.1.0/24 subnet, the router will not drop the packets but will forward them to the inside host defined in the NAT table.

In solution no. 2, we show another way to inform our ISP about the NAT pool in use by creating a loopback interface and assigning it an IP address in the range of our NAT pool. We have now just included the loopback address as part of our OSPF routes by including the `network 171.100.1.0 0.0.0.255 area 0` statement beneath our OSPF routing process. Notice that we have also removed the .1 address from our NAT pool and began our NAT pool addresses using host address .2 to eliminate overlap between the NAT pool and the IP address used on the loopback interface. Notice further that we have used the interface command `ip ospf network point-to-point` beneath the loopback interface. Normally, OSPF treats loopback interfaces as if they are an OSPF stub network and would send the full 32-bit entry of the interface as the route and not the entire subnet. In our example, the OSPF process would have sent 171.100.1.1/32 and not 171.100.1.0/24. In our case, this would not work since we need the entire 171.100.1.0/24 subnet to be propagated to our upstream ISP's router. The OSPF interface command tells OSPF to propagate the route for this interface as if it were a point-to-point network and not a stub network, which means it will propagate the entire 171.100.1.0/24 subnet via OSPF (the `ip ospf network point-to-point` command is available in version 11.3 and higher). Either of these methods works and it is mostly a matter of personal preference as to which to use.

> **NOTE**
> We realize that normally an organization would run Border Gateway Protocol (BGP) between its router and its ISP's router, and not OSPF. We chose OSPF as the routing protocol for this example to illustrate the use of the `ip ospf network point-to-point` command.

NAT Application: Example 3

In this example, the organization is the same as in Example 2, but the scenario is slightly different. Now that the organization has an Internet presence, it has decided to provide a Web server that can be accessed from the Internet so that people browsing the Web can learn about their organization. This server will reside on the internal network and be accessible from internal hosts, so it will have an IP address of 10.1.1.100. Since the Web server must be accessible from the Internet, this source IP address must be translated to an address from our inside global pool before being forwarded to our ISP router. We have chosen to use IP address 171.100.1.100 as the inside global address translation for the organization's Web server.

As in Example 2, Ethernet0 is connected to the internal network and the serial interface is connected via a PPP link to the ISP's router. On the internal network the company is using addresses from the 10.0.0.0/24 and the IP address range of the global pool is 171.100.1.0/24. In this example, we will assume that the ISP has a static route to our router for the IP address range 171.100.1.0/24 and that they are propagating this route to the Internet for us. (See Figure 8-6.)

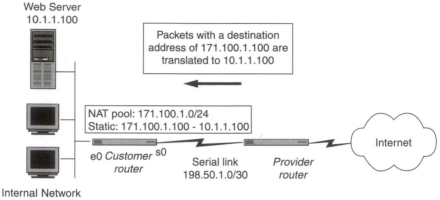

Web Server
10.1.1.100

Packets with a destination
address of 171.100.1.100 are
translated to 10.1.1.100

NAT pool: 171.100.1.0/24
Static: 171.100.1.100 - 10.1.1.100

e0 *Customer* s0
router

Serial link
198.50.1.0/30

Provider
router

Internet

Internal Network
10.0.0.0/8

Figure 8-6 NAT application schematic: example 3.

Solution

```
·interface ethernet0
  ip address 10.1.1.1 255.255.255.0
  ip nat inside
!
interface serial0
  IP address 198.50.1.1 255.255.255.252
  ip nat outside
!
ip access-list 1 permit 10.0.0.0 0.255.255.255
!
ip nat pool internet prefix-length 24
   address 171.100.1.1 171.100.1.99
   address 171.100.1.101 171.100.1.254
ip nat inside source static 10.1.1.100 171.100.1.100
ip nat inside source list 1 pool internet
```

Explanation

As in our other examples, we define the NAT inside and outside interfaces
first before any other NAT commands. We then need to configure the NAT
pool addresses and the NAT source list that will be allowed to obtain
addresses from the pool. This example differs from Example 2 in that now
we need to set aside IP address 171.100.1.100 for use by our Web server.
We must make a static mapping between the inside global and inside local
addresses. If we did not do this, there would be no way to ensure that the
NAT translation in the NAT table would map any particular IP address
from the NAT pool to our Web server. This would mean that from the
Internet, you would never know which IP address to use to reach the Web
server, which obviously would not be very useful.

Notice that we have created a static mapping between 10.1.1.100 and 171.100.1.100 in our configuration with the `ip nat inside source static` command. Notice also that the syntax of the NAT pool is different in this example. Cisco has extended the NAT syntax so you can split the range of IP addresses used by the NAT pool. We have defined two separate ranges, 171.100.1.1 to 171.100.1.99 and 171.100.1.101 to 171.100.1.254 so we can exclude the IP address 171.100.1.100 from the NAT pool since we are using it for a static translation. We use the `ip nat inside source list` command to define the IP addresses that will be allowed to obtain IP addresses from the NAT pool. Note that, up to this point, we have used only a standard IP access list to define the IP addresses. We could also use an extended IP access list, and we will see an example of this later in the chapter.

NAT Application: Example 4

In this example, an organization has a three-port router, one Ethernet port and two serial ports. Each of the serial ports is connected to a different ISP and each ISP has allocated our organization a separate class C address. ISP 1 has allocated 171.100.1.0/24 for the organization's use and ISP 2 has allocated 198.50.1.0/24 for the organization's use. The organization is going to take full routing from each ISP via the BPG routing protocol and allow the router to forward packets to whichever ISP has the best route to a particular destination. In order for packets to be routed back through the same ISP that was used as packets left the organization's router, the router will translate the source of outgoing packets from each provider's address space before sending the packet to the respective ISP. Packets sent to ISP 1's router will be translated to addresses from the ISP 1 address space and packets sent to ISP 2's router will be translated to addresses from the ISP 2 address space.

In addition to allowing internal hosts to obtain addresses from each respective provider's address space, depending on the route taken, this organization wants to provide a Web server that is accessible from either provider. What they would like is to have a static IP address assigned to the Web server from each provider's address space so that each provider can be used to reach the server's IP address. In other words, customers of ISP 1 will use an address from ISP 1 to reach the Web server and customers of ISP 2 will use an address from ISP 2 to reach the Web server. As in our previous example, the internal Ethernet interface uses the 10.0.0.0/24 address space and our Web server's inside local address is 10.1.1.100. It will appear as 171.100.1.100 from ISP 1 and as 198.50.1.100 from ISP 2. Each ISP will ensure that the appropriate DNS entries are in place to resolve our Web server's name to each respective IP address. (See Figure 8-7.)

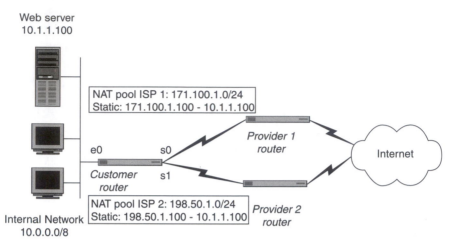

Figure 8-7   NAT application schematic: example 4.

Solution

```
interface ethernet0
 ip address 10.1.1.1 255.255.255.0
 ip nat inside
!
interface serial0
 description ISP-1
 IP address 171.99.1.1 255.255.255.252
 ip nat outside
!
interface serial1
 description ISP-2
 IP address 198.49.1.1 255.255.255.252
 Ip nat outside
!
ip access-list 1 permit 10.0.0.0 0.255.255.255
!
ip nat pool isp-1 prefix-length 24
 address 171.100.1.1 171.100.1.99
 address 171.100.1.101 171.100.1.254
ip nat pool isp-2 prefix-length 24
 address 198.50.1.1 198.50.1.99
 address 198.50.1.101 198.50.1.254
!
ip nat inside source static 10.1.1.100 171.100.1.100 extendable
ip nat inside source static 10.1.1.100 198.50.1.100 extendable
ip nat inside source route-map isp-1 pool isp-1
ip nat inside source route-map isp-2 pool isp-2
!
route-map isp-1 permit 10
  match ip address 1
  match interface serial0
!
```

```
route-map isp-2 permit 10
  match ip address 1
  match interface serial1
```

Explanation

This example is considerably more complicated than our previous examples, and there are several points of interest. We begin by defining our NAT inside and outside interfaces. In this case, we have two outside interfaces since our router has two Internet connections, one on each of our serial interfaces. The next step is to create our NAT pools that our internal clients will use to obtain inside global addresses. As stated earlier, we have two pools of addresses, one from each provider. We have therefore created two separate NAT pools named ISP 1 and ISP 2. Notice that in each NAT pool we have excluded the .100 host since we will use .100 from each NAT pool to create a static NAT mapping for our Web server. We have seen the syntax of the NAT pool statements in our earlier examples.

After creating our NAT pools, we then need to define our source lists that will tell the router what IP addresses are allowed to obtain addresses from our pools. Notice that instead of the `ip nat source list` command we are using the `ip nat source route-map` command. Using a route map instead of an access list alone allows us to define that a NAT pool will be selected not only by IP address, but also by things like the next hop IP address and the exit interface of the router. In our case, we will use the exit interface of the router. We have defined two route-map statements, `isp-1` and `isp-2`. The `isp-1` route-map matches on access list 1 *and* on interface serial0. This means that the route map will be matched if the IP packet matches list 1 and the destination interface is serial0. Packets exiting the router on interface serial0 are bound for ISP 1, so this matches our intent. The route map for `isp-2` is defined similarly. Our router will have routes from each provider that will tell it which interface to leave the router on, and depending upon our BGP configuration we will get some load sharing of outbound traffic. Notice that the way we have defined our NAT pools and our `ip nat inside source route-map` statements allows the router to select an address from each ISP's address space before sending the packet to the ISP's router. This will ensure that when the packets return, they will return through the same ISP that was used when it exited the internal network. This is true because normally each ISP only advertises IP addresses from its own address space to other providers. Packets from ISP 1's address space will flow back to ISP 1 and packets from ISP 2's address space will flow back to ISP 2.

The final step in the configuration is to allow devices on the Internet to access our Web server. We need a static NAT mapping between an inside global address and an inside local address. However, in this case we have defined not only one but two mappings to our Web server from two different inside global addresses. The key to this procedure is the use of the optional keyword `extendable`.

The `extendable` keyword tells the router to create an extended NAT mapping from each inside global address to the single inside local address using not only IP addresses but source and destination ports as well. For packets that flow from the NAT outside interfaces to the NAT inside, the static mapping will act as a template to create an extended translation. For packets flowing from the NAT inside to the NAT outside interfaces, the dynamic route maps will be used to create the extended translations. Without the `extendable` keyword, the router would not allow us to create multiple inside global addresses to a single inside local address.

NAT Application: Example 5

In this example, an organization uses a router with two interfaces, an Ethernet and a serial. Ethernet0 is connected to the internal network and the serial interface is connected via a PPP link to the ISP's router. On the internal network the company is using addresses from the 10.0.0.0/24 address space, which are not routable on the Internet. The company has been provided an IP address range 171.100.1.0/24 for their use and wants to create a globally accessible Web server. The company believes they will have a substantial number of connections to their Web server, but they only have low-end servers and do not wish to purchase additional servers as they have already spent a substantial amount of money on their existing hardware. The company would like to be able to use several servers and make it appear as if there is only one server to the outside world. In other words, they want packets sent to one inside global address to be translated to multiple inside local addresses. (See Figure 8-8.)

Solution

```
interface ethernet0
 ip address 10.1.1.1 255.255.255.0
 ip nat inside
!
interface serial0
 IP address 198.50.1.1 255.255.255.252
 ip nat outside
!
ip access-list 1 permit 171.100.1.100
!
ip nat pool web-farm 10.1.1.2 10.1.1.4 prefix-length 29 type rotary
ip nat inside destination list 1 pool web-farm
```

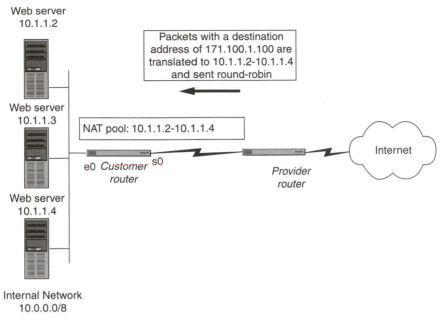

Figure 8-8 NAT application schematic: example 5.

Explanation

We begin by defining the interfaces that will participate in NAT and whether they are a NAT inside or outside interface by placing the appropriate commands beneath each interface. Once we have defined the appropriate NAT commands beneath each interface, we then define the NAT pool, except in this case the NAT pool Web-farm identifies the inside local addresses of all of our Web servers. Notice that in this case we have used the `prefix-length` parameter instead of the `netmask` parameter. A `prefix-length` of 29 is equivalent to a netmask parameter of 255.255.255.248. Notice also the use of the `rotary` keyword. This signals that we are going to use the IP addresses from the NAT pool in a round-robin fashion for translating inbound IP packets.

After defining our NAT rotary pool, we then define the IP addresses that will be selected for translation to our rotary pool. Instead of an `inside source list` we have defined an `inside destination list`. The `inside destination list` defines that packets with an IP destination matching access list 1 will be translated in a round-robin fashion to the pool of addresses defined in our rotary pool. In this case, access list 1 matches a single IP address, 171.100.1.100. Therefore, packets with a destination address of 171.100.1.100 will have their destination IP address changed to an address that the router will pick in a round-robin fashion from our rotary pool. This will allow us to use our three inside servers to all receive inbound packets with a destination address of 171.100.1.100. All three internal Web servers will share the load of requests sent to the single global address. It is important to note that the router will make no attempt to ensure that any of the three Web servers is actually active. If one of the Web servers is down, the router will still attempt to send packets to that Web server. If a more functional solution is desired, Cisco makes a product called a *Local Director* that can determine if the servers in the pool are actually active. Discussion of the Local Director product is beyond the scope of this book, so consult the Cisco documentation or contact your local reseller for more information.

NAT Application: Example 6

In this example, an organization uses a router with two interfaces, an Ethernet and a serial. Ethernet0 is connected to the internal network and the serial interface is connected via a PPP link to the ISP's router. On the internal network the company is using addresses from the 10.0.0.0/24 address space. The company has been allocated a single globally routable IP address from its provider, 171.100.1.1, which it has applied to the serial interface of their router. The company is using PAT to translate all of their inside local addresses to the single inside global address 171.100.1.1. Now the company wants to provide a Web and FTP server that can be accessed from the Internet and inbound Web server requests to be sent to

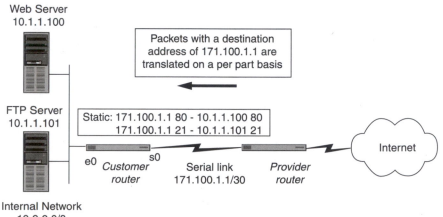

Figure 8-9   NAT application schematic: example 6.

the Web server at IP address 10.1.1.100 and inbound FTP requests to be sent to the FTP server at IP address 10.1.1.101. (See Figure 8-9.)

Solution

```
interface ethernet0
 ip address 10.1.1.1 255.255.255.0
 ip nat inside
!
interface serial0
 IP address 171.100.1.1 255.255.255.252
 ip nat outside
!
ip access-list 1 permit 10.0.0.0 0.255.255.255
!
ip nat inside source list 1 interface serial0 overload
ip nat inside source static tcp 10.1.1.100 80 171.100.1.1 80
ip nat inside source static tcp 10.1.1.101 21 171.100.1.1 21
```

Explanation

We begin by defining the interfaces that will participate in NAT and whether they are a NAT inside or outside interface by placing the appropriate commands beneath each interface. Normally, once we have defined out NAT interfaces, we would then define our NAT pool to specify the pool of inside global addresses in use. However, in this case there is only a single inside global address for our use, and we have applied that single inside global address to the serial0 interface of our router. Since there is only a single inside global address and it is applied to an interface of the router itself, we do not have to define a NAT pool. We simply use an alternative syntax for our `inside source list` which we have shown in our example. We define our source list so it uses the IP address of an interface on the router and we will overload this single IP address. This command alone will allow our internal hosts from the 10.0.0.0/24 network to obtain access to the Internet. The router will perform PAT and will create unique NAT mappings based on TCP/UDP port information. Once this step is completed, we then need to create static mappings for our internal Web and FTP servers.

Since we only have a single inside global IP address, we must define our static mappings based not only on IP address, but TCP or UDP port. In our example, we have defined that all IP packets with a destination address of 171.100.1.1 and a destination TCP port of 80 will be translated to inside host 10.1.1.100 on TCP port 80. We have also defined that packets with a destination address of 171.100.1.1 and a destination TCP port of 21 will be translated to inside host 10.1.1.101 on TCP port 21. This will allow us to provide Web and FTP services on different internal servers, even though we only have a single inside global address. Notice that because the syntax allows us to specify both the IP address and port of the inside servers, we could even provide multiple Web and FTP servers on the inside. For example, we could create a static mapping like this:

```
ip nat inside source static tcp 10.1.1.102 21 171.100.1.1 27
```

This translation would send all inbound packets with a destination address of 171.100.1.1 and a destination port of 27 to address 10.1.1.102 on the FTP port. Of course, we would have to ensure that external users were aware that they needed to contact our FTP server on a nonstandard port, but most modern FTP clients provide this ability. It should be obvious that there are many possible variations of port translation that an organization can use to provide services even with only a single globally routable IP address. The many variations available make this feature one of the more powerful ones available with Cisco NAT.

CHAPTER 9

Cisco Encryption and IPSec

T his chapter continues the discussion of technologies that are not access lists themselves but closely related to them, providing added security features. Specifically, two methods are reviewed for encrypting traffic in a Cisco network: *Cisco encryption technology* (CET) and IPSec. CET is a Cisco router-specific encryption framework that allows encryption of IP traffic between two or more Cisco routers. The specific implementation of CET is proprietary and only works between Cisco routers; however, the CET framework is composed of standards-based protocols. IPSec is a suite of standards and specifications that, taken together, constitute a framework that allows any IPSec-compliant device to securely communicate with any other IPSec-compliant device. Examples of devices created for IPSec-compliant implementations include Cisco routers, firewalls, Windows platforms, and various flavors of UNIX such as Linux, FreeBSD, and OpenBSD.

IPSec is the standard for intervendor cryptography and allows secure communications between widely disparate devices. Theoretically, any device with an IP stack and standards-compliant IPSec software should be able to communicate securely with any other device running standards-compliant IPSec software. The IPSec standards have been developed by the Internet community and laid out in several RFCs that address the many different components. Many different RFCs relate to IPSec, and each covers a specific area. A good starting point for research into the IPSec RFCs is RFC 2411, the IPSec document road map.

Both CET and IPSec technologies facilitate secure communications across unsecured networks such as the Internet. While IPSec is clearly the future of intervendor secure communication, CET is still a viable alternative for networks where a Cisco-specific solution is acceptable and is slightly easier to configure than IPSec, so we will include examples of its use along with IPSec later in this chapter.

Overview

This chapter begins with a brief discussion of cryptography and its role in securing data communication, followed by a list of terms used in cryptography that are helpful to know as we proceed with the chapter's examples. The chapter concludes with a brief overview of CET and IPSec, describing the components of each technology and how they can be implemented in a network to provide secure communication. This brief introduction is intended only to provide a very short overview and facilitate discussion of the examples of CET and IPSec. Cryptography is a fascinating and very complex field of study, and the examination of the principles, algorithms, and mathematics involved can literally fill entire bookshelves. This chapter focuses on the actual implementation of the technologies and gives only a brief overview of the underlying principles. For those interested in further study of cryptography, we highly recommend *Applied Cryptography* by Bruce Schneier. Additional details regarding IPSec can be found in the RFC's addressing IPSec technologies, beginning with RFC 2411, the IPSec documentation road map.

Basic Cryptography

First we discuss cryptography in general and why it is important. *Cryptography* is defined as the science of reading or writing coded messages. We expand this definition and discuss cryptography theory in the next section.

Encryption in Theory

A *coded message* is one that has undergone some set of operations, normally called an *algorithm*, so that the order of the words, letters, and numbers in the message are scrambled and no longer resemble the original message. The algorithm will specify the operations to be performed on the message to scramble the letters so that it is unreadable. A simple algorithm might be shift all the letters in the message to the right by three letters. A more complex algorithm might be give each letter a number from 1 to 26. Shift each odd-numbered letter to the left by either two or four positions, shift each even-numbered letter to the right by a number from one to three positions, alternating the number of shifts for each letter. (Note that both of these algorithms are extremely trivial and are easily broken.) The goal of every cryptographic algorithm is to take the original message, referred to as *plaintext*, and produce an encrypted or enciphered message, called *ciphertext*. For example, a plaintext message might be

```
The eagle has landed
```

and the corresponding ciphertext might be

```
Xtyhif .f&d2ghuflkfl{yxaz
```

The ciphertext should bear as little a resemblance as possible to the original plaintext. If this were not the case, careful analysis by individuals who study cryptography, called *cryptographers*, and by people who study the science of breaking cryptography, called *cryptanalysts*, could result in breaking the coding scheme used and retrieving the original message. This is obviously bad if you only wanted certain individuals to be able to read the original plaintext message. The purpose of using cryptography is to prevent anyone but the intended recipient of the enciphered message from decoding the message and retrieving the original plaintext. If the plaintext message can be derived from the ciphertext through analysis, the entire process has been worthless and your security has been completely compromised.

Encryption in Practice

This is all very straightforward, but you may ask, "How does it actually work in practice?" A good question. Typically, two things are needed to create a ciphertext message from a plaintext message: an algorithm and a key. The *algorithm* is the set of steps performed on the original message to produce the ciphertext message. The algorithm is typically well known and has been studied by cryptographers and cryptanalysts for years looking for weaknesses. Weaknesses in an algorithm will usually result in the algorithm producing similar enciphered text from similar plaintext. If similar inputs to the algorithm produce similar outputs, cryptanalysts can use well-known techniques to analyze the similarities between the outputs to reconstruct unknown plaintext messages from known ciphertext.

We should note that the terms cryptographer and cryptanalyst are not necessarily equivalent. A cryptographer studies the science of cryptography, while a cryptanalyst attempts to break cryptographic algorithms. Of course, a cryptographer may also be a cryptanalyst and vice versa. Here we will refer generically to cryptographers even though the context may refer to someone who examines algorithms to attempt to break them.

Returning to our discussion of cryptography, we noted previously that cryptographic algorithms are studied for years by cryptographers looking for weaknesses. You may wonder how secrecy is maintained if the cryptographic algorithm is so well known. This is where a secret key value plays a crucial role. Although the encryption algorithm may be well known, the key is kept secret. Since the algorithm is known, the key plays the critical role in preventing the ciphertext from being deciphered by anyone except the intended recipients. A secret key value is used as some form of input to the algorithm so that even though an attacker may know every step in an algorithm, without the key he or she cannot complete crucial steps in the algorithm process.

Encryption Example

Let's take a very simple example. The algorithm we'll use is shift the letters of the message x number of positions to the right. This is a small variation on the well-known Caesar cipher, which shifts each letter three positions to the right and is one of the oldest known cryptographic algorithms. In our example, the number x is the key and will be a number between 1 and 25 since we're using the English alphabet and there are only 26 letters. In this example, we'll set the value of x to 5:

Plaintext: the quick fox jumped
Ciphertext: ymj vznhp ktc ozruji

In this case, the algorithm is known, so our security is entirely based on the key. We assume that we know the key (that x is 5) and that the recipient of the message knows the key, but anyone eavesdropping on the message doesn't know the key even though they probably know the algorithm.

> **NOTE**
> In real-world cases, the algorithm used may not be known. If an eavesdropper doesn't know the algorithm used in advance, the job is harder, but far from impossible. There are very few well-known encryption algorithms in widespread use. An eavesdropper who didn't know the algorithm could just try all the well-known algorithms until a useful one occurred.

If we assume that an eavesdropper knows the algorithm, it is obvious that our security lies entirely with the key. The attacker will try to use all possible keys to decrypt the message. Hopefully, the time it takes to determine the key is too long for the information to be of use to the attacker or the resources (skill, money, computing power, etc.) required to determine the key exceed the attacker's ability. If the message can be decrypted in a month using a machine that costs $1 million to build, but the message is only worth $100,000 and it is only useful for 24 h, we don't care if the message is decrypted. By the time the key is discovered the message will be worthless to the eavesdropper and the cost to recover the message is so prohibitive that no one will try to recover it in the first place. Of course, this assumes that the attacker hasn't already built a $1 million machine.

Note that in our simple example it would take a person only a few minutes to determine the key by hand. Just start by using 1 for the key, then 2, then 3, etc. Once the number 5 is reached the code is broken. Even if we chose 25 as the key, it would still only take a few minutes to run through all possible keys manually. This is an extremely simple example of what is called a *simple substitution cipher* or a *monoalphabetic cipher*, and it's obviously not very secure. You just replace a single letter with another letter based on a shift in the letters. There are variations on this theme that involve shifting letters in such a way that a single letter of plaintext can map to several different letters of ciphertext, but for our purposes these details aren't as important as understanding the concept of an algorithm and a key. We will not discuss particular encryption algorithms in this chapter except to note the specific algorithms that are used for CET and IPSec. Suffice it to say that the algorithms used in modern cryptography are considerably more complicated than our simple example and that the algorithms themselves have been examined by cryptographers over a period of many years and have been deemed to be secure, provided an appropriate key length is used.

The Importance of Good Keys

Generally, the longer the key, the more difficult it is to break an encryption scheme because more possibilities must be examined to perform an exhaustive key search to find the right key to decipher a message. An exhaustive search of all available keys is called a *brute force* attack. No magic is involved; you just try to decrypt the message using every possible key until you find the right one that produces the original plaintext. This sounds very simple and, in fact, it is and it's very easy to automate as we saw in our simple example. This may lead you to suspect that breaking cryptography is easy. In point of fact, it is not. At least, it's not easy to break good algorithms with long keys. In this context, a good algorithm is one that has been examined by cryptographers and has been determined to contain no weaknesses that would provide information to an attacker that shortens the key search. A weakness in a cryptographic algorithm can shorten the key search significantly, sometimes enough to make finding the key through a brute force attack feasible.

Given a sufficiently long key and a good algorithm, the time required to try all possible keys through a brute force attack is much longer than the age of the universe. Given a 128-bit key and enough computing power to try 1 million keys per second, someone would still be trying to force the right key long after the sun has gone supernova (at which point I'm probably not concerned that they've broken my key). Even given the tremendous advances in computing power being made every year, a few orders of magnitude increase in processing speed is not much when dealing with numbers like 10^{30} and higher.

When dealing with long keys, such as a 128-bit long one, the number of possible key combinations is 2^{128}, which translates roughly to 3.5×10^{30}. As a point of reference, the age until the Sun goes supernova is estimated to be 10^9 and the age of the universe is estimated at 10^{10}. The point here is that a key of sufficient length makes a brute force attack infeasible, and an attacker would have to try to exploit a weakness in the algorithm itself or develop new mathematical techniques. It's often easier to just bribe someone who knows the key to tell you what it is or develop some form of blackmail to force him or her to give you the key.

A final point: you may have noticed that we have made several remarks about a good algorithm being examined and verified by cryptographers. Unfortunately, not all cryptographic algorithms undergo this scrutiny. Some cryptography schemes rely on the idea that the algorithm is unknown to any eavesdroppers. Typically, these schemes are developed by vendors with the intent of either being first to market with a new cryptography implementation or to increase the speed of cryptographic functions since good cryptography algorithms usually require a lot of computing power to manipulate very large numbers and complex algorithms. You should be wary of cryptography that uses unknown algorithms.

A vendor who claims its cryptography is just as good as the algorithms that have been examined by leading cryptographers may be correct, but it's not likely. Many vendors who implement cryptography are not cryptographers and do not have a strong background in theoretical mathematics, so they are not qualified to judge whether an algorithm is sufficiently strong. An algorithm may appear unbreakable to an untrained observer, but may be trivial to an experienced cryptographer. Many vendor algorithms have claimed to have strong cryptography but were discovered to be extremely weak once professional cryptographers examined them. Only trust vendor implementations that rely on well-known and trusted encryption algorithms.

Cryptography Definitions

In this section, we present some of the terms used in cryptography that will aid discussion of the examples presented later. The terms presented here are not an exhaustive list, and only includes the terms that we feel will be beneficial to a discussion of CET and IPSec.

Building Blocks

Cryptography is built upon the two fundamental ideas introduced previously: algorithms and keys. All of the terms discussed in this chapter are either an encryption algorithm, an implementation of a particular algorithm, an encryption scheme that centers around algorithms, or a system for exchanging secret keys. The universe of cryptography centers around the creation and implementation of algorithms and the creation and exchange of secret keys. If you keep this in mind, all of the terms discussed will be much clearer.

Although the math of cryptography can be mind numbingly difficult, the principles involved are actually not difficult to grasp once the foundation of algorithms and keys are understood. Unless you are a mathematician and wish to prove the correctness of the algorithms used by your cryptography systems, there is little need to fully understand the exact mechanics of why certain algorithms produce strong cryptography. It can be useful, though, to know the basic procedures involved and it is certainly useful to know the common terms used in the field and how they relate to the building blocks of algorithms and keys.

Symmetric Key Encryption

So far, we have discussed algorithms in a general sense as if all algorithms performed more or less the same types of functions. This is not the case. Earlier we showed an example algorithm that was very simple. The algorithm performs an operation on the plaintext using a single key value, and to reverse the operation you just perform the opposite operation using the same key. In our letter shift example, we shifted the letters x number of positions to the right where x is our key number between 1 and 25. To reverse the encryption we just shift the letters x positions to the left using the same key value. This sort of cryptography is called *symmetric key encryption* since the same key is used in both the encryption and decryption phases. It is also called *secret key encryption* since it involves a single, secret key.

The strength of the encryption relies on the key being known only by the required parties. It works well as long as the key is kept secret and is known only by the parties involved. Symmetric key encryption schemes are very strong, but they don't scale very well. You need to have a separate key for each encrypted connection to a different party. If you are talking to Bob using one key, you need to use a different key to talk to Mary if you don't want Bob and Mary to be able to decrypt each other's messages.

Symmetric key encryption also raises the problem of how to exchange the secret keys to begin with. You can't just send the keys across the network, since the reason for using cryptography in the first place is because the network is unsecured. You must have an alternative method of exchanging the keys, which may become cumbersome when dealing with a large number of peers. Another kind of cryptography scheme addresses these issues, and it is called *asymmetric key encryption*. This scheme is discussed in our next definition.

Asymmetric Key Encryption

In contrast to symmetric key encryption in which only a single key is used, asymmetric key encryption uses two complimentary keys. One key, called the *public key*, may be advertised to anyone who wants it. The other key, called the *private key*, is known only by the intended recipient of the message encrypted with the public key. Typically, a single individual will have his or her own private key/public key combination. Basically, the process is as follows. The public key value is given to anyone who wants it. Once someone has the public key, this key can be used to encrypt a message to be sent to the owner of the public/private key combination. Only the private key can decrypt the message encrypted with the public key, and only the owner of the public key/private key combination has the private key, so the secrecy of the message is maintained. Once the message has been encrypted with the public key, it can only be decrypted with the private key. The public key cannot be used to decrypt the message it just encrypted, so it does not matter who has the public key as long as the private key is kept secret. This form of encryption is also known as *public key encryption*.

This process may seem a little like magic if you are only familiar with symmetric key encryption. You may wonder why you can't just reverse the process of encrypting the message with the public key to obtain the original plaintext. The answer has to do with what is called *modulo arithmetic*. When you divide any integer by any other integer, you are left with a quotient and a remainder. For example, 7 divided by 4 gives a quotient of 1 and a remainder of 3. Modulo arithmetic is only interested in the remainder portion, so 7 mod 4 = 3. The reason why this is important to public key cryptography is that modulo arithmetic involves a process where, even if the result is known—in our case 3—it is impossible (or at least exceedingly difficult) to know what the original value was that produced the remainder of 3. In the equation $x \bmod y = z$, even if you know y and z, there is no method other than brute force to obtain x. There will be many, many values for x that produce the same value of z given the same y value. For example, if y is 4 and z is 3, all of the following values are possible x values: 7, 11, 15, 19, 23, 27, etc. There is no way to know which of these possible values of x is the real number that produced the remainder of 3. This is one of the basic principles of public key cryptography. Modulo arithmetic involves a process where information about the original value is lost and cannot be retrieved using the same key once the algorithm produces the ciphertext. In our example, you know the algorithm and you know the public key was 4 and the encrypted value is 3, but this doesn't tell you what the original number was.

This is all well and good, but given these constraints you may wonder how anyone could retrieve the original value of x since key information has been lost by the modulo arithmetic process. The answer is that the deck has been stacked. The private key value is derived from the public key value by a special modulo arithmetic process that allows you to use the private key to obtain the plaintext message from the ciphertext by reversing the encryption procedure using the private key. This process works only because of the mathematical relationship between the public and private key that was determined before the public key was used in the encryption process. The public and private keys are usually very large prime numbers, 100 to 200 digits long, and the relationship between them is unique. Each private key can decrypt only its respective public key and vice versa. Since the numbers used are very large, it is extremely unlikely that any two public key/private key combinations will be identical. Therefore, for all intents and purposes, everyone can have a unique private key/public key combination.

Because the public key/private key combination is unique, any person can give out his or her public key but can be assured that any messages encrypted with the public key can be decrypted only by the private key. Obviously, if the private key is lost, the messages could only be decrypted by a brute force attack. If strong cryptography is used, those messages can probably never be decrypted unless the values that were used to produce the original public key/private key numbers have been preserved. Likewise, if the private key is stolen, all messages encrypted with the public key can now be decrypted by the attacker. It goes without saying that keeping the private key safe and secret is incredibly important.

One last point is worth noting about public key encryption. In practice, public key encryption is much slower than private key encryption due to the amount of processing that must be done. It was seen very early after the development of public key cryptography that one could use public key encryption to exchange symmetric encryption secret keys dynamically on a session-by-session basis. A *session* is defined as a single conversation between two end points on a data network. Basically, all that is necessary is for one end point to pick a random secret key and encrypt it with the other end point devices' public key. The encrypted secret key is then sent to the end point where it is decrypted using the private key known only to that end point. No one else can decrypt the secret session key since no one else has the end point's private key. Once the secret session key is known by each end point, the end points can then use this key for standard symmetric key encryption that can be done very fast in hardware.

This is how most modern cryptography systems operate. They exchange a secret key using public key cryptography and then use that secret key. It solves the problem of getting a secret key to each end party securely and also solves the problem of maintaining many different secret keys. The secret keys are chosen dynamically on a per-session basis and then destroyed after the session ends. The only thing that is necessary to make this procedure work is that each end station has its own public key/private key combination. Note that this description of the process of exchanging a private key using public key encryption is very simplified and, in practice, many additional steps may be performed. However, no matter how many additional steps are performed, the basic principles of the secret key exchange are the same.

Hash Function

A *hash function* is a one-way algorithm that takes a message of arbitrary length and produces a fixed-length scrambled digest version. A *digest* is typically a shortened version of text that contains only the most relevant parts of the text, and this is more or less what a hash function produces. A hash contains elements of the original text that uniquely identify the original message, but key parts of the text have been removed and modified so that it is extremely difficult, if not impossible, to obtain the original message from the hash. This is the one-way part of the definition. You can run the algorithm on a given amount of text to obtain a fixed-length hash value, but you cannot obtain the original text from the hash. Recall our earlier discussion of how one-way algorithms are made possible using modulo arithmetic. A hash algorithm is really just a public key cryptography algorithm without the key. Once the algorithm produces the hash, the process cannot be reversed because there are no keys.

The function of a hash is to uniquely identify the text. It's like a fingerprint for each unique message. Different messages should produce different values and the same message should produce the exact same hash. Hash values are used for things like maintaining integrity of messages. If I send you a message and give you the hash of the message, you can run the same hash algorithm that I used on the message you receive and compare it to the hash value you received. If the computed hash value of the message that was sent is not the same as the hash value received, you know that the message was tampered with during transmission. Hash values are also useful for digitally signing messages. Digital signatures are discussed next.

Digital Signature

A *digital signature* is a hash value that has been encrypted with a user's private key. It can be used much like a normal signature to verify identity, but it also verifies the integrity of the message to which the signature is attached. The procedure is very simple:

1. Jay creates a message for Ellen.
2. Jay uses one of several well-known hash algorithms to create a hash value based on the message created in step 1.
3. Jay encrypts this hash value with his private key.
4. Jay attaches the encrypted hash value to the original message and sends the entire message to Ellen.
5. Ellen removes the attached encrypted hash value and decrypts it using Jay's public key.
6. Ellen then runs the same hash algorithm as Jay on the original message to obtain a hash value.
7. Ellen compares the computed hash value to the deciphered hash value obtained in step 5.

If the hash values match, Ellen knows that the message has not been altered and was sent by Jay since only Jay has access to her private key. If the message has been altered or if someone else encrypted the hash with his or her private key, the procedure fails and Ellen knows not to trust the message. This procedure works because only Jay has access to her private key and each message produces a unique hash value.

Certificate Authority

A *certificate authority* is an entity, usually a computer, that stores public keys. Actually what it stores are objects called *certificates* that include information about users or devices, including their public keys. The certificate includes identifying information about the owner of a particular public key such as name, address, company, etc. You can think of a certificate as a driver's license with a key attached. The purpose of a certificate is twofold:

1. Identify the public key of a user or device.
2. Verify that the supposed owner of a public key is indeed the real owner of the public key.

The *certificate authority* (CA) is a trusted third party that keeps track of all certificates and ensures that if someone claiming to be Bill Gates places a certificate into the CA database, he or she is, in fact, Bill Gates and not an imposter. By using a CA, you have a central repository of certificates that allows you to obtain other users' public keys and verify the identity of those users. Without a CA, you would have to obtain the public key directly from the user, and if someone happened to be impersonating the user, your secure communication might be sent to the wrong person. Software to create your own CA is available from many vendors, and some vendors will run a CA service for you. A CA is useful when using public key cryptography because it provides a central repository for users' and devices' public keys. It also provides authentication assurance that when you obtain a public key from the CA for Bob Jones, it is really the public key of Bob Jones and not someone else.

The Data Encryption Standard (DES)

DES is a symmetric key algorithm developed in 1977 by the National Bureau of Standards. It can use key lengths of 40 and 56 bits. Another encryption scheme, called 3DES or triple DES, uses the same DES algorithm but instead of a single encryption step it performs encryption, then decryption, then encryption again, usually with a different key in each step. This process significantly increases the difficulty of a brute force attack. The 56-bit DES has been broken in about 12 h using a brute force attack, so 3DES is recommended if you need very strong encryption. Cisco's implementation of IPSec supports 3DES, but CET does not.

The Digital Signature Standard (DSS)

DSS is a digital signature algorithm developed by the National Institute of Standards and Technology. It produces a digital signature as we discussed earlier by encrypting a message hash with a user's private key. DSS is used by CET but not by IPSec.

The Internet Security Association and Key Management Protocol (ISAKMP)

ISAKMP is a framework for specifying a methodology for exchanging secret keys and negotiating security parameters between hosts. ISAKMP defines the general mechanics to be used so a secret key can be exchanged across an unsecured network, as discussed in the section on public key cryptography. ISAKMP specifies such information as the location of messages in packets and the general framework of how the communication process will take place, but it does not specify the protocols and algorithms that will be used.

The Internet Key Exchange (IKE)

IKE is a protocol that actually implements the specifications of a key exchange, as outlined in the ISAKMP framework. It is derived from other key exchange protocols such as Oakley and SKEME. IKE is used to authenticate keys between peers and to establish a shared security policy between peers. IKE is used to verify things, such as the identity of a peer who requests an encryption session, and to establish what algorithms and keys will be used by the peers. IKE is used by IPSec but not by CET.

The Rivest, Shamir, Adleman Algorithm (RSA)

RSA is a public key cryptography algorithm named after Rivest, Shamir, and Adleman, the people who created it. It facilitates the exchange of secret keys detailed in the section on asymmetric key encryption. It can also be used to create a digital signature.

Diffie-Hellman

Diffie-Hellman is a public key cryptography algorithm that facilitates the exchange of secret keys across an unsecured network. The algorithm is named after Diffie and Hellman who published the first public research on public key encryption in 1977. It can be used in much the same way as RSA, although its primary purpose is to facilitate the exchange of secret session keys across an unsecured network.

MD5

MD5 is a one-way hash algorithm that produces a 128-bit hash value from a message of arbitrary length.

SHA

SHA is a one-way hash algorithm that produces a 160-bit hash value. It is similar to MD5 but is considered stronger than MD5.

You will encounter many additional terms in cryptography. Try to classify the terms into basic concepts. Remember that everything centers around algorithms and keys. The term may designate a symmetric key algorithm, like DES, or an asymmetric algorithm, like RSA, or even a message digest algorithm, like MD5 or SHA. It may also be just a framework for key exchange such as ISAKMP. Always compare the terms to the concepts you understand and don't get lost in the details of a particular implementation.

CET Overview

Now that we understand some of the most widely used cryptography terms, we can begin our specific discussion of CET.

Definition

CET was Cisco's initial implementation of cryptography, and it allows you to establish secure connections between all Cisco router platforms with the appropriate software. CET was introduced in IOS version 11.2, but underwent significant changes in 11.3. Most of the changes were in the command structure used to enable CET, and the commands from 11.3 are not backward-compatible with 11.2. Keep this in mind if you ever have to revert from 11.3 code revision to 11.2.

The CET implementation is proprietary, so you can only create secure tunnels between Cisco routers. However, the algorithms used are DSS and DES, which are well-known cryptography standards so you can feel secure using CET. One downside to CET is that it only supports up to 56-bit DES and not 3DES. This may be a problem for some implementations considering that DES has already been cracked in a fairly short amount of time. While many hundreds of machines were involved in the cracking of DES, the computing power available doubles every 18 months and prices continue to decrease. Also, it is naive to believe that security organizations, such as the NSA, do not have extremely powerful machines that can crack DES much faster than 12 h, possibly in minutes or even seconds. You must consider whether using DES is secure enough for your particular environment.

On the plus side, CET is easier to configure than IPSec and is generally less CPU intensive, so it can run on lower-end routers at higher speeds. This does not mean, however, that it is not CPU intensive. The encryption process can be extremely CPU intensive, depending on the amount of encryption performed, so if you have a lower-end router like a 1600 or 2500, you will not be able to encrypt much more than 128 kbps. Higher-end platforms, like the 3600 and 7200 series routers, can encrypt megabits per second, so if you require these kinds of speeds, you will need to consider using a high-end router.

Implementation

As stated earlier, CET is very easy to configure. In fact, only three steps are involved:

1. Manually generate DSS key pairs on each router.
2. Exchange public keys with peers.
3. Create an extended access list defining what traffic will be encrypted, create a crypto map defining peer routers, and apply the map to an interface.

Each of these steps will be briefly covered in this section.

Step 1

In step 1, we must generate a public key/private key combination for each router. Recall our discussion earlier on public key cryptography and the use of public and private keys. These keys will be used to exchange secret session keys between routers that will be used by the DES algorithm to encrypt sessions between routers.

```
2621#conf t
Enter configuration commands, one per line. End with CNTL/Z.
2621(config)#crypto key generate dss test
Generating DSS keys ....
 [OK]

2621(config)#exit
2621#
```

We have now created our public and private keys. On a 2600 series router this took about 1 s. We can look at our public key but not our private key. The private key is stored in a separate area of NVRAM and cannot be viewed. We use the command show crypto key mypubkey dss to display our public key:

```
2621#show crypto key mypubkey dss
Key name: test
 Serial number: FA755D90
 Usage: Signature Key
 Key Data:
  CF12BED2 F9B079BB 7F8C82B4 0F36C3E3 7A497850 D9EAC785 A04A0E94
    211D3D2B
  F1DAADEB 3FCF31B0 045C75C1 E53993B6 F1C4B41B 4C561895 74C85D95
    3E1B6074
2621#
```

Once this step is completed on each router, all that is needed is to exchange the public keys between each router that will participate in encryption.

Step 2

In step 2 we must exchange our public key with the peer router with which we will create encrypted connections. We can do this either manually or dynamically. To perform the manual process, view the public key on each router with the show crypto key mypubkey dss command shown earlier and then copy the text that is shown in the screen into a memory buffer. Then, use the command crypto key pubkey-chain dss command and paste the copied text into each peer router's configuration. The dynamic process is much easier, you simply use the command crypto key exchange dss on each peer router. One router waits in passive mode to be contacted by the peer router:

```
2621#conf t
Enter configuration commands, one per line. End with CNTL/Z.
```

```
2621(config)#crypto key exchange dss passive
Enter escape character to abort if connection does not complete.
Wait for connection from peer [confirm]
Waiting ....
```

The other router contacts its peer to begin exchanging public keys:

```
3620#conf t
Enter configuration commands, one per line. End with CNTL/Z
3620(config)#crypto key exchange dss 192.168.1.1 test2
Key name: test2
 Serial number: FA755D90
 Usage: Signature Key
 Key Data:
  CF12BED2 F9B079BB 7F8C82B4 0F36C3E3 7A497850 D9EAC785 A04A0E94
    211D3D2B
  F1DAADEB 3FCF31B0 045C75C1 E53993B6 F1C4B41B 4C561895 74C85D95
    3E1B6074

Wait for peer to send a key [confirm]
```

Once the key exchange process is completed, we need to define an access list on each router and a crypto map specifying each peer router.

Step 3

In step 3 we first create an extended access list that will specify what traffic we will allow to be encrypted. It is normal to specify the source IP address range as your local LAN subnets and the destination IP addresses as the remote router LAN subnets. After creating the access list, we must then create a crypto map that specifies the peer router's hostname or IP address and the access list to be used for encrypting traffic to this peer. Finally, we must apply the crypto map to an interface. Normally, the crypto map is applied to the interface closest to the destination peer router. An example of these steps is shown here:

```
Crypto map test 10
  Set peer 192.168.1.2
  Match address 101
!
interface ethernet0
  ip address 10.1.1.1 255.255.255.0
!
interface serial0
  ip address 192.168.1.1 255.255.255.0
  crypto map test
!
access-list permit ip 10.1.1.0 0.0.0.255 50.1.1.0 0.0.0.255
```

These are all the steps necessary to configure CET on a Cisco router. A few additional commands that are useful for diagnosing information about the encryption processes when using CET are listed here:

```
Show crypto engine connections active
Show crypto engine connections dropped-packets
Show crypto Cisco connections
```

IPSec Overview

We now provide a basic overview of the protocols associated with IPSec. IPSec is not a single protocol or algorithm, but a suite of specifications that together compose an encryption standard that can be used for inter-vendor cryptography implementations. IPSec implements security at the IP layer, so it is independent of any upper-layer applications or transport layer protocols. The upper layers do not have to be aware of the security implemented at the IP layer, so no modifications above the IP layer are necessary.

IPSec functions by encapsulating information in the IP datagram with a new IPSec header, much like a normal IP header encapsulates the upper-layer TCP or UDP information. The new IPSec header contains information that allows authentication of each IP packet. The contents of the original IP packet may or may not be encrypted, depending on the needs of the particular implementation. IPSec can be configured to encapsulate the entire IP datagram or only the upper-layer information. If it is configured to encapsulate the entire IP datagram, it is said to operate in *tunnel mode*. If IPSec is configured to encapsulate only the upper-layer information, it is said to operate in *transport mode*. In addition to the IPSec mode, there are two forms of IPSec headers. The first type of header is called an *authentication header* (AH), and the second type is called the *encapsulating security payload* (ESP). The AH header is used only for authenticating IP packets, and performs no encryption of the original IP packet. The ESP header does perform encryption and can also perform authentication of the original IP packet much like the AH header.

We will discuss the specifics of the IPSec headers and the packet formats later in this section. For now, it is only important to understand that IPSec functions like many standard tunnel protocols in that it wraps a new header around the original IP datagram, as shown in Figure 9-1.

IPSec Motivation

Before discussing the specific characteristics of IPSec, it is important to understand why you would want to use IPSec and why IPSec was developed in the first place. The IPSec standard was created because the Internet community wanted a vendor-independent way for IP devices to:

1. *Verify the origin of an IP datagram.* As we have noted previously, it is very easy for an attacker to send IP packets with a forged source IP

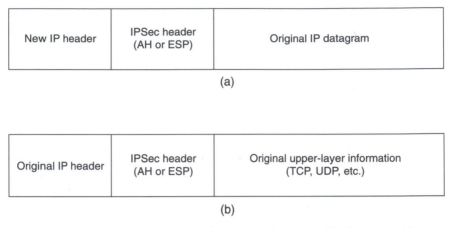

Figure 9-1 IPSec wrapping a new header around the original IP datagram. (*a*) Tunnel mode. (*b*) Transport mode.

address. Since this attack is very easy, reliance on IP addresses for access control is very weak. Many attacks have taken advantage of trust between machines based on IP addresses by forging source IP addresses. IPSec allows a device to authenticate the source of the IP datagram based on criteria that are much stronger than the source IP address. This feature of IPSec is called *origin authentication*.

2. *Verify the integrity of the IP datagram.* In addition to verifying the source of an IP datagram, a desire exists to ensure that the IP datagram was not altered during transmission across a network. With IPSec you can ensure that no alteration was performed on an IP packet. This feature of IPSec is called *connectionless integrity*.

3. *Ensure that the contents of IP datagrams cannot be read in transit.* In addition to authentication and integrity, it is desirable to ensure that unauthorized parties cannot read the contents of IP datagrams while the datagram is transiting a network. This assurance is created by encrypting the packet before placing it on a network. By encrypting the packet you ensure that an attacker cannot decipher the contents of the packet even if he or she were able to capture it with a sniffer program.

4. *Ensure that authenticated packets are not resent.* Finally, even if an attacker cannot send forged packets, cannot alter the packets, and cannot read the contents of the packets, he or she might try to disrupt communication by capturing legitimate packets and then resending them, resulting in transactions being completed multiple times or just confusion by the upper-layer applications that rely on the information in the duplicated packets. IPSec can ensure that duplicate packets are detected and rejected. This feature is called *antireplay*.

The current IP header cannot supply any of these services. In fact, many network attacks take advantage of one or more of these weaknesses in the IP protocol. IPSec was created to alleviate these weaknesses. We should note that the next generation of IP, IPv6, has IPSec support built into its specification, whereas in current IPv4 implementations it is an add-on. In the next section, the fundamental characteristics of IPSec are discussed.

IPSec Fundamentals

IPSec is built on two fundamental concepts:

1. Security protocols
2. Key management

Each of these fundamental principles is discussed further in the following sections.

Security Protocols

The security protocols provide all of the following services: origin authentication, connectionless integrity, encryption, and antireplay. They do this through the use of the two kinds of encapsulation headers: the *authentication header* (AH) and the *encapsulating security payload* (ESP). The functions provided by each header are summarized in Table 9-1. Each header may be used in either tunnel mode or transport mode. Tunnel mode encapsulates the entire IP datagram and transport mode encapsulates only the upper-layer information. The format of each header is presented in Figures 9-2 and 9-3 along with a brief explanation of each field in the header.

Table 9-1   Features of the IPSec Security Headers

	AH	ESP
Origin authentication	x	x
Connectionless integrity	x	x
Antireplay	x	x
Encryption		x
Traffic flow confidentiality		x

Bit: 0   31

Next Header	Payload Length	Reserved
Security Parameter Index (SPI)		
Sequence Number		
Authentication Data (variable)		

Figure 9-2   AH header format.

AH Header

- *Next header (8 bits)*. Identifies the type of header that follows this header, typically either IP if in tunnel mode or TCP/UDP if in transport mode.
- *Payload length (8 bits)*. Length of the AH in 32-bit words minus 2. The default length of the AH data field is 96 bits, which is three 32-bit

Bit: 0   31

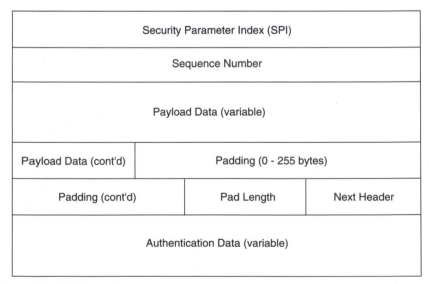

Figure 9-3   ESP header format.

words. The fixed portion of the AH is three 32-bit words, for a total of six 32-bit words. This would give a payload length of $6 - 2 = 4$.

- *Security parameter index (32 bits)*. This is a bit string used to identify each *security association* (SA).

- *Sequence number (32 bits)*. A counter value used for antireplay purposes. The counter increases with each new packet in an SA sent up to a maximum value of $2^{32} - 1$. Once the maximum value is reached, a new SA is negotiated and the counter is reset.

- *Authentication data (variable)*. A variable-length field that contains the *message authentication code* (MAC) for the packet. A MAC is very similar to a digital signature. It is a hash value created from the original packet and then encrypted, but instead of a user's private key for the encryption, the algorithm uses a shared secret key.

In transport mode the AH authentication data (the MAC) is calculated based on the contents of the IP payload (all upper-layer information) and selected portions of the IP header that do not change as the packet is routed, such as source and destination IP addresses. In tunnel mode, the AH authentication data is calculated based on the entire original IP packet and selected portions of the new IP header that do not change as the packet is routed. IP fields that change as the packet is routed, such as the TTL value, are not used to calculate the authentication data. As we noted earlier, no encryption is performed when using the AH header, so the contents of the packet can be viewed as it transits a network.

ESP Header

- *Security parameter index (32 bits)*. A bit string used to identify each security association.

- *Sequence number (32 bits)*. A counter value used for antireplay purposes. The counter increases with each new packet in an SA sent up to a maximum value of $2^{32} - 1$. Once the maximum value is reached, a new SA is negotiated and the counter is reset.

- *Payload data (variable)*. The original upper-layer information if in transport mode or the entire original IP packet if in tunnel mode that has been encrypted.

- *Padding (0 to 255 bytes)*. The padding is used for several purposes:
  1. It is useful if the encryption algorithm used requires that the plaintext be a multiple of a certain number of bytes.
  2. The ESP format requires the pad length and next header fields be aligned within a 32-bit word, so the padding ensures this requirement is met.

3. It allows the masking of the true length of the original upper-layer information or IP packet. This prevents an attacker from performing traffic analysis based on the size of the packets. This feature is called *traffic flow confidentiality*.

- *Pad length (8 bits)*. The number of pad bytes.

- *Next header*. As with the AH header, this identifies the next header in the payload.

- *Authentication data (variable)*. As with the AH header, this is the variable-length field that contains the message authentication code for the packet. However, the AH field in an ESP header does not include any portion of the IP header in its hash calculation. When in transport mode, it does not include fields in the original IP header; when in tunnel mode, it does not include fields in the new IP header.

An important point to note about the AH and the ESP headers is that they do not specify what algorithms to use to create the contents of the authentication data and payload data fields. Several different MAC algorithms and encryption algorithms can be used. This means that as new algorithms are developed, they can be incorporated into the IPSec standard without significant architectural changes. Currently, MD5 and SHA are the two supported MAC algorithms used to create the authentication data field. The encryption algorithms for the ESP payload include DES, 3DES, RC5, and IDEA. We will see later how to select which algorithms to use.

Security Association

In addition to the IPSec headers, another important concept related to the IPSec security protocols is a security association. An SA can be thought of as a security tunnel between two IPSec peers. A separate SA can be created for different types of traffic flows. For example, you could have an SA between two hosts for TCP traffic and a separate SA between the same two hosts for UDP traffic. You could even have separate SA's for each TCP or UDP port in use. Each SA is uniquely identified by three parameters:

1. *Security parameter index (SPI)*. The SPI is simply a bit string assigned to each SA. As we have seen, the SPI is carried in the AH or ESP header. The SPI allows the receiving IPSec peer to differentiate the SA to which a packet belongs.

2. *IP destination address*. The destination of the IPSec datagram.

3. *Security protocol identifier*. Whether the IPSec header is AH or ESP.

IPSec uses these three pieces of information to identify each SA connection between peer devices. As noted, two devices may have many SAs between them, and the SPI is used to uniquely identify them since the destination address and the security protocol, AH or ESP, may be the same. Note that each SA can use a different security protocol. You may have some traffic between two IPSec peers that you only want to use the AH header for authentication purposes and other traffic that you want to be encrypted. IPSec is flexible enough to permit these kinds of situations.

Security Protocol Database

IPSec uses a database called the *security protocol database* (SPD) to determine what IPSec parameters to apply to a particular class of IP traffic. The SPD defines what types of IP traffic will require processing by IPSec and which ones will not. For those IP packets that require processing by IPSec, the SPD defines whether the packets will use an AH or ESP header and also defines what algorithms will be used for the different kinds of packets. It is through the SPD that an IPSec device creates SAs. An IPSec device consults its SPD for each IP packet to determine if IPSec will process the packet and, if so, the SA to which the packet belongs.

In the Cisco IPSec implementation, extended access lists perform most of the functions of the SPD to classify the various kinds of packets that will be processed by IPSec. The match between traffic classified by an access list and the type of security protocol and algorithms to be used is performed by a crypto map. Several different algorithms can be used by the AH and ESP security protocols, so you must specify the algorithms that you will use. We will see examples of this later.

Key Management

Now that we understand the IPSec security protocols, we will briefly examine key management. As we have discussed, cryptography centers around algorithms and keys. The IPSec security protocols deal with the algorithms used and the security protocol header formats. Key management focuses on how you can exchange the secret keys to be used by the IPSec algorithms across an unsecured network. Typically, each SA will require at least two keys, one for data transmission in each direction. If you plan on using both the AH and ESP headers for an SA, you'll need four keys, two for each SA for each security protocol header.

These keys are secret-session keys used with either the MAC algorithm to create the authentication data or with the ESP encryption process to create the payload data. Because we cannot simply send the keys across the unsecured network, a method is needed to ensure that each end of an SA has the secret keys it needs to complete IPSec processing. Each IPSec device can be informed of the keys it requires through a manual or an automated process. The manual process is very cumbersome and requires an administrator to manually configure each IPSec host with the keys needed for each SA. This process is normally suitable only for testing purposes. The automated process makes use of a key management protocol called the *Internet key exchange* (IKE).

IKE takes care of the complexity of exchanging secret keys for all of the algorithms used by IPSec. By offloading the key management functions to a common key management protocol, it again makes it easy to incorporate new algorithms into the IPSec suite of protocols. IKE uses public key cryptography algorithms to securely exchange secret keys across an unsecured network. IKE is a protocol that operates within the ISAKMP framework. Much of the Cisco terminology refers to IKE and ISAKMP as if they were the same term. In most of the Cisco commands, you use ISAKMP as the keyword and not IKE, so we will refer to IKE as ISAKMP for the remainder of this chapter. For our purposes, the differences between IKE and ISAKMP are not of great importance and you can think of them as referring to the same process. The central point to understand is that ISAKMP allows the exchange of secret-session keys across an unsecured network and that these secret-session keys are used by the AH and ESP security protocols for authentication and encryption.

Implementing IPSec

Now that we understand the basics of IPSec, we will review the procedures to enable it on a Cisco router. Although IPSec is not as easy to configure as CET, the process is not very complicated and is straightforward once you understand the basic principles of IPSec. There are two basic steps needed to configure IPSec:

1. Enable ISAKMP for key exchange.
2. Enable IPSec.

Each of these steps involves several additional steps that we discuss in detail in this section. Note that, strictly speaking, it is not necessary to use ISAKMP for key exchange. As stated previously, you can manually configure the encryption and MAC keys on each IPSec peer. This procedure is very cumbersome and we will not cover configuring IPSec in this manner.

Enable ISAKMP

The first step required for ISAKMP is to create a policy on each IPSec peer. The ISAKMP policy specifies the security parameters that will be negotiated with each IPSec peer. These policies specify the encryption parameters needed to protect ISAKMP negotiations. Each ISAKMP negotiation needs to be protected from eavesdroppers, so the process begins by each peer agreeing on a common set of encryption parameters that will be used to secure further ISAKMP negotiations. If the ISAKMP negotiation process were not protected, each IPSec peer would not be able to determine that it was negotiating with the real peer. An attacker could come between IPSec peers and spoof each end of the connection and obtain all the necessary information to eavesdrop on all later ISAKMP negotiations, compromising your IPSec communication. The parameters for an ISAKMP policy are listed here:

- *Encryption algorithm.* DES, 3DES.
- *Hash algorithm.* SHA, MD5.
- *Authentication method.* RSA signatures, RSA nonces, preshared keys.
- *Diffie-Hellman group.* 768-bit or 1024-bit (group 1 or group 2).
- *Security association lifetime.* Default 86,400 s (1 day).

Creation of a sample ISAKMP policy is shown here, with the default values of each parameter:

```
2621#conf t
Enter configuration commands, one per line. End with CNTL/Z.
2621(config)#crypto isakmp policy 1
2621(config-isakmp)#encryption des
2621(config-isakmp)#hash sha
2621(config-isakmp)#authentication rsa-sig
2621(config-isakmp)#lifetime 86400
2621(config-isakmp)#group 1
2621(config-isakmp)#
2621#
```

The encryption and hash algorithms, which we have seen before, are the same sort of algorithms used by the IPSec security protocols. The authentication method is new however. The authentication method defines how ISAKMP will encrypt its messages for key negotiation. As noted previously, public key encryption is useful for exchanging a secret-session key. In order to use public key encryption, however, we must first create a public/private key combination on each IPSec device. Alternatively, we can use a shared secret key on each IPSec peer. ISAKMP will use this shared secret key to encrypt its key exchange procedures. Our examples will only cover the use of the shared secret key for ISAKMP negotiation. The reader should consult the Cisco documentation for details on the use of public key encryption for ISAKMP key exchange.

The group parameter specifies whether a 768-bit (group 1) or 1024-bit (group 2) Diffie-Hellman modulus will be used during the key exchange process. (A derivative of the Diffie-Hellman algorithm is used by ISAKMP.) Using group 2 is more secure, but requires more processing on the IPSec peer and is not supported by all IPSec implementations. If your devices can support it, group 2 is the preferred method. The lifetime value can be adjusted to suit your environment, with a shorter lifetime generally being more secure but again requiring more processing on each IPSec peer. We recommend a lifetime of 1 to 6 h if your IPSec peers can support renegotiating the ISAKMP SA that often.

Once the ISAKMP policy is defined, the only other step required for ISAKMP is to specify the shared secret key to be used for each peer.

```
2621#conf t
Enter configuration commands, one per line. End with CNTL/Z.
2621(config)#crypto isakmp key thisisatest address 10.1.4.1
2621(config)#crypto isakmp key thisisatest2 address 10.50.8.3
2621(config)#
2621#
```

You can use the same or different keys for each peer. Using the same key makes configuration easier since you don't have to keep track of the separate keys used by each peer, but it is not as secure as using separate keys for each peer. In either case, each end of an IPSec connection must have the same shared secret key for ISAKMP processing to be successful.

A few other commands that are useful for examining and monitoring your ISAKMP negotiation process are listed here:

```
Show crypto isakmp sa
Show crypto isakmp policy
Clear crypto isakmp [connection-id]
Debug crypto isakmp
```

Enable IPSec

Once you have successfully configured ISAKMP, four basic steps are needed to complete the IPSec-specific portion of a configuration:

1. Create an access list that will define what traffic will be selected for processing by IPSec.

2. Create the transform sets that define what security policies will be used for each access list created in step 1.

3. Create a crypto map that matches the access lists in step 1 and the transform sets in step 2 to a particular IPSec peer.

4. Apply the crypto map to an interface.

Each of these steps is examined in this section.

Step 1

We create an access list that specifies the traffic to be processed by IPSec. Typically, the access list is configured so that IPSec processes all traffic between local LAN subnets:

```
Access-list 101 permit ip 150.100.1.0 0.0.0.255 172.50.1.0 0.0.0.255
```

Step 2

We create the transform sets that specify what security protocols and algorithms will be used when communicating with a particular peer. You can specify AH for authentication and ESP for encryption and/or authentication. You must specify at least one security protocol. Many configurations use ESP for both encryption and authentication:

```
Crypto ipsec transform-set test esp-3des esp-md5
```

Step 3

We create the crypto map that will match the access list and transform sets created to a specific IPSec peer. You can specify multiple peer IP addresses per map entry, but you can only specify a single transform set and access list match per entry:

```
Crypto map testing 10 ipsec-isakmp
   Match address 101
   Set transform-set test
   Set peer 171.50.1.1
   Set peer 10.1.8.1
Crypto map testing 20 ipsec-isakmp
   Match address 102
   Set transform-set test2
   Set peer 150.8.3.1
```

Step 4

The fourth and final step is to apply the crypto map created in step 3 to a router interface. Typically, the crypto map is applied to the interface closest to the IPSec peer:

```
Interface serial0
   Crypto map testing
```

Once these steps have been completed, ISAKMP and IPSec processing should proceed normally. Note that it is important that both the policy parameters created with ISAKMP and the transform set parameters created with IPSec match on each end of the IPSec connection. If a common set of parameters does not exist, ISAKMP negotiation will fail.

Now that we understand the basics of CET and IPSec, we present several examples of each of these technologies.

Encryption Application: Example 1

In this example, an organization has two routers, each with two interfaces, an Ethernet and a serial. The routers are located at two different sites

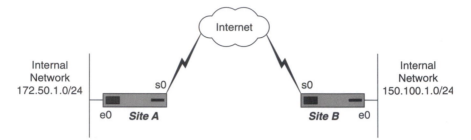

Figure 9-4 Encryption network schematic: example 1.

and each router has a connection to the Internet via its serial interface. The organization wants to use the Internet to connect the two sites, but wants to ensure that the data transmitted from one site to another are encrypted for transport across the Internet. At site A the company is using IP addresses from the 172.50.1.0/24 address space and at site B the company is using IP addresses from the 150.100.1.0/24 address space. The company has no plans to create additional sites in the next 2 to 3 years and does not require any non-Cisco equipment to create encrypted connections to either site router. Since the routers are low-end 2500 routers, only 56-bit DES will be used. Additionally, the company wants a solution that is simple to configure and maintain (Figure 9-4).

Solution

```
Router A
Hostname site-a
!
crypto map site-b 10 cisco
  set peer 205.15.1.1
  match address 101
!
interface ethernet0
  ip address 175.50.1.1 255.255.255.0
!
interface serial0
  ip address 205.15.5.1 255.255.255.252
  crypto map site-b
!
ip access-list 101 permit ip 172.50.1.0 0.0.0.255 150.100.1.0 0.0.0.255

Router B
Hostname site-b
!
crypto map site-a 10 cisco
  set peer 205.15.5.1
  match address 101
!
interface ethernet0
  ip address 150.100.1.1 255.255.255.0
```

```
!
interface serial0
   ip address 205.15.1.1 255.255.255.252
   crypto map site-a
!
ip access-list 101 permit ip 150.100.1.0 0.0.0.255 172.50.1.0 0.0.0.255
```

Explanation

In this example, we chose to implement CET instead of IPSec. Only two routers are involved, so exchanging keys is not difficult. Also, 3DES is not required since the company has decided to use 56-bit DES for the encryption. CET is somewhat easier to configure than IPSec as well, and the company wants the configuration to be as simple as possible while still providing good cryptography. We assume for this example that the public/private keys on each router have been created and exchanged as demonstrated earlier.

The configuration of each router is very straightforward. We first define access list 101 on each router to determine what traffic will be encrypted. In this example, the access lists on each router define that all traffic going from the LAN interface on one router will be encrypted when it is going to the LAN interface on the other router. No other traffic will be encrypted such as traffic to and from the Internet. We could also have excluded particular hosts on each router's subnet from the encryption process if we wished by using deny entries in our access list in conjunction with our permit. After defining each access list, we need to define a crypto map that will specify the peers with which we are establishing encryption sessions and the access lists used for each peer. Since there is only one peer for each router, only one peer and one access list are needed. Finally, we apply the crypto map to the serial interface of each router. Typically, you want to apply the crypto map to the interface closest to the peer router, which is the serial interface on each router in this example.

Encryption Application: Example 2

In this example, the organization is similar to the one in Example 1, with two routers, each of which has two interfaces, an Ethernet and a serial. The organization has requirements very similar to those in Example 1, except that they now wish to pass IPX traffic from one site to another. They want this traffic, as well as the IP traffic, to be protected by encryption. Additionally, this organization uses subnets of the 10.0.0.0/8 private network on the LAN interfaces at each site. They are opposed to using NAT as they have some applications that do not work with NAT. They need a way to have traffic from both private IP addresses and IPX networks cross the Internet securely. At site A the company is using IP

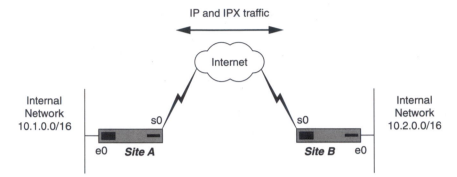

Figure 9-5   Encryption network schematic: example 2.

addresses from the 10.1.0.0/16 address space, and at site B the company is using IP addresses from the 10.2.0.0/16 address space (Figure 9-5).

Solution

```
Router A
Hostname site-a
!
crypto map site-b 10 cisco
  set peer 205.15.1.1
  match address 101
!
interface tunnel 0
  tunnel source serial0
  tunnel destination 205.15.1.1
  ip address 10.100.1.1 255.255.0.0
  ipx network ab
  crypto map site-b
!
interface ethernet0
  ip address 10.1.1.1 255.255.0.0
  ipx network aa
!
interface serial0
  ip address 205.15.5.1 255.255.255.252
  crypto map site-b
!
ip access-list 101 permit ip host 205.15.5.1 host 205.15.1.1

Router B
Hostname site-b
!
crypto map site-a 10 cisco
  set peer 205.15.5.1
  match address 101
!
interface tunnel 0
  tunnel source serial0
```

```
    tunnel destination 205.15.5.1
    ip address 10.100.2.1 255.255.0.0
    ipx network ab
    crypto map site-a
!
interface ethernet0
    ip address 150.100.1.1 255.255.255.0
    ipx network bb
!
interface serial0
    ip address 205.15.1.1 255.255.255.252
    crypto map site-a
!
ip access-list 101 permit ip host 205.15.1.1 host 205.15.5.1
```

Explanation

As in Example 1, we chose to implement CET instead of IPSec. The configuration of CET is simpler than that of IPSec and 56-bit DES is adequate for this organization's encryption needs. As before, we assume that the public/private keys on each router have been generated and exchanged as demonstrated earlier. In spite of the similarities with Example 1, there are some significant differences in this case.

First, we have created a new interface named tunnel 0, which is a tunnel interface that will allow us to encapsulate IPX packets in IP packets for transmission across the Internet. Only IP packets are routed across the Internet, so if we did not encapsulate the IPX packets in an IP packet, IPX packets could not traverse the Internet from site A to site B. The configuration of the tunnel interface is straightforward, we must specify a source and destination interface for the tunnel. These addresses will be the tunnel end points. Packets created for use by the tunnel interface will use the source address defined in this step as the source address of all packets sent through the tunnel.

We should note that packets are not physically sent through the tunnel interface. The tunnel interface is only a logical construct. Logically, a packet is sent through the tunnel interface at which point a new IP header is wrapped around the existing layer 3 header. The original layer 3 header could be IPX, Appletalk, DECnet, or even IP. All packets logically sent through the tunnel interface receive the new IP header and are then routed to the appropriate physical interface. Since these packets all receive a new IP header, all packets routed through the tunnel interface have the same source IP address. Once the tunneled packet arrives at the other end of the tunnel, the router strips off the IP header created by the tunnel interface and then sends the original packet to the appropriate interface. In our case, packets sent through the tunnel interface are given a new IP header with the address of our serial interface. On router A the address will be 205.15.5.1 and on router B the address will be 205.15.1.1.

In addition to the source and destination addresses configured on the tunnel interface, we have also defined an IPX and IP network address. Notice that the IPX and IP networks match on each end of the tunnel interface. This is required. As far as each router is concerned, the two tunnel interfaces are connected. Note that they are connected only logically and not physically. There could be any number of physical hops between routers A and B, but the tunnel interfaces consider themselves to be connected on a point-to-point link, just as if you had a physical point-to-point link between the two routers. Notice that the tunnel interface is configured with an IP address from the 10.0.0.0/8 network. This is fine since the IP packets routed through the tunnel interface end up with an IP source address of the serial interface on each router, which is a routable address.

The crypto map statements are the same in this example as in Example 1. In fact, there are only two small changes from the perspective of CET process. We have modified access list 101 so that it matches packets for encryption that have a source and destination address of the serial interfaces on our routers. We can do this because, as we stated, each packet routed through the tunnel interface will end up with a source address of the serial interface of its respective router. Keep in mind that this is not NAT. No translation is taking place on the original IP header. A new IP header is being wrapped around the original header. The new IP header is removed by the router at the other end of the tunnel for further forwarding as needed. The other small change to the CET process is that we have applied the crypto map, as well as the physical interface, to the tunnel interface. The only other changes made to the configuration are the addition of IPX network numbers on each router's Ethernet0 interfaces.

Note that we could perform a very similar configuration using IPSec encryption instead of CET. The only changes needed would be to the encryption-specific portions of the configuration. None of the tunnel or other interface configuration parameters would need to be changed, since only the crypto map statement enables the encryption on each interface, so that changing the configuration is very simple if the organization decided to use IPSec in the future.

Encryption Application: Example 3

In this example, an organization has five sites connected to the Internet. One site acts as the hub site where all the data information is stored, and the remaining sites are branch offices. Each site has a router with two interfaces, an Ethernet and a serial. The serial connection at each site is used to connect to the Internet. The organization wishes to configure encryption on each of the four branch offices and the hub site so that each branch office can communicate securely with the hub. The branch

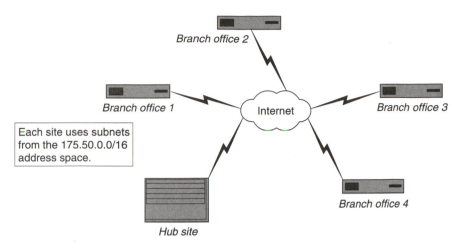

Figure 9-6 Encryption network schematic: example 3.

offices do not need encrypted connections to each other. The organization also has plans to allow users dialing into their ISP from home to connect back to the hub site, so they would like to use standards-based encryption if possible. They are also very security conscious and want to use the strongest encryption available. Each site is using a subnet of the 175.50.0.0/16 address space and each serial interface is using an IP address from the 205.18.1.0/24 subnet (Figure 9-6).

Solution

NOTE
Since all branch office sites are configured similarly, we only show the configuration for the hub site and one branch office.

```
Hub Router
Hostname hub
!
crypto isakmp policy 1
  encryption 3des
  hash md5
  authentication pre-share
crypto isakmp key itsasecret address 205.18.1.10
crypto isakmp key itsasecret address 205.18.1.20
crypto isakmp key itsasecret address 205.18.1.30
crypto isakmp key itsasecret address 205.18.1.40
!
crypto ipsec transform-set test esp-3des esp-md5-hmac
!
```

```
crypto map test 1 ipsec-isakmp
  set peer 205.18.1.10
  set peer 205.18.1.20
  set peer 205.18.1.30
  set peer 205.18.1.40
  set transform-set test
  match address 101
!
interface ethernet0
  ip address 175.50.1.1 255.255.255.0
!
interface serial0
  ip address 205.18.1.1 255.255.255.0
  crypto map test
!
access-list 101 permit ip 175.50.0.0 0.0.255.255 175.50.0.0 0.0.255.255

Branch Office 1
Hostname branch-1
!
crypto isakmp policy 1
  encryption 3des
  hash md5
  authentication pre-share
crypto isakmp key itsasecret address 205.18.1.1
!
crypto ipsec transform-set test esp-3des esp-md5-hmac
!
crypto map test 1 ipsec-isakmp
  set peer 205.18.1.1
  set transform-set test
  match address 101
!
interface ethernet0
  ip address 175.50.10.1 255.255.255.0
!
interface serial0
  ip address 205.18.1.10 255.255.255.0
  crypto map test
!
access-list 101 permit ip 175.50.0.0 0.0.255.255 175.50.0.0 0.0.255.255
```

> **NOTE**
> In practice, it would be unlikely that all of the serial interfaces on your Internet-connected routers would be from the same IP subnet; we used a common subnet in this example to facilitate discussion.

Explanation

In this example, we chose to implement IPSec. IPSec meets the organizational requirements for an open cryptography standard and can use 3DES as its encryption algorithm. Both of these features were required by the specifications of this example. Since only five routers are involved, we have decided to use a shared secret key for the ISAKMP key exchange process. Either a shared secret key or a CA is required to allow the peers to authenticate each other prior to allowing IPSec security associations to be created between peers.

We begin by defining our ISAKMP key exchange policy. This is the policy that defines the parameters that allow ISAKMP to negotiate a key exchange with each peer router. These parameters must match on each router or the ISAKMP protocol will not be able to negotiate connections with each peer router. We have defined that we are using the MD5 algorithm as our hash function and that authentication will be done by using preshared keys. All other values are left at their default settings.

Next, we must define the shared key that will be used with each IPSec peer. We could use a separate key with each peer router, but in this case we have chosen to use the same secret key with each peer, `itsasecret`. The shared secret key at each end of an IPSec connection must match exactly. If the keys do not match, key negotiation will fail. After setting up the shared secret key for each peer, we must then define the transform sets that can be used. The transform set defines what encryption algorithms the router will accept and whether it will use ESP or AH. In our case, we have selected 3DES for our ESP encryption and MD5 as our hash algorithm for our ESP authentication. You can specify several different transform sets and the routers will attempt to negotiate until a common set of transforms is found.

Once we have defined the transform sets, we must create a crypto map. The creation of the crypto map is similar to the method in Example 1 with CET, but with additional parameters. In addition to specifying a peer IP address and the access list to use for encryption, we must also specify what transform sets may be used for this peer. In our example, we have specified only a single transform set so we will use the transform set `test`. We have created access list 101, which will be used to specify which traffic will be encrypted between the peer routers. Since we are subnets of 175.50.0.0/16 address space at each location, we have specified that all traffic to and from any subnet of this address space will be encrypted. The final step is to apply the crypto map to an interface. As with CET, we apply the crypto map closest to the location of our peer router, in this case the serial interfaces of each router.

Encryption Application: Example 4

In this example, an organization has two sites connected to the Internet over low-speed 128-kbps links and low-end 1600 routers. The organization wants a secure connection between these two sites using standards-

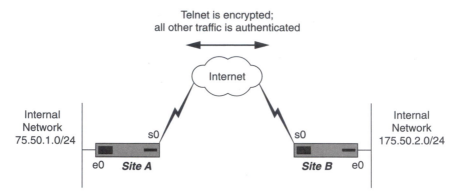

Figure 9-7 Encryption network schematic: example 4.

based encryption. They are very concerned about the extra processing that will be required and want to alleviate as much extra processing overhead as possible. They only require telnet sessions to be encrypted to protect their passwords in transit, but they would like all of their traffic between the sites to be authenticated. Each site is using a subnet of the 175.50.0.0/16 address space (Figure 9-7).

Solution

```
Router A
Hostname site-a
!
crypto isakmp policy 1
  encryption des
  hash md5
  authentication pre-share
!
crypto isakmp key itsasecret address 205.15.1.1
!
crypto ipsec transform-set encrypt esp-des esp-md5-hmac
crypto ipsec transform-set authent ah-md5-hmac
!
crypto map test 10 ipsec-isakmp
  set peer 205.15.1.1
  set transform-set encrypt
  match address 101
crypto map test 20 ipsec-isakmp
  set peer 205.15.1.1
  set transform-set authent
  match address 102
!
interface ethernet0
  ip address 175.50.1.1 255.255.255.0
!
interface serial0
  ip address 205.15.5.1 255.255.255.252
```

```
   crypto map test
!
ip access-list 101 permit tcp 175.50.1.0 0.0.0.255 175.50.2.0 0.0.0.255
eq 23
ip access-list 102 permit ip 175.50.1.0 0.0.0.255 175.50.2.0 0.0.0.255

Router B
Hostname site-b
!
crypto isakmp policy 1
  encryption des
  hash md5
  authentication pre-share
!
crypto isakmp key itsasecret address 205.15.5.1
!
crypto ipsec transform-set encrypt esp-des esp-md5-hmac
crypto ipsec transform-set authent ah-md5-hmac
!
crypto map test 10 ipsec-isakmp
  set peer 205.15.5.1
  set transform-set encrypt
  match address 101
crypto map test 20 ipsec-isakmp
  set peer 205.15.5.1
  set transform-set authent
  match address 102
!
interface ethernet0
  ip address 175.50.2.1 255.255.255.0
!
interface serial0
  ip address 205.15.1.1 255.255.255.252
  crypto map test
!
ip access-list 101 permit tcp 175.50.2.0 0.0.0.255 175.50.1.0 0.0.0.255
eq 23
ip access-list 102 permit ip 175.50.2.0 0.0.0.255 175.50.1.0 0.0.0.255
```

Explanation

In this example, we chose to implement IPSec. IPSec meets the organizational requirements for an open cryptography standard while CET does not. Since only two routers are involved, we have decided to use a shared secret key for the ISAKMP key exchange process. Either a shared secret key or a CA is required to allow the peers to authenticate each other prior to allowing IPSec security associations to be created between peers.

We begin by defining our ISAKMP key exchange policy, the policy that will define the parameters allowing ISAKMP to negotiate a key exchange with each peer router. These parameters must match on each router or the ISAKMP protocol will not be able to negotiate connections with each peer router. We have defined that we are using the MD5 algorithm as our hash function and that authentication will be done by using preshared keys.

We have further specified that DES will be used for the ISAKMP encryption to minimize processing overhead.

Next, we must define the shared key that will be used with each IPSec peer. We have defined that each peer will use the shared secret key `itsasecret`. This key must be the same on each IPSec peer router. After defining our shared secret key, we must define the algorithms that IPSec will use by creating one or more transform sets. In this example, we have created two transform sets, `encrypt` and `authent`. In the `encrypt` transform set we have defined that we will use ESP for both encryption and authentication. In the `authent` transform set we have defined authentication only. We will use each transform set for a different kind of traffic.

After defining our transform sets, we must also create access lists that classify the traffic that will use each transform set. The specification of this example was that only telnet should be encrypted. Considering this, we have created two access lists on each router. Access list 101 will match on telnet sessions from one LAN segment to another, and access list 102 will match on any IP traffic between the two LAN segments. After creating our access lists, the final step is to create our crypto map. In this example, we have created a crypto map named `test`. The `test` crypto map defines two sets of map entries. The first entry uses access list 101 and matches only telnet traffic from one subnet to another. The second entry uses access list 102 and matches on all IP traffic, so it will match any traffic that doesn't match the first set of crypto map options.

Notice that we have defined the same peer under each set of options, but that we are using different transform sets, depending on whether we want encryption or only authentication. When creating multiple crypto map entries, the entries are considered in numeric order from lowest to highest, so entry 10 will be considered before entry 20. IPSec will check access list 101 to see if the IP traffic matches, meaning it is a telnet session. If the traffic does not match access list 101, IPSec considers the next crypto map entry and will check access list 102, which matches any IP traffic. We could have created many additional crypto map entries, each specifying a different access list and a different series of transform sets.

CHAPTER 10

Traffic Policing
and
Queuing

The final chapter completes the discussion of technologies that are not access lists but closely related to them and provide additional value-added features. Specifically, we examine ways to manipulate traffic flows in a network by using various queuing and traffic management techniques. The Cisco IOS provides many features that help to control the traffic flows in a network. For example, various queuing methods can be enabled to grant certain classes of traffic priority over other classes of traffic on congested data lines. Particular traffic flows can be limited by strictly defining the amount of data a particular flow can send through a router interface by using traffic policing. Several different methods will be examined that control the flow of data traffic in your network through a combination of queuing and traffic shaping or policing technologies.

Queuing Technologies

We begin with a discussion of a series of congestion management features referred to collectively as *queuing technologies*. These congestion management features allow you to control congestion on a router interface by determining the order in which packets are transmitted out that interface based on priorities placed on those packets. Use of different queuing techniques can control to a greater or lesser degree the traffic allowed to be transmitted through a router interface in preference to other traffic. Queuing techniques are only useful in situations where more data are available to transmit than can be sent out a router interface. In other words, they are only useful when transmission congestion occurs on a router interface. If there is no congestion on a router interface, configuring queuing on that interface will serve little purpose.

For example, you may have traffic entering a router on a high-speed LAN interface attempting to exit the router on a low-speed WAN interface. In such a situation, it is likely that there will be too much traffic for the router to transmit on the low-speed WAN interface without some traffic being dropped. When there is more traffic to transmit out an interface than that interface can accommodate, a period of congestion is said to occur. As an example, if there is 1024 kbps (about 1 Mbps) of data traffic arriving inbound from a LAN interface destined to a WAN interface and the WAN interface can only transmit at a rate of 512 kbps, approximately 512 kbps of traffic must be dropped. We say approximately because the router will attempt to hold some of the traffic in a buffer in lieu of dropping it. If the amount of traffic entering the router were simply a burst and not a constant amount of traffic, the router would be able to buffer a small amount of the traffic without dropping it. However, the router's interface buffers are limited and once those buffers fill, traffic must be dropped. Queuing techniques allow you to classify which traffic is given preference so that more important traffic, however you define "important," is transmitted while traffic of lesser importance is dropped.

This is a central point to understand. The only reason to use one of the available queuing methods is because you have some traffic that is higher priority than other traffic. If you do not care which traffic is dropped, there is little reason to configure queuing methods. The router will simply send the traffic on a first in, first out (FIFO) method and any traffic that cannot be sent will be dropped, no matter what kind of traffic it is. In most environments, some data traffic needs to have priority over other traffic, so it is a good idea to understand the different queuing mechanisms available to manage periods of congestion.

Another point to grasp is that queuing methods are only needed when a router interface experiences periods of congestion because the amount of data to transmit is greater than the speed of the interface. This normally only happens on low-speed WAN interfaces. Congestion is much less of a problem in the LAN environment where you are dealing with interfaces that support megabits of data per second (1 million bits). In the WAN environment, many times you have only kilobits of data per second (1000 bits), and congestion is much more likely to occur.

Queuing Methods

In this section the four queuing techniques that you can use on a Cisco router are presented. Each queuing method will be presented, followed by a discussion of the specifics of why and when you might want to use each queuing method. At the end of this section, examples illustrating the use of these queuing methods are presented.

Types of Queues

The four types of queues are

1. First in, first out (FIFO)
2. Weighted fair queuing (WFQ)
3. Custom queuing (CQ)
4. Priority queuing (PQ)

First In, First Out (FIFO)

FIFO queuing is exactly what it sounds like. The router simply sends packets out an interface in the order in which they arrived. If the interface is congested, the router will attempt to buffer as much data as it can while traffic is transmitted out the interface. FIFO does not classify traffic in any way; there is only a single queue and all traffic is treated equally. When using FIFO, bursty traffic sources can consume all of the available buffer space on an interface at the expense of other traffic.

FIFO is the default queuing method for interfaces with speeds greater than 2.048 Mbps (E1), so it is the default for all LAN type interfaces (token ring, Ethernet, FDDI, etc.). FIFO is the fastest queuing method, and works well on interfaces that experience little congestion such as LAN interfaces. LAN interfaces typically have little congestion because of the high transmission rates. Conversely, WAN interfaces typically experience congestion due to their relatively low speeds compared to LAN interfaces. In the WAN, 1 Mbps and higher is considered high speed, while the slowest LAN technology currently in use is 4-Mbps token ring. (There are older LAN technologies that are slower than 4 Mbps, but these are very rare.) In modern LAN environments, 10-Mbps speeds are widespread, and 100-Mbps speeds are very common.

Weighted Fair Queuing (WFQ)

WFQ uses a scheduling method that provides a fair allocation of bandwidth to all network traffic. WFQ applies a priority to traffic to classify this traffic into conversations and determine how much bandwidth each conversation needs relative to other conversations. WFQ uses a flow-based algorithm that moves interactive traffic to the front of the queues to reduce response time and fairly shares the remaining bandwidth among high-traffic flows. Interactive traffic, such as telnet, will get priority over bulk transfer traffic such as FTP. Packets with the same source IP address, destination IP address, and source or destination TCP/UDP port are classified as belonging to the same traffic flow. WFQ will allocate an equal share of bandwidth to each flow, but will give priority to low-bandwidth flows. That is, the queues for low-bandwidth flows will be serviced before the queues for high-bandwidth flows.

Basically, each identified flow is allocated its own queue. A limited number of these dynamic queues can be created, and the default is 256. Each dynamic queue has a limited number of messages that can be held, called the *congestive-message threshold*. The default congestive-messages threshold is 64 messages per queue. New messages for high-bandwidth flows are discarded once the message threshold has been reached. Low-bandwidth flows, however, are allowed to continue to queue data. Consequently, low-bandwidth queues may sometimes contain more messages than specified by the congestive-threshold number.

WFQ is also aware of IP precedence settings and can allocate additional bandwidth for higher-precedence traffic. Each category of traffic is allocated a percentage of traffic based on its IP precedence setting as it relates to the total precedence of all traffic flows. For example, assume that there is one traffic flow for each IP precedence level 0 through 7. The ratio of bandwidth allocated for each queue is found by adding 1 to the precedence level and dividing that number by the total precedence for all flows. For each precedence level,

$$\text{Precedence } 0 + 1 = 1$$
$$\text{Precedence } 1 + 1 = 2$$

and so on for each subsequent precedence level.

$$\text{Total precedence levels} = 1 + 2 + 3 + 4 + 5 + 6 + 7 + 8 = 36$$

(We have one flow for each precedence, 0 through 7.)

So the packet ratio for flows with an IP precedence of 0 is $\frac{1}{36}$. The packet ratio for flows with an IP precedence of 1 is $\frac{2}{36}$ and so on. If we had 10 flows with precedence level 2 and one flow for each of the other precedence levels, our calculation is

$$1 + 2 + 3(10) + 4 + 5 + 6 + 7 + 8 = 43$$

IP precedence level 0 gets a ratio of $\frac{1}{43}$, level 2 gets $\frac{2}{43}$, and each level 3 precedence gets $\frac{3}{43}$ and so on. These numbers are ratios that determine the amount of available bandwidth each precedence level will get. It is easy to see that although each level gets some of the bandwidth, the higher-precedence flows get a higher percentage of the bandwidth because of the higher ratio (that is, $\frac{8}{36}$ is higher than $\frac{1}{36}$).

WFQ is enabled on an interface with the command:

```
fair-queue [congestive-discard-threshold [dynamic-queues
[reservable-queues]]]
```

Example:

```
Interface serial0
 Fair-queue 64 256
```

As mentioned, the default values for the discard threshold and the number of dynamic queues are 64 and 256, respectively. The reservable queues are related to RSVP (Reservation Protocol). RSVP is not covered in this book. WFQ is the default queuing method for all interfaces with speeds of 2.048 Mbps (E1) and below, so no additional configuration is needed to enable it if the interface is a standard Cisco router serial interface. As mentioned earlier, the default queuing method for higher-speed interfaces is FIFO.

Custom Queuing

The third type of queuing available is called *custom queuing* (CQ). CQ allows you to create up to 16 queues and specify the number of bytes to forward from each queue each time a queue is serviced. This process allows you to allocate resources to applications that require a certain, fixed amount of bandwidth. Additionally, you can specify the maximum number of packets in each queue, allowing you to further control the amount of traffic available to each queue. CQ works by specifying the number of bytes or packets that will be serviced for each class of traffic. CQ services each queue in a round-robin fashion by cycling through each queue. If a queue is empty, CQ simply moves on to the next queue. As each queue is serviced, CQ empties packets from the queue until either the byte count limit of the queue is reached or the queue is empty. The bandwidth available for each queue is specified indirectly in terms of the byte count and length of the queue.

There are 17 queues available for CQ. Queue 0 is a system queue, and is used by the router for any system-related packets such as signaling packets. Queues 1 to 16 are used to specify the class of traffic allocated to each queue. Traffic can be classified based on protocol, packet size, and protocol access list. For example, you can place all IP traffic in queue 1, or you could specify that all IP traffic with a packet size less than 500 bytes is allocated to queue 2. You could even specify that all IP traffic that matches IP access list 101 is allocated to queue 3. Several commands can be used to specify the classes of traffic allocated to each queue and to specify the byte count or the number of packets available for each queue. Generally, a particular `queue-list` command is associated with a `list-number`, which is just an integer used to reference the queue commands, much like an access-list number.

```
queue-list list-number interface interface-type interface-number
    queue-number
```

Example

```
queue-list 1 interface ethernet0 2
```

The above example assigns packets arriving on the Ethernet0 interface to queue number 2. The list number is 1, which is used as a reference to group-related sets of queue commands.

```
queue-list list-number protocol protocol-name queue-number queue-keyword
    keyword-value
```

Example

```
queue-list 1 protocol ip 3 gt 1024
```

This example assigns IP packets with a size greater than 1024 bytes to queue 3.

```
queue-list list-number queue queue-number byte-count byte-count-number
```

Example

```
queue-list 1 queue 2 byte-count 5000
```

This command allows you to set the number of bytes that each queue will be allowed to transfer each time the queue is serviced. In this example, the number of bytes for queue 2 is set to 5000. The default value is 1500.

```
queue-list list-number queue queue-number limit limit-number
```

Example

```
queue-list 1 queue 4 limit 30
```

This command allows you to set the number of packets that can be stored in a queue. In this example, queue number 4 is allowed to hold 30 packets. The default value is 20 and the range of available values is 0 to 32,767. A value of 0 means that an unlimited number of packets may be queued.

Once the queues have been created and assigned appropriate byte-count and packet-limit values, you must apply the queue to a particular interface. This is done with the interface command `custom-queue-list`:

```
Interface serial0
    custom-queue-list 1
```

An important point to understand when using CQ is that even if a packet exceeds the byte-count limit of a queue, at least one packet will be sent from the queue each time the queue is serviced as long as there are packets in the queue. So, for example, if there were only 500-byte packets in queue 1 and the byte-count limit was 100 for that queue, CQ would remove a single packet from that queue each time it cycled through all queues. If the byte count limit were 600, it would service two packets. This is important because different protocols use different packet sizes. Even within the same protocol, such as IP, packet sizes can vary widely based on the application used. For this reason, it is important to "normalize" the queue byte count, that is, allocating an appropriate byte count based on the average packet size for the protocol in conjunction with the desired percentage of bandwidth you wish to allocate.

For example, assume you have two traffic flows and you want to assign 75 percent of the bandwidth to traffic flow A and 25 percent of the bandwidth to traffic flow B. Traffic flow A has an average packet size of 100 bytes, and traffic flow B has an average packet size of 300 bytes. In order to assign 75 percent of the bandwidth to traffic flow A, you need to take into account that the byte size is one-third of the byte size of traffic flow B. The easiest way to normalize the traffic is to divide the percentage of traffic we wish to allocate for a flow by the average packet size:

$$\text{Flow A} = \frac{75}{100} = 0.75$$

$$\text{Flow B} = \frac{25}{300} = 0.083$$

If we divide each number by 0.083 (the lowest number), we get

$$\text{Flow A} = 9.036$$
$$\text{Flow B} = 1.0$$

Rounding up for flow A, we see that we need to allocate 10 packets to flow A for each packet for flow B. Multiplying by the number of bytes per packet for each flow tells us we need to allocate 10,000 bytes for flow A's queue and 300 bytes for flow B's queue. Similar conversions can be done for each traffic flow for which you want to create a queue.

Custom queuing is very useful in situations where you want to allocate a specific, fixed portion of the available bandwidth for a particular traffic flow, but would still like to allocate some bandwidth for other traffic flows. If, for example, you wanted to allocate approximately 50 percent of the available bandwidth for SNA and leave the rest for other traffic. In some situations, you want to allocate a guaranteed amount of bandwidth for certain traffic flows, even at the expense of all other flows. A queuing method for these situations is discussed next.

Priority Queuing

Priority queuing (PQ) works very similarly to CQ, except that in PQ an individual queue is allowed to dominate over other queues. The four queues, in order of priority, are: high, medium, normal, and low. All traffic in a higher-priority queue is serviced before a lower-priority queue is serviced. This means that if there are always packets in the high-priority queue, the lower-priority queues will never be serviced and traffic using those queues would fail. You can classify how traffic is placed into a queue based on protocol, protocol access list, incoming interface, or packet size. Interface keepalives are always placed in the high-priority queue; all other traffic, including router updates, must be explicitly allocated or they are placed in the normal queue. Several commands are available to configure priority queuing:

```
priority-list list-number protocol protocol-name {high | medium | normal
  | low}
queue-keyword keyword-value
```

Example

```
Priority-list 1 protocol ip high list 101
```

This command allows you to assign a particular protocol (IP, IPX, AppleTalk, etc.) to one of the priority queues. You can optionally specify a `queue-keyword` such as `list` to specify the use of an access list to match packets. Other keywords include:

gt	greater than a certain byte count
lt	less than a certain byte count
tcp	TCP port to match (either source or destination)
udp	UDP port to match (either source or destination)
fragments	IP fragments

In this example we are assigning IP packets matching access list 101 to the high queue.

```
priority-list list-number interface interface-type interface-number
  {high | medium | normal | low}
```

Example

```
Priority-list 1 interface ethernet0 medium
```

This command allows you to assign packets arriving on a particular router interface to a queue. This example assigns packets arriving on the Ethernet0 interface to the medium queue.

```
priority-list list-number default {high | medium | normal | low}
```

Example

```
priority-list 1 default normal
```

This command allows you to assign the default queue for packets that do not match explicit queue definitions. The normal queue is usually the default.

```
priority-list list-number queue-limit [high-limit [medium-limit
   [normal-limit [low-limit]]]]
```

Example

```
priority-list 1 queue-limit 30 50 50 30
```

This command allows you to change the packet-limit counts for each of the queues. The default values for the queues are 20, 40, 60, and 80. In this example we have set the high queue limit to 30, the medium queue limit to 50, the normal queue limit to 50, and the low queue limit to 30.

Once the queues have been created and assigned appropriate values, you must apply the queue to a particular interface. This is done with the interface command `custom-queue-list`:

```
Interface serial0
   Priority-group 1
```

Following are some examples that use queuing techniques.

Queuing Application: Example 1

An organization has two sites connected across a WAN. Site A is the hub site that contains all of the servers accessed from site B. Site A uses its WAN link to site B to access corporate resources, but also accesses the Internet through site A for casual Web browsing. The corporation would like to ensure that Web traffic sent across the WAN link to the remote site is given a lower priority than other traffic from site A to site B. But they do want the Web traffic to be guaranteed a certain amount of bandwidth (Figure 10-1).

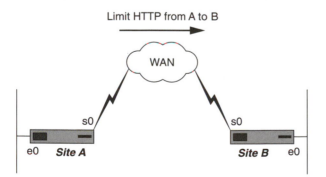

Figure 10-1 Sites A and B communicating across a WAN link with the Web traffic limited from A to B.

Solution

```
Router A
Hostname site-a
!
interface serial0
  ip address 205.15.5.1 255.255.255.252
  custom-queue-list 1
!
queue-list 1 protocol ip 1 list 101
queue-list 1 queue 1 byte-count 3000
queue-list 1 protocol ip 2 list 102
queue-list 1 queue 2 byte-count 1500
!
ip access-list 101 deny tcp any eq www any
ip access-list 101 permit ip any any
!
ip access-list 102 permit tcp any eq www any
```

Explanation

In this example, we chose to implement custom queuing. CQ allows us to assign a larger percentage of bandwidth to certain classes of traffic, while still ensuring that the other classes of traffic are serviced in a reasonable amount of time. We first created two access lists, 101 and 102. Access list 101 will match all traffic, except packets with a source port of http (Web). Access list 102 will match only packets with a source port of http. After defining our access lists, we have specified several entries for our queue-list number 1. We have specified the protocol as IP and assigned access list 101 to queue 1 and access list 102 to queue 2. We have additionally assigned a byte size of 3000 to queue 1 and 1500 to queue 2 which effectively gives queue 1 twice the bandwidth of queue 2. Notice that we have only configured the queuing on site A. The queuing affects traffic as it leaves a router interface, so configuring a queue on router B would have little effect since the traffic is going from router A to router B.

In this example, we assume that the packet sizes for Web and non-Web traffic are about the same. If the packet sizes were not the same, we would have to normalize the byte sizes for each queue as discussed earlier. Instead of CQ, we could have attempted to just allow WFQ to perform its standard queuing and see if the performance was acceptable. The advantage of WFQ is that it does not require any additional configuration, but it may not provide the needed performance. You should perform testing in your own environment to determine if WFQ provides the performance desired or if other queuing methods are needed.

Queuing Application: Example 2

In this example, the same organization as in Example 1 has two sites connected across a WAN. However, in this example a critical application that

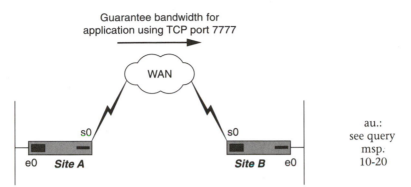

Figure 10-2 Sites A and B communicating across a WAN link. The bandwidth to the application using TCP port 7777 is guaranteed.

uses TCP port 7777 must be allocated a dedicated amount of bandwidth, even to the detriment of other traffic flows (Figure 10-2).

Solution

```
Router A
Hostname site-a
!
interface serial0
  ip address 205.15.5.1 255.255.255.252
  priority-group 1
!
priority-list 1 protocol ip high tcp 7777
priority-list 1 protocol ip normal
priority-list 1 queue-limit 40 40 60 80
```

Explanation

In this example, we chose to implement priority queuing. PQ allows us to give absolute priority to certain classes of traffic over others. As long as there are packets in a higher-priority queue, that queue will be serviced, even if packets in lower-priority queues must be dropped. In this example, no access lists were created. Instead, we have just used the parameters available with PQ to define that any packets with a TCP source or destination port of 7777 are placed into the high-priority queue. All other IP packets are placed into the normal queue. In actuality, the normal queue is the default queue, so we did not need to explicitly place the IP packets into the normal queue; they would be placed into the normal queue by default.

We have also adjusted the number of packets that are allowed per queue with the `queue-limit` command. Normally, the number of packets in each queue is 20, 40, 60, and 80, respectively. We have specified that 40 packets are allowed in the high queue, ensuring that the application using TCP port 7777 will be able to monopolize the available bandwidth if needed. Notice that, again, we have defined the queue only on router A, since this is the source of the traffic flowing toward router B, and we can only affect how the traffic is queued on an outbound interface.

This completes our coverage of the various queuing techniques. In the next section, the use of the traffic-shaping and -policing capabilities of the Cisco IOS are explored.

Traffic Policing

Traffic policing is the general term given to technologies that allow a device to limit strictly the amount of traffic allowed to be received or sent over an interface. Traffic-policing software ensures that only the specified amount of traffic can be sent or received, and all other traffic may be dropped. In Cisco IOS, the traffic-policing software is called *committed access rate* (CAR). CAR services limit the input or output transmission rate on an interface, based on various criteria. CAR is typically configured at the edge of a network such as an Internet connection between ISP's or between an ISP and a customer. CAR can limit traffic based on IP precedence, incoming interface, or IP access list (CAR is only available for IP). The action that CAR takes when traffic exceeds its allocated limit, such as dropping the traffic or resetting its precedence value, can be configured. You can configure CAR either for all IP traffic or you can define different policies for different classes of IP traffic.

Configuring CAR

When defining CAR, you first determine the average bits per second (bps) considered the normal rate of traffic for the flow you are classifying. Then, you define a *normal burst* rate and an *exceed burst* rate. Traffic is allowed to burst above the normal rate up to the normal burst rate. Any traffic that exceeds the normal rate plus the normal burst rate might be discarded. The probability increases as the traffic flow increases until the value of the normal rate plus the exceed burst is reached. Once the traffic flow exceeds the value of the normal rate plus the exceed burst rate, all traffic is discarded. For example, let's say the normal rate is 512,000 bps, the normal burst is 56,000 bps, and the exceed burst is 64,000 bps. Traffic rates up to 564,000 bps (512,000 + 56,000) still conforms to the thresholds. Traffic rates between 564,001 and 576,000 bps exceed the thresholds and might be discarded. All traffic above 576,000 bps will be discarded by CAR.

If you are defining CAR for all IP traffic, only a single interface command is required:

```
rate-limit {input | output} [access-group [rate-limit] acl-index] bps
  burst-normal burst-max conform-action action exceed-action action
```

Example

```
Interface serial0
  rate-limit input 512000 56000 64000 conform-action transmit
    exceed-action drop
```

If you are defining CAR for multiple classes of traffic, you must define CAR access lists that classify the traffic to be policed by CAR in addition to applying CAR to an interface:

```
access-list rate-limit acl-index {precedence | mac-address | mask
  prec-mask}
```

Example

```
Access-list rate-limit 100 4000.1e01.3245
```

Alternatively, a standard or extended IP access list can be used instead of a rate-limit access list. The conform and exceed actions can be one of the following:

- Continue (continue with the `next rate-limit` command).
- Drop.
- Set-prec-continue (set IP precedence and continue with `next rate-limit` command).
- Set-prec-transmit (set IP precedence and transmit packet).
- Transmit.

In the next section, an example of the use of CAR is presented.

CAR Application Example

In this example, an organization is providing Internet service to several different customers. The provider has a Fast Ethernet interface through which three different customers access the Internet. They wish to limit the amount of traffic that each customer is allowed to receive based on contract levels. Each customer has contracted to receive only 10 Mbps. The provider will allow each customer to burst up to 1 Mbps over this rate, but all traffic rates higher than this should be dropped (Figure 10-3).

Solution

```
Provider router
Hostname provider
!
```

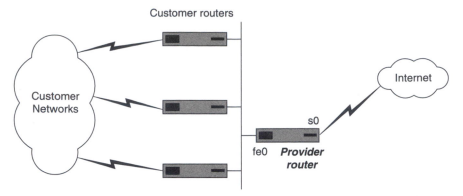

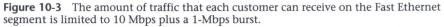

Figure 10-3 The amount of traffic that each customer can receive on the Fast Ethernet segment is limited to 10 Mbps plus a 1-Mbps burst.

```
interface fastethernet0
  ip address 205.15.5.1 255.255.255.0
  rate-limit output access-group rate-limit 100 10000000 1000000 1000000
conform-action transmit exceed-action drop
rate-limit output access-group rate-limit 101 10000000 1000000 1000000
conform-action transmit exceed-action drop
rate-limit output access-group rate-limit 102 10000000 1000000 1000000
conform-action transmit exceed-action drop
!
access-list rate-limit 100 00e0.1245.1111
access-list rate-limit 101 00e0.1245.2222
access-list rate-limit 102 00e0.1245.3333
```

Explanation

In this example, we use CAR to limit the amount of traffic allowed out of the provider router Fast Ethernet interface to each customer router. First we identify the three separate routers, so we will need to create three separate rate-limit statements. If we used only one rate-limit statement, the combined traffic of all three routers would not be able to exceed 10 Mbps, which is not what we want. Notice that we have defined three separate rate-limit statements under the Fast Ethernet interface, one for each customer router.

Notice that each of the rate-limit statements specifies a normal rate of 10 Mbps and a burst and exceed burst of 1 Mbps. Notice also that each rate-limit statement specifies a different access list. We have also defined three rate-limit access lists, each specifying the MAC address of one of the customer routers. Obviously, we would need to know the MAC addresses of the routers, but this information is easily obtained either by examining each customer router or getting it from the arp cache on the provider router.

CAR allows you to limit strictly the amount of bandwidth sent or received out an interface. This can be very useful, but sometimes you don't want to just drop traffic but to prioritize the traffic and queue it according to the different classes of traffic. Traffic shaping, which allows for the queuing of traffic to smooth traffic flows, is examined in the next section.

Traffic Shaping

Traffic-shaping (shaping) technology is closely related to traffic policing (policing). Both shaping and policing classify traffic according to defined parameters and attempt to manipulate the flow of traffic based on these classifications. The difference is that shaping attempts to buffer the traffic and transmit it in a controlled fashion without packet loss, smoothing or "shaping" the traffic flow. Policing, in many cases, will simply drop traffic that does not conform or will set the IP precedence and attempt to transmit the packet. Policing does not attempt to buffer the traffic and is, therefore, susceptible to bursty traffic monopolizing limited bandwidth. Shaping attempts to smooth traffic flows and prevent individual traffic flows from monopolizing the bandwidth. As with CAR, you define an average bit rate, a burst size, and an exceed burst size. Unlike CAR, traffic shaping is only used for traffic that is outbound on a router interface. Traffic shaping allows the router to queue certain traffic flows to attempt to prevent packet loss, even when the traffic rate exceeds its specified limits.

There are two kinds of traffic shaping: *generic traffic shaping* (GTS), which is suitable for use on any type of interface, and *frame-relay traffic shaping* (FRTS), which is suitable only for frame-relay interfaces. You can use GTS on a frame-relay interface and configure it to adapt to received congestion messages (BECN's) and slow down its sending rate.

Configuring GTS

To configure GTS, first define an access list, which is typically an extended IP access list:

```
Access-list 101 permit udp any any
```

Then, define a `traffic-group` command under the interface where the traffic that you wish to shape will leave the router, specifying the average bit rate, the burst size, and the exceed burst size:

```
Interface serial0
 Traffic-shape group 101 64000 8000 6000
```

Alternatively, you can shape the traffic for the entire interface using the `traffic-shape rate` command:

```
Interface serial0
  Traffic-shape rate 64000 8000 6000
```

If you are configuring GTS on a frame-relay interface using the `traffic-shape rate` command, you can also use the `traffic-shape adaptive` command to allow the router to lower the traffic rate in response to received BECNs:

```
Interface serial0
  Traffic-shape rate 64000 8000 6000
  Traffic-shape adaptive 32000
```

When the BECN bit is set in a frame-relay packet, it indicates congestion in the frame-relay cloud. The `traffic-shape adaptive` command causes the router to lower the traffic rate to a value between the average configured with the `traffic-shape rate` command and the `traffic-shape adaptive` command. This allows GTS to respond to congestion in the frame-relay network dynamically. We will see in the next section that frame-relay traffic shaping can respond to congestion messages from the frame-relay network as well.

GTS shapes traffic using a WFQ queuing scheme, discussed earlier in this chapter. The queuing method used with GTS cannot be altered. We will see in the next section that FRTS can use both CQ and PQ when configuring frame-relay traffic shaping.

Configuring FRTS

FRTS is much like GTS since it allows the router to shape traffic flows through an interface to attempt to have the traffic conform to configured rate levels. FRTS is specific to frame relay and a number of parameters are related only to frame relay. Typically, FRTS is configured in situations where you have sites that communicate with one another over a frame-relay network, and the bandwidth at each site has a wide disparity. For example, if you have a site with a 768-kbps link sending data to a site with only a 64-kbps link, it is easy for the site with the larger bandwidth to overwhelm the site with the smaller bandwidth. FRTS shapes the traffic so that a limited amount of traffic is allowed to flow to the site with the smaller bandwidth. FRTS also allows the queuing techniques discussed earlier so that some traffic is given preference over other traffic. This can be useful on a public frame-relay network where data rates are not guaranteed. You can specify that your critical traffic gets priority over other, less critical traffic flows.

To configure FRTS you need to first define a map class that will be configured beneath a particular frame-relay interface or subinterface. The map class allows you to define whether you will use custom or priority queuing and specify values such as the CIR, Bc, and Be. These values are used by

FRTS to adjust its traffic based on parameters set in the frame-relay network. CIR is the amount of traffic that is guaranteed by the network expressed in bits per second. Bc is the committed burst size, which is typically the same value as the CIR expressed in bits. Be is the exceed burst size, which is the number of bits that you are allowed to burst above the committed burst.

```
Map-class frame-relay map-class-name
```

Example

```
Map-class frame-relay test
```

The `map-class` command is applied in interface configuration mode. All of the following FRTS commands are defined beneath the `map-class` command:

```
Frame-relay custom-queue-list list-number
```

Example

```
Frame-relay custom-queue-list 1

Frame-relay priority-group list-number
```

Example

```
Frame-relay priority-group 2
```

These commands allow you to define CQ or PQ if you choose to use one of these queuing methods. If you do not select one of these methods, FIFO queuing is used.

```
Frame-relay traffic-rate average [peak]
```

Example

```
Frame-relay traffic-rate 16000 64000
```

This command allows you to set the average and peak rate of traffic that will be shaped by FRTS. BECN feedback is enabled by default, so the router will drop its sending rate back to 16,000 bps in response to received BECNs. Typically, the peak value will be the same as your Bc value or very close to it.

```
frame-relay cir [out] bps
```

Example

```
Frame-relay cir 64000

frame-relay bc [out] bps
```

Example

```
Frame-relay bc 64000

frame-relay be [out] bps
```

Example

```
Frame-relay be 256000
```

These commands allow you to set your CIR, Be, and Bc values as mentioned earlier.

Here is a complete example of a FRTS map-class command; only relevant portions of the configuration are shown:

```
Interface serial0
 Frame-relay traffic-shaping
 !
interface serial 0.1 point-to-point
 frame-relay class test
 !
map-class frame-relay test
 frame-relay traffic-rate 16000 64000
 frame-relay cir 56000
 frame-relay be 64000
```

There are many different options available for FTRS, and the interested reader should consult the Cisco documentation for more information on all of the available options.

We now present some examples of traffic policing and shaping.

Traffic-Shaping Application: Example 1

In this example, an organization has three sites, a hub site and two spoke sites. The spoke sites make use of the hub site to access their business

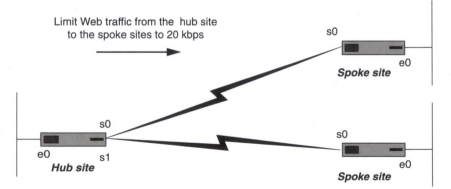

Figure 10-4 Web traffic to the spoke sites is limited to 20 kbps.

applications as well as for Internet access. The organization has a 64-kbps link from the hub site to each of the spoke sites, and they want to limit the amount of Web traffic to each spoke site to 20 kbps since they have had problems with heavy Web surfers saturating their WAN links. No other traffic needs to be limited (Figure 10-4).

Solution

```
Hub Router
Hostname hub
!
interface serial0
  ip address 205.15.5.1 255.255.255.252
  traffic-shape group 101 20000
!
interface serial1
  ip address 208.30.1.1 255.255.255.252
  traffic-shape group 101 20000
!
ip access-list 101 permit tcp any eq www any
```

Explanation

In this example, we implemented GTS to shape the traffic from the hub site to each of the spoke sites. We have configured an access list 101 that matches on Web traffic going from the hub site to the spoke sites. On each serial interface we have defined traffic shaping that will limit the Web traffic to 20-kbps average rate, with no burst rate. All other traffic will be forwarded normally.

Traffic-Shaping Application: Example 2

In this example, an organization has two sites connected over a frame-relay network. The bandwidth at site A is 768 kbps and the bandwidth at site B is 256 kbps. The organization wants to ensure that the traffic from site A does not overwhelm the lower-speed line at site B (Figure 10-5).

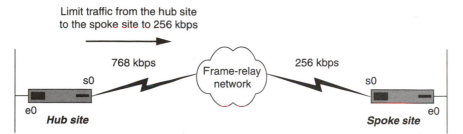

Figure 10-5 Traffic from site A to site B is limited so that the lower-speed link at site B does not experience congestion.

Solution

```
Hub Router:
Hostname hub
!
interface serial0
  encapsulation frame-relay
  frame-relay traffic-shaping
!
interface serial0.0 point-to-point
  frame-relay interface-dlci 110
  frame-relay class test
!
map-class frame-relay test
  frame-relay traffic-rate 200000 256000
  frame-relay cir 200000
  frame-relay be 256000
```

Explanation

In this example, we implemented FRTS to throttle the traffic sent from the hub site to the spoke site. We have configured a frame-relay map class called test. Beneath the test map class we have configured the average traffic rate at 200 kbps and the burst rate at 256 kbps. This will cause the hub router to throttle traffic sent to the spoke site if the traffic rate rises above 256 kbps. We have also defined the CIR value as 200 kbps and the Be rate as 256 kbps to match the settings on the `traffic-rate` command. Notice that we have configured the `frame-relay traffic-shaping` command beneath the serial0 interface and applied the map class to the subinterface.

APPENDIX A

Determining Wildcard Mask Ranges

In this section, we present an algorithm that can be used to determine the correct wildcard mask ranges when attempting to summarize an arbitrary range of IP addresses. We will first present the algorithm and then show a detailed example of how it can be used.

The algorithm is presented below. Key sections of the algorithm are referenced by an index number.

```
      Convert the octet you are summarizing from decimal to binary

      Set the beginning IP address to BEGIN
      Set the ending IP address to END
  1 While BEGIN < END do
      2 Find the lowest order bit in BEGIN that is 1, this is the FOUND
        bit
      3 If there is a binary 1 in END that is a higher order bit than
        the HIGHEST order bit in BEGIN then
            All bits to the right of the FOUND bit are included in the
            range.
      4 Else
            5 Find the highest order bit in END less than the FOUND
              bit. This is the NEW-FOUND bit.
            6 If none found then
                All bits to the right of the FOUND bit are included
            7 Else
                  8 If all bits lower than NEW-FOUND in END are 1 then
                    All bits lower than NEW-FOUND including NEW-FOUND
                    are included in the range
                  9 Else IF there is at least 1 bit in END that is a
                    higher order bit than FOUND that is a 1 while the
                    corresponding bit in BEGIN is 0 then
                        All bits lower than NEW-FOUND including NEW-
                        FOUND are included in the range
```

```
        10 Else
                All bits to the right of NEW-FOUND are included
                in the range
        11 Set MASK equal to the value of the range found
        12 BEGIN and MASK represent a contiguous range
        13 Set BEGIN equal to BEGIN + MASK + 1
        14 Return to While
```

The use of this algorithm is best illustrated with an example. In this section we will summarize the range of IP addresses between 175.100.38.0/24 and 175.100.92.0/24. We will show how the wildcard masks for each access-list entry was created.

We begin by concentrating on the third octet of the beginning and ending IP address networks. The first two octets match, so we are not concerned with them. The last octet is the host octet, so we are not concerned with it either.

The first step is to represent the value of the beginning and ending numbers in binary.

```
        38 = 00100110
        92 = 01011100
```

Phase 1

```
        Begin    = 00100110 (38)
        End      = 01011100 (92)
        (1) While begin is less than end do
```

BEGIN is less than END, so we continue.

```
        (2) Find the lowest order bit in BEGIN that is 1, this is the FOUND bit
```

The lowest order bit in BEGIN that is 1 is in bit position 2 going from right to left, 00100110. Bit position 2 is the FOUND bit position.

```
        (3) If there is a binary 1 in END that is a higher order bit than the
        HIGHEST order bit in BEGIN
```

We see that bit position 7 in END is a binary 1:

```
        01011100
```

The highest bit position in BEGIN that is a binary 1 is in position 6:

```
        00100110
```

Therefore this condition is met.

```
        Then All bits to the right of the FOUND bit are included in the range.
```

The FOUND bit is in position 2, so bits in position 1 are included in the range.

```
(11) Set MASK equal to the value of the range found.
```

Only the bits in position 1 are included in the range, so the value of MASK is 2 raised to the 0th power or 1. In binary, the value of each bit is 2 raised to the $n-1$ power where n is the bit position.

```
(12) BEGIN and MASK represent a contiguous range
```

BEGIN is 00100110 or 38, MASK is 1. Using these numbers we can create an access-list entry:

```
access-list 100 permit ip 175.100.38.0 0.0.1.255
```

Notice that we used the BEGIN and MASK values in the 3rd octet of the IP address and wildcard mask for this access-list entry.

```
(13) Set BEGIN equal to BEGIN + 1 MASK + 1
```

BEGIN = 38 + 1 + 1 = 40

```
(14) Return to While
```

Repeat the process

Phase 2

```
Begin    = 00101000 (40)
End      = 01011100 (92)
(1) While begin is less than end do
```

BEGIN is less than END, so we continue.

```
(2) Find the lowest order bit in BEGIN that is 1, this is the FOUND bit
```

The lowest order bit in BEGIN that is 1 is in bit position 4 going from right to left, 00101000. Bit position 4 is the FOUND bit position.

```
(3) If there is a binary 1 in END that is a higher order bit than the
HIGHEST order bit in BEGIN
```

We see that bit position 7 in END is a binary 1:

```
01011100
```

The highest bit position in BEGIN that is a binary 1 is in position 6:

```
00101000
```

Therefore this condition is met.

```
Then All bits to the right of the FOUND bit are included in the range.
```

The FOUND bit is in position 4, so bits in positions 1–3 are included in the range.

```
(11) Set MASK equal to the value of the range found.
```

The bits in positions 1–3 are included in the range, so the value of MASK is 2 to the 2nd power, 2 to the 1st power, and 2 to the 0th power. This is 4 + 2 + 1 = 7.

```
(12) BEGIN and MASK represent a contiguous range
```

BEGIN is 00101000 or 40, MASK is 7. Using these numbers we can create an access-list entry:

```
access-list 100 permit ip 175.100.40.0 0.0.7.255
```

```
(13) Set BEGIN equal to BEGIN + 1 MASK + 1
```

BEGIN = 40 + 7 + 1 = 48

```
(14) Return to While
```

Repeat the process

Phase 3

```
Begin    = 00110000 (48)
End      = 01011100 (92)
```

```
(1) While begin is less than end do
```

BEGIN is less than END, so we continue.

```
(2) Find the lowest order bit in BEGIN that is 1, this is the FOUND bit
```

The lowest order bit in BEGIN that is 1 is in bit position 5 going from right to left, 00110000. Bit position 5 is the FOUND bit position.

```
(3) If there is a binary 1 in END that is a higher order bit than the
HIGHEST order bit in BEGIN
```

We see that bit position 7 in END is a binary 1:

```
01011100
```

The highest bit position in BEGIN that is a binary 1 is in position 6:

```
00110000
```

Therefore this condition is met.

```
Then All bits to the right of the FOUND bit are included in the range.
```

The FOUND bit is in position 5, so bits in positions 1–4 are included in the range.

```
(11) Set MASK equal to the value of the range found
```

The bits in positions 1–4 are included in the range, so the value of MASK is 2 to the 3rd power, 2 to the 2nd power, 2 to the 1st power, and 2 to the 0th power. This is 8 + 4 + 2 + 1 = 15.

```
(12) BEGIN and MASK represent a contiguous range
```

BEGIN is 00110000 or 48, MASK is 15. Using these numbers we can create an access-list entry:

```
access-list 100 permit ip 175.100.48.0 0.0.15.255
```

```
(13) Set BEGIN equal to BEGIN + 1 MASK + 1
```

BEGIN = 48 + 15 + 1 = 64

```
(14) Return to While
```

Repeat the process

Phase 4

```
Begin    = 01000000 (64)
End      = 01011100 (92)
(1) While begin is less than end do
```

BEGIN is less than END, so we continue.

```
(2) Find the lowest order bit in BEGIN that is 1, this is the FOUND bit
```

The lowest order bit in BEGIN that is 1 is in bit position 7 going from right to left, 01000000. Bit position 7 is the FOUND bit position.

```
(3) If there is a binary 1 in END that is a higher order bit than the
HIGHEST order bit in BEGIN
```

We see that bit position 7 in END is a binary 1:

```
01011100
```

The highest bit position in BEGIN that is a binary 1 is in position 7:

```
01000000
```

Therefore this condition is **NOT** met. We now operate on the **4 ELSE** condition.

```
(5) Find the highest order bit in END less than the FOUND bit. This is
the NEW-FOUND bit.
```

The FOUND bit is in position 7 of BEGIN: 01000000. The highest order bit in END less than the FOUND bit is in position 5: 01011100. Bit position 5 is the NEW-FOUND bit.

```
(6) If none found
```

A bit was found, so we execute the **7** ELSE portion

```
(8) If all bits lower than NEW-FOUND bit in END are 1
```

The NEW-FOUND bit position is 5, so we examine the bits in END to the right of the 5th bit: 01011100. We can see that not all of the bits are 1, so we execute the **9** Else IF.

```
(9) Else IF there is at least 1 bit in END that is a higher order bit
than FOUND that is a 1 while the corresponding bit in BEGIN is 0
```

The FOUND bit is position 6, so we are looking for bits in END that are in bit positions higher than 6 that are 1 where the corresponding bit in BEGIN is 0. By examining the bits higher than the 6th position in END, we see that there is no bit position that meets the criteria. There is a binary 1 in bit position 7 in END: 01011100 but there is a corresponding binary 1 in bit position 7 in BEGIN: 01000000. This condition is not met, so we execute the **10** Else.

```
(10) Else all bits to the right of NEW-FOUND are included in the range
```

The NEW-FOUND bit is in position 5, so bits 1–4 are included in the range

```
(11) Set MASK equal to the value of the range found
```

The bits in positions 1-4 are included in the range, so the value of MASK is 2 to the 3rd power, 2 to the 2nd power, 2 to the 1st power, and 2 to the 0th power. This is $8 + 4 + 2 + 1 = 15$.

```
(12) BEGIN and MASK represent a contiguous range
```

BEGIN is 01000000 or 64, MASK is 15. Using these numbers we can create an access-list entry:

```
access-list 100 permit ip 175.100.64.0 0.0.15.255
```

```
(13) Set BEGIN equal to BEGIN + MASK + 1
```

BEGIN = $64 + 15 + 1 = 80$

```
(14) Return to While
```

Repeat the process

Phase 5

```
Begin    = 01010000 (80)
End      = 01011100 (92)
(1) While begin is less than end do
```

BEGIN is less than END, so we continue.

> (2) Find the lowest order bit in BEGIN that is 1, this is the FOUND bit

The lowest order bit in BEGIN that is 1 is in bit position 5 going from right to left, 01010000. Bit position 5 is the FOUND bit position.

> (3) If there is a binary 1 in END that is a higher order bit than the HIGHEST order bit in BEGIN

We see that bit position 7 in END is a binary 1:

> 01011100

The highest bit position in BEGIN that is a binary 1 is in position 7:

> 01010000

Therefore this condition is **NOT** met. We now operate on the **4** ELSE condition.

> (5) Find the highest order bit in END less than the FOUND bit. This is the NEW-FOUND bit.

The FOUND bit is in position 5 of BEGIN: 01010000. The highest order bit in END less than the FOUND bit is in position 4: 01011100. Bit position 4 is the NEW-FOUND bit.

> (6) If none found

A bit was found, so we execute the **7** ELSE portion

> (8) If all bits lower than NEW-FOUND bit in END are 1

The NEW-FOUND bit position is 4, so we examine the bits in END to the right of the 4th bit: 01011**100**. We can see that not all of the bits are 1, so we execute the **9** Else IF.

> (9) Else IF there is at least 1 bit in END that is a higher order bit than FOUND that is a 1 while the corresponding bit in BEGIN is 0

The FOUND bit is position 5, so we are looking for bits in END that are in bit positions higher than 5 that are 1 where the corresponding bit in BEGIN is 0. By examining the bits higher than the 5th position in END, we see that there is no bit position that meets the criteria. There is a binary 1 in bit position 7 in END: 01011100, but there is a corresponding binary 1 in bit position 7 in BEGIN: 01000000. This condition is not met, so we execute the **10** Else.

> (10) Else all bits to the right of NEW-FOUND are included in the range

The NEW-FOUND bit is in position 4, so bits 1–3 are included in the range

```
(11) Set MASK equal to the value of the range found
```

The bits in positions 1–3 are included in the range, so the value of MASK is 2 to the 2nd power, 2 to the 1st power, and 2 to the 0th power. This is $4 + 2 + 1 = 7$.

```
(12) BEGIN and MASK represent a contiguous range
```

BEGIN is 01010000 or 80, MASK is 7. Using these numbers we can create an access-list entry:

```
access-list 100 permit ip 175.100.80.0 0.0.7.255
```

```
(13) Set BEGIN equal to BEGIN + MASK + 1
```

$BEGIN = 80 + 7 + 1 = 88$

```
(14) Return to While
```

Repeat the process

Phase 6

```
Begin    = 01011000 (88)
End      = 01011100 (92)
(1) While begin is less than end do
```

BEGIN is less than END, so we continue.

```
(2) Find the lowest order bit in BEGIN that is 1, this is the FOUND bit
```

The lowest order bit in BEGIN that is 1 is in bit position 4 going from right to left, 01011000. Bit position 4 is the FOUND bit position.

```
(3) If there is a binary 1 in END that is a higher order bit than the
HIGHEST order bit in BEGIN
```

We see that bit position 7 in END is a binary 1:

```
01011100
```

The highest bit position in BEGIN that is a binary 1 is in position 7:

```
01011000
```

Therefore this condition is **NOT** met. We now operate on the **4 ELSE** condition.

```
(5) Find the highest order bit in END less than the FOUND bit. This is
the NEW-FOUND bit.
```

The FOUND bit is in position 4 of BEGIN: 01011000. The highest order bit in END less than the FOUND bit is in position 3: 01011100. Bit position 3 is the NEW-FOUND bit.

```
(6) If none found
```

A bit was found, so we execute the 7 ELSE portion

```
(8) If all bits lower than NEW-FOUND bit in END are 1
```

The NEW-FOUND bit position is 3, so we examine the bits in END to the right of the 3rd bit: 01011100. We can see that not all of the bits are 1, so we execute the 9 Else IF.

```
(9) Else IF there is at least 1 bit in END that is a higher order bit
than FOUND that is a 1 while the corresponding bit in BEGIN is 0
```

The FOUND bit is position 4, so we are looking for bits in END that are in bit positions higher than 4 that are 1 where the corresponding bit in BEGIN is 0. By examining the bits higher than the 4th position in END, we see that there is no bit position that meets the criteria. There is a binary 1 in bit position 7 and 5 in END: 01011100, but there is a corresponding binary 1 in bit positions 7 and 5 in BEGIN: 01011000. This condition is not met, so we execute the 10 Else.

```
(10) Else all bits to the right of NEW-FOUND are included in the range
```

The NEW-FOUND bit is in position 3, so bits 1–2 are included in the range

```
(11) Set MASK equal to the value of the range found
```

The bits in positions 1–2 are included in the range, so the value of MASK is 2 to the 1st power and 2 to the 0th power. This is $2 + 1 = 3$.

```
(12) BEGIN and MASK represent a contiguous range
```

BEGIN is 01011000 or 88, MASK is 3. Using these numbers we can create an access-list entry:

```
access-list 100 permit ip 175.100.88.0 0.0.3.255
```

```
(13) Set BEGIN equal to BEGIN + MASK + 1
```

BEGIN = $88 + 3 + 1 = 92$

```
(14) Return to While
```

Repeat the process

Phase 7

```
Begin    = 01011100 (92)
End      = 01011100 (92)
(1) While begin is less than end do
```

BEGIN is **NOT** less than END, so we exit the loop.

Since BEGIN is now equal to END, we are done but we still have to add the last entry to cover the 175.100.92.0/24 network:

```
access-list 100 permit ip 175.100.92.0 0.0.0.255
```

We have now completed the summarization process. Collecting all of the access-list entries we have created, we now have the complete access list:

```
access-list 101 permit ip 175.100.38.0 0.0.1.255 any
access-list 101 permit ip 175.100.40.0 0.0.7.255 any
access-list 101 permit ip 175.100.48.0 0.0.15.255 any
access-list 101 permit ip 175.100.64.0 0.0.15.255 any
access-list 101 permit ip 175.100.80.0 0.0.7.255 any
access-list 101 permit ip 175.100.88.0 0.0.3.255 any
access-list 101 permit ip 175.100.92.0 0.0.0.255 any
```

APPENDIX B

Creating Access Lists

We now turn our attention to the creation and operation of access lists. The basic syntax of an access list is:

```
Access-list [1-1199] [permit|deny] [protocol|protocol-keyword]
    [source source-wildcard|any] [source port] [destination destination-
    wildcard|any] [destination port] [precedence precedence#] [options]
```

We will discuss each of these fields in detail next. Actual commands are in bold, and the other statements are English equivalents of the command syntax. Each section of the command is separated on its own line with a number to facilitate discussion. In practice, each access-list entry normally appears on a single line in the router configuration.

```
Access-list
[access list number 1-1199]
[permit or deny]
[some protocol]
[source address and mask]
[source port number or range]
[destination address and mask]
[destination port number or range]
[options]
```

A few words need to be said about the above command structure. First, not all the fields are required. Only fields 1, 2, and 4 are required in every type of access list. Most access lists also include fields 3 and 6. Each field is discussed below:

```
[access list number 1-1199]
```

The actual number that is used varies, depending on the type of access list used. Different types of access lists use different numbers. An IP access list, for example, uses a different number than an IPX access list. There are many different types of access lists.

`[permit or deny]`

A permit or deny statement is always required. This is how you specify whether the packets that match an access-list entry are to be allowed or denied access.

`[some protocol]`

Quite a few different protocols can be filtered using an access list. A short list includes IP, IPX, AppleTalk, DECnet, VINES, and XNS. It is also possible to filter on MAC layer addresses. Within most protocol stacks, there are usually additional protocols that can be filtered. For example, filters can also be created for TCP, UDP, and ICMP, all of which use IP at the network layer.

`[source address and mask]`

The source address and mask of the packets are always required. The source address is normally the layer 3 address of the packet, unless the access list is a MAC layer filter. The mask portion tells the router how much of the address to match when filtering packets. The concept is similar to a subnet mask. For instance, you may want to match all packets originating from the 10.10.0.0 255.255.0.0 subnet. The mask allows you to tell the router to match only the first two octets of the address. If no mask is specified, an exact match is assumed. If 10.10.0.0 is typed, the access-list entry would only match packets with a source address of 10.10.0.0 (a very unlikely source address). Although the principle is the same, the syntax of this mask is different than a network mask. In addition to the use of an actual address, many protocols also support the use of the "any" keyword.

`[source port number or range]`

This field is used when filtering on layer 4 information. It allows you to specify a particular higher-layer port. If the access list protocol is TCP, for example, you could specify a source TCP port of 25 (SMTP). You can also use symbols like GT for "greater than," LT for "less than," and RANGE to create specific ranges of port numbers.

`[destination address and mask]`

This field has the same parameter structure as the source address and mask.

```
[destination port number or range]
```

This field has the same parameter structure as the source port number or range.

```
[options]
```

This field allows a variety of additional fields to be matched in the access-list entry. The contents of the field vary depending on the type of access list. A typical option for a TCP access list would be "established," indicating the access-list entry would examine the packet to see if the ACK or RST bit is set. The "log" option is also common, indicating that matches of the access-list entry should be logged to the router's buffer or a syslog server. Other options include filtering on TOS and IP precedence.

Standard Access Lists

The basic format of a standard IP access list is:

```
Access-list [1-99] [permit|deny] [ip address] [mask] [log]
```

> **NOTE**
> The log keyword is available only in IOS 11.3 and later versions.

Each access list is given a unique number that is used to inform the IOS of the type of access list you are defining. This number is also used in all subsequent references to the access list. Standard IP access lists are defined within the range 1–99. In IOS version 11.2, named access lists were introduced, allowing you to define names for your access lists. These lists were created so you can delete specific entries in the access list without recreating the entire list. Additional entries, however, are still added to the end of the access list.

APPENDIX D

Extended IP Access Lists

Extended IP access lists provide much greater functionality and flexibility than standard IP access lists. Extended access lists provide the capability to filter by source address as in standard access lists, but they can also filter by destination address and upper layer protocol information. Very complex packet filters can be built with extended access lists. Extended access lists are numbered from 100–199 and their format is

```
Access-list [100-199] [permit|deny] [protocol|protocol-keyword]
    [source source-wildcard|any] [destination destination-wildcard|any]
    [precedence precedence# [tos tos] [log]
```

A list of possible protocols includes

- IP
- TCP
- UDP
- ICMP
- IGMP
- GRE
- IGRP
- EIGRP
- IPINIP
- OSPF
- NOS
- Integer in the range 0 through 255

To match any Internet protocol, use the keyword IP. Some of the protocols, such as TCP, UDP, and ICMP, have more options that are supported by alternate syntax. Extended access lists allow you to filter by IP precedence and type of service fields as well, although few organizations actually use these features. Additionally, you can log access-list matches by using the optional LOG keyword at the end of an access-list entry. Log entries will be sent to whatever logging facility you have enabled on the router.

APPENDIX E

Glossary

access control list   A list defining the kinds of access granted or denied to users of an object.

address   In data communication, this is a designated identifier.

address class   Traditional method of assigning blocks of addresses to organizations.

address mask   A bit mask used to select bits from an IP address for subnet addressing.

address resolution   Conversion of an IP address into a corresponding physical address, such as Ethernet or token ring.

address resolution protocol (ARP)   A TCP/IP protocol used to dynamically bind a high-level IP address to low-level physical hardware addresses. ARP works across single physical networks and is limited to networks that support hardware broadcast.

address space   Addresses used to uniquely identify network-accessible units, sessions, adjacent link stations, and links in a node for each network in which the node participates.

addressing   In data communication, the way in which a station selects the station to which it is to send data. An identifiable place.

AppleTalk   A networking protocol developed by Apple Computer for use with its products.

application layer   According to the ISO OSI model, this is layer 7. It provides application services.

ARPANET   The world's first packet-switching network. For many years it functioned as an Internet backbone.

autonomous system (AS)   An internetwork that is part of the Internet and has a single routing policy. Each Autonomous System is assigned an Autonomous System Number.

bandwidth   The quantity of data that can be sent across a link, typically measured in bits per second.

baud   A unit of signaling speed equal to the number of times per second that a signal changes state. If there are exactly two states, the baud rate equals the bit rate.

carrier-sense multiple access with collision detection (CSMA/CD)   A protocol utilizing equipment capable of detecting a carrier that permits multiple access to a common medium. This protocol also has the ability to detect a collision, because this type of technology is broadcast-oriented.

classless inter-domain routing (CIDR)   A method of routing used to enable the network part of IP addresses to consist of a specified number of bits.

collision   An event in which two or more devices simultaneously perform a broadcast on the same medium. This term is used in Ethernet networks, and also in networks where broadcast technology is implemented.

collision detection   Term used to define a device that can determine when a simultaneous transmission attempt has been made.

congestion   A network state caused by one or more overloaded network devices. Congestion leads to datagram loss.

connected   To have a physical path from one point to another.

connection   A logical communication path between TCP users.

connection-oriented internetworking   A set of subnetworks connected physically and thus rendered capable of connection-oriented network service.

connection-oriented service   A type of service offered in some networks. This service has three phases: connection establishment, data transfer, and connection release.

cracker   Someone who attempts to break into computer systems, often with malicious intent.

data circuit-terminating equipment (DCE)   Equipment required to connect a DTE to a line or to a network.

data-link control (DLC)   A set of rules used by nodes at layer 2 within a network. The data link is governed by data-link protocols such as Ethernet or token ring for example.

data-link control (DLC) protocol   Rules used by two nodes at a data-link layer to accomplish an orderly exchange of information. Examples are Ethernet, channel, FDDI, and token ring.

data-link layer   Layer 2 of the OSI reference model. It synchronizes transmission and handles error correction for a data link.

data-link level   The conceptual level of control logic between high-level logic and a data-link protocol that maintains control of the data link.

data terminal equipment (DTE)   A source or destination for data. Often used to denote terminals or computers attached to a wide area network.

DECnet   Digital Equipment Corporation's proprietary network protocol. Versions are identified by their phase number—such as Phase IV and Phase V.

directed broadcast address   In TCP/IP-based environments, an IP address that specifies all hosts on a specific network. A single copy of a directed broadcast is routed to the specified network where it is broadcast to all machines on that network.

DIX Ethernet   Version of Ethernet developed by Digital, Intel, and Xerox.

domain name server   In TCP/IP environments, it is a protocol for matching object names and network addresses. It was designed to replace the need to update /etc/hosts files of participating entities throughout a network.

domain name system (DNS)   The online distributed database system used to map human-readable machine names into IP addresses. DNS servers throughout the connected Internet implement a hierarchical name space that allows sites freedom in assigning machine names and addresses. DNS also supports separate mappings between mail destinations and IP addresses.

dotted-decimal notation   A phrase typically found in TCP/IP network conversations. Specifically, this refers to the addressing scheme of the Internet protocol (IP). It is the representation of a 32-bit address consisting of four 8-bit numbers written in base-10 with periods separating them.

encapsulate   Generally agreed on in the internetworking community to mean surrounding one protocol with another protocol for the purpose of passing the foreign protocol through the native environment.

Ethernet   A data-link-level protocol. It (Version 2.0) was defined by Digital Equipment Corporation, Intel Corporation, and the Xerox Corporation in 1982. It specified a data rate of 10 Mbits/s, a maximum station distance of 2.8 km, a maximum number of stations of 1024, a shielded coaxial cable using baseband signaling, functionality of CSMA/CD, and a best-effort delivery system.

exterior gateway protocol (EGP)   Routers in neighboring Autonomous Systems use this protocol to identify the set of networks that can be reached within or via each Autonomous System. EGP is being supplanted by BGP.

filter   A device or program that separates data, signals, or material in accordance with specified criteria.

firewall   A system that controls what traffic may enter and leave a site.

frame   One definition generally agreed on as being a packet as it is transmitted across a serial line. The term originated from character-oriented protocols. According to the meaning in OSI environments, it is a data structure pertaining to a particular area of data. It also consists of slots that can accept values of specific attributes.

hierarchical routing   From a TCP/IP perspective, this type of routing is based on a hierarchical addressing scheme. Most TCP/IP routing is based on a two-level hierarchy in which an IP address is divided into a network portion until the datagram reaches a gateway that can deliver it directly. The concept of subnets introduces additional levels of hierarchical routing.

hop count   (1) A measure of distance between two points in the Internet. Each hop count corresponds to one router separating a source from a destination (for example, a hop count of 3 indicates that three routers separate a source from a destination). (2) A term generally used in TCP/IP networks. The basic definition is a measure of distance between two points in an internet. A hop count of n means that n routers separate the source and the destination.

interior gateway protocol (IGP)   Any routing protocol used within an internetwork.

International Organization for Standardization (ISO)   An organization of national standards-making bodies from various countries established to promote development of standards to facilitate international exchange of goods and services, and develop cooperation in intellectual, scientific, technological, and economic activity.

Internet   According to different documents describing the Internet, it is a collection of networks, routers, gateways, and other networking devices that use the TCP/IP protocol suite and function as a single, cooperative virtual network. The Internet provides universal connectivity and three levels of network services: unreliable, connectionless packet delivery; reliable, full-duplex stream delivery; and application-level services such as electronic mail that build on the first two. The Internet reaches many universities, government research labs, and military installations and over a dozen countries.

Internet address   According to TCP/IP documentation, it refers to the 32-bit address assigned to the host. It is a software address that on local ("little i") internets is locally managed, but on the central ("big I") Internet is dictated to the user (entity desiring access to the Internet).

Internet Assigned Numbers Authority (IANA) The authority responsible for controlling the assignment of a variety of parameters, such as well-known ports, multicast addresses, terminal identifiers, and system identifiers.

Internet control message protocol (ICMP) A protocol that is required for implementation with IP. ICMP specifies error messages to be sent when datagrams are discarded or systems experience congestion. ICMP also provides several useful query services. Specific to the TCP/IP protocol suite. It is an integral part of the Internet protocol. It handles error and control messages. Routers and hosts use ICMP to send reports of problems about datagrams back to the original source that sent the datagram. ICMP also includes an echo request/reply used to test whether a destination is reachable and responding.

Internet gateway routing protocol (IGRP) A proprietary protocol designed for Cisco routers.

Internet group management protocol (IGMP) A protocol that is part of the multicast specification. IGMP is used to carry group membership information.

Internet packet exchange (IPX) A Novell protocol that operates at OSI layer 3. It is used in the NetWare protocols; it is similar to IP in TCP/IP.

Internet protocol (IP) A protocol used to route data from its source to its destination. A part of TCP/IP protocol.

IP Internet protocol. The TCP/IP standard protocol that defines the IP datagram as the unit of information passed across an internet and provides the basis for connectionless, best-effort packet delivery service. IP includes the ICMP control and error message protocol as an integral part. The entire protocol suite is often referred to as TCP/IP because TCP and IP are the two fundamental protocols.

IP address The 32-bit dotted-decimal address assigned to hosts that want to participate in a local TCP/IP internet or the central (connected) Internet. IP addresses are software addresses. Actually, an IP address consists of a network portion and a host portion. The partition makes routing efficient.

IP datagram A term used with TCP/IP networks. It is a basic unit of information passed across a TCP/IP internet. An IP datagram is to an internet as a hardware packet is to a physical network. It contains a source address and a destination address along with data.

link A medium over which nodes can communicate using a link-layer protocol.

link-state protocol A routing protocol that generates routes using detailed knowledge of the topology of a network.

logical link control (LLC)   According to OSI documentation, a sublayer in the data-link layer of the OSI model. The LLC provides the basis for an unacknowledged connectionless service or connection-oriented service on the local area network.

loopback address   Address 127.0.0.1, used for communications between clients and servers that reside on the same host.

MAC address   A physical address assigned to a LAN interface.

MAC protocol   A Media Access Control protocol defines the rules that govern a system's ability to transmit and receive data on a medium.

maximum transfer unit (MTU)   The largest amount of data that can be transferred across a given physical network. For local area networks implementing Ethernet, the MTU is determined by the network hardware. For long-haul networks that use aerial lines to interconnect packet switches, the MTU is determined by software.

multicast   A technique that allows copies of a single packet to be passed to a selected subset of all possible destinations. Some hardware supports multicast by allowing a network interface to belong to one or more multicast groups. Broadcast is a special form of multicast in which the subset of machines to receive a copy of a packet consists of the entire set. IP supports an internet multicast facility.

multicast address   According to Apple documentation, an Ethernet address for which the node accepts packets just as it does for its permanently assigned Ethernet hardware address. The low-order bit of the high-order byte is set to 1. Each node can have any number of multicast addresses, and any number of nodes can have the same multicast address. The purpose of a multicast address is to allow a group of Ethernet nodes to receive the same transmission simultaneously, in a fashion similar to the AppleTalk broadcast service.

multicasting   A directory service agent uses this mode to chain a request to many other directory service agents.

multicast IP address   A destination IP address that can be adopted by multiple hosts. Datagrams sent to a multicast IP address will be delivered to all hosts in the group.

NetBEUI   Local area network protocol used for Microsoft LANs.

NetBIOS   A network programming interface and protocol developed for IBM-compatible personal computers.

network   A collection of computers and related devices connected together in such a way that collectively they can be more productive than standalone equipment.

network address   In general, each participating entity on a network has an address so that it can be identified when exchanging data. According to IBM documentation, in a subarea network, an address consists of subarea and element fields that identify a link, link station, PU, LU, or SSCP.

network layer According to ISO documentation, it is defined as OSI layer 3. It is responsible for data transfer across the network. It functions independently of the network media and the topology.

octet Eight bits (a byte).

open shortest path first (OSPF) A routing protocol based on the least cost for routing.

packet A term used generically in many instances. It is a small unit of control information and data that is processed by the network protocol.

physical address An address assigned to a network interface.

physical layer A term used in OSI circles. It refers to the lowest layer defined by the OSI model. However, layer 0 would be the lowest layer in such a model. This layer (layer 0) represents the medium, whether hard or soft.

point-to-point protocol (PPP) A protocol for data transfer across serial links. PPP supports authentication, link configuration, and link monitoring capabilities and allows traffic for several protocols to be multiplexed across the link.

presentation layer According to the OSI model for networks, this is layer 6. Data representation occurs here. Syntax of data such as ASCII or EBCDIC is determined at this layer.

protocol An agreed-upon way of doing something.

proxy ARP In TCP/IP networks, this is a technique where one machine answers ARP requests intended for another by supplying its own physical address.

RARP *See* reverse address resolution protocol.

Request for comments (RFC) Proposed and accepted TCP/IP standards.

reverse address resolution protocol (RARP) A TCP/IP protocol for mapping Ethernet addresses to IP addresses. It is used by diskless workstations that do not know their IP addresses. In essence, it asks "Who am I?" Normally, a response occurs and is cached in the host.

routing The moving of data through paths in a network.

routing information protocol (RIP) A simple protocol used to exchange information between routers. The original version was part of the XNS protocol suite.

routing policy Rules for which traffic will be routed and how it should be routed.

routing table A table containing information used to forward datagrams toward their destinations.

segment   A Protocol Data Unit consisting of a TCP header and optionally, some data. Sometimes used to refer to the data portion of a TCP Protocol Data Unit.

session layer   According to the OSI reference model, this is layer 5. It coordinates the dialog between two communicating application processes.

shortest path first   A routing algorithm that uses knowledge of a network's topology in making routing decisions.

sliding window   A scenario in which a protocol permits the transmitting station to send a stream of bytes before an acknowledgment arrives.

stub network   A network that does not carry transit traffic between other networks.

subnet address   A selected number of bits from the local part of an IP address, used to identify a set of systems connected to a common link.

subnet mask   A configuration parameter that indicates how many bits of an address are used for the host part. It is expressed as a 32-bit quantity, with 1s placed in positions covering the network and subnet part of an IP address and 0s in the host part.

switch   A layer 2 device that enables many pairs of LAN devices to communicate concurrently.

T1   A digital telephony service that operates at 1.544 megabits per second. DS1 framing is used.

T3   A digital telephony service that operates at 44.746 megabits per second. DS3 framing is used.

Telnet   The TCP/IP TCP standard protocol for remote terminal service.

10Base T   An Ethernet implementation using 10 Mbits/s with baseband signaling over twisted-pair cabling.

time to live (TTL)   A technique used in best-effort delivery systems to avoid endlessly looping packets. For example, each packet has a "time" associated with its lifetime.

token   The symbol of authority passed successively from one data station to another to indicate which station is temporarily in control of the transmission medium.

token ring   A network with a ring topology that passes tokens from one attaching device to another.

token-ring network   A ring network that allows unidirectional data transmission between data stations by a token-passing procedure.

transmission control protocol (TCP)   The TCP/IP standard transport-level protocol that provides the reliable, full-duplex, stream service on which many application protocols depend. It is connection-oriented in that before transmitting data, participants must establish a connection.

transport layer   According to the OSI model, it is the layer that provides an end-to-end service to its users.

trivial file transfer protocol (TFTP)   A TCP/IP UDP standard protocol for file transfer that uses UDP as a transport mechanism. TFTP depends only on UDP, so it can be used on machines such as diskless workstations.

well-known-port   A term used with TCP/IP networks. In TCP/IP, applications and programs that reside on top of TCP and UDP, respectively, have a designated port assigned to them. This agreed-on port is known as a well-known-port.

APPENDIX F

Acronyms
and Abbreviations

AAI	Administration authority identifier
AARP	AppleTalk address resolution protocol
AC	Access control
ACK	Positive acknowledgment
ACL	Access control list
ADSP	AppleTalk data stream protocol
AEP	AppleTalk echo protocol
ANS	American National Standard
ANSI	American National Standards Institute
ARP	Address resolution protocol
ARPA	Advanced Research Projects Agency
ARQ	Automatic repeat request
ARS	Automatic route selection
ASCII	American Standard Code for Information Interchange
bps	bits per second
BOC	Bell Operating Company
BRI	Basic rate interface

BSD	Berkeley standard distribution
BTU	Basic transmission unit
CCITT	Consultative Committee in International Telegraphy and Telephony
CO	Central office
CODEC	Coder/decoder
CPE	Customer premises equipment
CSMA/CD	Carrier-sense multiple access with collision detection
CSU	Channel service unit
DA	Destination address
DAD	Draft addendum
DARPA	Defense Advanced Research Projects Agency
DEC	Digital Equipment Corporation
DES	Data Encryption Standard
DIS	Draft International Standard
DIX	DEC, Intel, and Xerox
DNS	Domain name service (also system)
DoD	U. S. Department of Defense
DSU	Digital services unit
E-mail	Electronic mail
ECC	Enhanced error checking and correction
EIA	Electronic Industries Association
FCC	Federal Communications Commission
FCS	Frame-check sequence
FDX	Full-duplex
FRAD	Frame relay access device
FTP	File transfer protocol in TCP/IP
Gb	Gigabit
Gbps	Gigabits per second
GB	Gigabyte

GUI	Graphical user interface
HDLC	High-level data-link control
HDX	Half-duplex (also HD)
hex	Hexadecimal
IAB	Internet Architecture Board
ICMP	Internet control message protocol
IEEE	Institute of Electrical and Electronic Engineers
I/O	Input/output
IP	Internet protocol
IPX	Internetwork packet exchange
IRSG	Internet Research Steering Group
IRTF	Internet Research Task Force
IS	International Standard
ISO	International Standards Organization
ISP	Internet Service Provider
IT	Information technology
ITC	Independent telephone company
ITU	International Telecommunication Union
kbs	Kilobits
kbps	Kilobits per second
kB	Kilobyte
kHz	Kilohertz
LAN	Local area network
LE	Local exchange
LEC	Local exchange carrier
LLC	Logical link control
Mb	Megabits
Mbps	Megabits per second
MB	Megabyte
MBps	Megabytes per second

MS	Management services; message store
MTU	Maximum transfer unit
NCP	Network Core Protocol
ns	Nanosecond
NSF	National Science Foundation
NSFNET	National Science Foundation Network
OS	Operating System
OSE	Open-systems environment
OSF	Open Software Foundation
OSI	Open-systems interconnection
OSPF	Open shortest path first
PCM	Pulse-code modulation
PDN	Public data network
PDU	Protocol data unit
PING	Packet Internet Groper
POP	Point of presence
POTS	Plain old telephone service
PRI	Primary rate interface
PSDN	Packet-switched data network
RBOC	Regional Bell Operating Company
RFC	Request for comment
RFP	Request for proposal
RFQ	Request for price quotation
RIF	Routing information field
RIP	Router information protocol
RISC	Reduced instruction-set computer
s	Second
SA	Source address (field); subarea; sequenced application
SNMP	Simple network management protocol

SPX	Sequenced packet exchange
TA	Terminal adapter
TC	Transport connection or technical committee
TCP	Transmission control protocol
TCP/IP	Transmission control protocol/Internet protocol
TDM	Time-division multiplexing; topology database manager
Telnet	Remote log-on in TCP/IP
TFTP	Trivial file transfer protocol
TTL	Time to live
VAC	Value-added carrier
VAN	Value-added network
VAS	Value-added service
VT	Virtual terminal

Index

About the Authors

Gil Held is an award-winning lecturer and author. He is the author of more than 40 books covering computer and communications technology. A member of the adjunct faculty at Georgia College and State University, Gil teaches courses in LAN performance and was selected to represent the United States at technical conferences in Moscow and Jerusalem.

Kent Hundley (CCNA) is a Senior Network Consultant for Lucent Netcare Professional Services, a global provider of network integration and management services. He specializes in complex network and security issues for Fortune 500 companies.